Dear Clarissa.

May you grow continually through
life's joys and struggles.

Water from the Well

Water from the Well

Reflections on Being a Jew at the End of History

Rebbetzin Holly Pavlov

Edited by Bluma Trapp

TARGUM/FELDHEIM

Published by:
TARGUM PRESS, INC.
22700 W. Eleven Mile Rd.
Southfield, MI 48034
E-mail: targum@netvision.net.il
Fax: 888-298-9992
www.targum.com

Distributed by:
FELDHEIM PUBLISHERS
208 Airport Executive Park
Nanuet, NY 10954

Printing plates by Frank, Jerusalem
Printed in Israel by Chish Press

Letter of Approbation for *Mirrors of Our Lives*

Rabbi CHAIM P. SCHEINBERG
Rosh Hayeshiva "TORAH ORE"
and Morah Hora'ah of Kiryat Mattersdorf

הרב חיים פינחס שיינברג
ראש ישיבת "תורה אור"
ומורה הוראה דקרית מטרסדורף

סיון תשס"ס
פעיה"ק ירושלים תובב"א

In every generation, through the study of Torah, Jews have identified with and become connected to the *Avos* and *Imahos*, our great Patriarchs and Matriarchs, who are the very soul of the Jewish people. *Mirrors of Our Lives: Reflections of Women in Tanach* is a book that will give the English speaking public a deeper understanding of the foundation on which our nation is built.

Rebbetzin Holly Pavlov has devoted her life to the field of educating women and in *kiruv levavos*, bringing Jews closer to Torah and mitzvos. The excellence of her teaching and the success of her *kiruv* work at She'arim College of Jewish Studies for Women can now be found in her superb book on the matriarchs. The guidance provided by these Torah ideas will not only elevate and strengthen the reader; they will give practical tools that can be utilized in everyday life.

May HaShem bless her with renewed strength and continued success in teaching *Am Yisroel* and in bringing those who have wandered away closer to Torah.

הכו"ח לכבוד התורה ולומדי'

חיים פנחס שיינברג

Dear Friends:

I have read the manuscript of *Water from the Well* by Rebbetzin Holly Pavlov and have found it interesting, informative, and inspiring.

Rebbetzin Pavlov presents various episodes from Tanach, exploring their breadth and depth through the various Midrashim and commentaries. She then culls from them insights and guidance that are rooted in sound Torah sources and Torah *hashkafah*. Finally, she derives from them practical aids for facing the experiences of life in our complex world.

As Rebbetzin Pavlov herself conveys, the woman's role is predominately to dig a well, to remove the obstructions that hinder the Torah from manifesting itself in the world and in individuals.

Water from the Well will serve as an excellent drill to help dig the wells of one's heart and bring forth Torah true ideas and ideals.

I have been acquainted with Rabbi and Rebbetzin Pavlov and their family for many years. They are a true family, dedicated to *klal Yisrael* in disseminating Torah, *emunah*, and *yiras Shamayim*. The Pavlovs are the founders and guiding force of She'arim College of Jewish Studies for Women in Jerusalem.

May Hashem grant the Pavlovs life and health to continue in their holy word for many more years to come.

Sincerely,

With Torah blessings,

Rabbi Zev Leff

This book is dedicated to the memory of
our fathers, our teachers

Moshe ben Yosef ע״ה
Chananya ben Nachum ע״ה

And יב״ל, in honor of our mothers,
our teachers,

Chana Etis bas Moshe Aaron
Faiga Bluma bas Azriel

whose wisdom continues to inspire us,
whose life lessons take on new dimensions as we
ourselves experience what they have taught us,
whose love underlines all we do,
and whose presence remains strong in our lives.

Holly and Yosef Pavlov

לעלוי נשמת

יונינא בת ויילא

In memory of our dear student

Yanina Kuklenko

whose soul thirsted for truth,
who found herself and her voice in Torah,
who clung to Hashem with trust and
devoted herself to acts of chesed,
and
who inspired us with her deep *emunah*.

She'arim College of Jewish Studies for Women
Rabbi and Rebbetzin Pavlov

Contents

Preface 11

Acknowledgments 15

How to Read This Book 17

CHOSENNESS 19

Laughter Is Serious Business 21

Building the Nation 35

Shame: A Jewish Approach 55

Initiative: The Legacy of Leah 70

LIFE IN EXILE 103

Are We Really Free to Choose? 105

Crying Out in Solitude 125

Longing for Guidance 142

Lowliness, Sin, and Transformation 157

Trusting God in the Dark of the Night 175

God Hides, We Seek 188

Water from the Well 205

Footsteps of the Mashiach 219

Preface

When I was a child, I learned Jewish history. I felt small in the face of the courage I read about — the bravery and self-sacrifice of the Jews who lived before me. They were so often given only terrible choices: to be true to their Torah or to their instinct to survive. Loyalty to Torah usually came with consequences that included exile from country to country, or subjugation by the perpetrators of the Inquisition, the Crusades, the Holocaust, and all other pogroms, persecutions, and massacres.

I was amazed by how many Jews chose spiritual commitment over physical survival. I wondered how they lived under such oppression, forgoing an easier life if it meant conversion. I marveled at the strength of their beliefs and their trust in God. I asked, how were they able to make the choice to sanctify God's name, to give their lives and the lives of their children for the sanctification of God's name?

Mostly, I wondered if I would have such strength of conviction. Would I, given a choice of conversion or death, choose Torah? The question disturbed me. Would I opt for an easier life in this world over eternal life in the next? Might I fail my people or my God because of fear or a faith not strong enough for the test?

When I grew up, I moved with my husband and children to Israel. I realized that there are times when we are given the choice whether to sanctify God's name or not. And there are also times when the knife, the gun, the bomb chooses the Jew, and his death sanctifies God's name. In these moments, God Himself selects the person and his "mission." Yet there is still choice — we choose to live in Israel, to ride a bus, to serve in the army. We choose to go to public places, to send our children to school — all the time knowing that there is danger, a chance that this may be a last good-bye.

How do we make such choices and go on living joyfully? Being in Israel over twenty-two years, I am beginning to learn how. I have discovered that crises bring opportunity for growth, for a fuller awareness of God, for a more profound love of Torah, and for a true appreciation of each moment of life. Moreover, it is only through the struggle that our trust in God grows, that our commitment to Torah is solidified.

Of course, one does not need to live in Israel to appreciate our vulnerability as people. It often seems that, although we wish it otherwise, life is more about struggle than joy and, in fact, joy comes to punctuate the struggle, and not the other way around. The darkness is the backdrop against which to see the light.

In fact, without the struggle, we cannot learn to appreciate life and truly trust God. Without struggle, we remain unaware of all the good in our lives. So that suffering is a gift — the means to grow and develop into more spiritually connected people.

It is when we become intensely aware of the fragility of our lives that we come to examine them. We then search for the meaning of our existence. Life becomes richer, moments become significant, and simple — and not so simple — events assume purpose.

But what purpose? What is the purpose of our lives, if so much is about struggle and adversity? What do we have to gain from or, better yet, contribute to the world?

Many say that in this period of history our suffering is intensified. I certainly see many around me struggling with financial pressure, difficult relationships, illness, childlessness, singleness/loneliness, children born with impairments — all the things in life over which we have little or no control. Is it that as we reach the end of history, as we approach the Messianic era, life has become more difficult, our pain much greater? I am not sure this is true, as suffering is nothing new in Jewish history.

Yet something is indeed different in our era. Something has changed in the way we suffer. We have lost a sense of why life is so, why we struggle so much. Perhaps we are farther than any other generation from a sense of our purpose. We see no end to the suffering, and worse, we see no purpose.

Perhaps it is also because we have a greater sense of entitlement to a happily-ever-after and are perplexed when there is no happy ending. Our lives, in so many ways, are easier than those of previous generations, and that ease makes suffering so much more incongruous with our expectations. This mind-set is a source of great suffering in itself, a force that greatly aggravates whatever challenges we're given.

If only we could see ourselves as bigger than just the lead character in the drama of our own lives. If only we could understand that it's not all about us, but that we are part of a greater story that began before we were born, continues after we die, and involves an entire nation. If only we could stop feeling we are owed anything and get on with discovering and fulfilling our unique missions in life. Learning Torah can correct this deficit in perspective, reminding us of the bigger picture and our place in it.

While a clearer sense of mission will not eliminate our suffering, a Torah perspective will assign it purpose and direction. Seeing ourselves as part of a process, of the growth of the nation, as a chain that leads to the Messianic era, will ease our way, enabling us to bear our burdens with greater strength.

This book is a reflection of my own attempts to understand our reality. Through teaching and mentoring the thousands of women who come to learn in She'arim, as well as those I meet during my lecture tours abroad, I have listened to the voice of personal struggle. The struggles are diverse yet similar in that they are tests designed to stretch a person.

Every essay in this book is an effort to see our struggles in the context of this larger story, to see crises as an opportunity to foster trust, to accept that God is guiding us, although we don't always see Him directly. I write in order to frame our lives — both the dark and the light — in terms of a vision that goes beyond the individual.

The lives of our ancestors are our models for this reframing. Those men and women who formed the Jewish people walked this path before us. They built the Jewish people, not easily, not without crisis and pain and fear. But despite the difficulties they faced, they built the Jewish people with vision, and through that vision, they rose above their anxieties and trusted God.

It is to them we turn as our teachers, to show us how to live our lives, how to punctuate them with joy, how to see the light through the dark, how to walk to the end of history.

Acknowledgments

It has been one of my life's blessings to be a teacher: to be able to interact with students, to hear their questions, to probe their minds, to listen to their struggles, and to learn with and from them. I always tell them that I teach them that which I need to learn, so that they are my study partners in the text and in life. The truth is more complicated than that — in sharing their life's journeys and struggles, successes and failures with me, they have taught me more than I have taught them, for they have exposed me to worlds I could not know and to questions I would not have. For this, I thank them.

I work with an extraordinary staff. They are exceptional in their devotion to She'arim and to our students. Each of them is dedicated far beyond their assigned hours and duties, acknowledging that her/his real employer is God, and not only the seminary for which they work. It is simply a privilege to work with them, to be inspired by them, and to learn from them. They have shared with me freely from their wisdom and allowed me to work through ideas with them, thus contributing greatly to this book. Thank you to Gitty Appel, Rabbi Yosef Benarroch, Tziporah Breines, Rabbi Avraham Brussel, Rivi Brussel, Rabbi Yosef Cowan, Nina Fixler, Sandie Freishtat, Barbara Friedman, Rachel Hershberg, Malka Kaganoff, Esti Klebanow, Gila Manolson, Annette Migdal, Rabbi Dov Nossel, Rachel Preuffer, Miriam Shaul, Ariela Sher, Reva Sperling, Chaya Tavin, Shoshana Raff, and Rabbi Moshe Weiden.

Bluma Trapp, senior editor of this book and founder of Blossom Editing Services, was a student of mine who, in editing this book, became my colleague. She has a keen eye for detail and helped me develop ideas and flesh out thoughts that were not fully developed. Her advice was always excellent and my book is certainly a better product because of her input. Sara Granovettor edited several articles in this book, always prodding me to greater clarity and encouraging me to continue.

My son Chananya was my research assistant. His breadth of knowledge and understanding were of great benefit in helping me solidify many of the ideas in these essays. Of course, it was also a source of personal *nachas*.

The staff of Targum has been excellent in bringing this book to production. Working with Chaya Baila Gavant was a pleasure, as I value her professionalism and sensitivity. A special thanks goes to Diane Liff, who designed the inspiring cover.

How do we thank those who gave us life, raised us, and taught us the fundamental values with which we live our lives? My mother, Mrs. Nita Quint, and my father, Mr. Maurice Quint (*a"h*), imbued me with a love of learning, compassion for others, and a sense of responsibility. My in-laws, Mrs. Faye Pavlov Lipshitz and Mr. Chananya Pavlov (*a"h*), raised their children with a love of Torah and respected each one for his individuality. I must also thank my dear aunt Esther Babad who has always been proud of my accomplishments, attended my classes — in her nineties she traveled to She'arim by bus! — and who has been a third *bubby* to my children and grandchildren. I use this opportunity to thank them for everything. Your love and attention has not gone unnoticed.

To my wonderful children and their spouses — Arona and Reuven Pokroy, Ariela and Uri Sher, Aliza and Chananya Pavlov, Brachy and Levi Pavlov, Elan, Eliyahu, and Miriam — who have taught me how much joy a child (and child-in-law) can give a parent. In their adulthood, they have become my closest friends and remain my biggest supporters. May they be blessed to see their children walking in the footsteps of our great matriarchs and patriarchs. May their children bring them the same *nachas* that they bring me.

I cannot adequately thank my dear husband, Yosef, for everything that he has done for me and everything that he has encouraged me to do. He has always had confidence in my abilities, but more importantly he has taught me how to be a better person and Jew. His wisdom, patience, and understanding have instructed and guided me in my life and my life's work.

Finally, I wish to express my gratitude to the Master of the Universe, who "in His wisdom, opens gates" for us to enter. In hindsight, I see how often I was led through a gate that I did not anticipate, only to find a world of challenge and growth before me. Each gate led to another and each provided a new opportunity for personal development. It is with tremendous gratitude that I thank Him for leading me on this journey.

How to Read This Book

Torah, the Sages say, is like water. And learning Torah is like digging a well — the deeper we go, the more water we find. There is no end to the water that hides beneath the surface of the earth, and so we dig, using our intellect and emotion as the shovel to unearth hidden wisdom.

Those who have dug before us provide guidance and skill for this venture. Our great rabbis and commentators over the centuries gave us the map with which to find our treasured water. In fact, as we learn, we find ourselves in a dialogue with them. What do you think, Rashi? And you, Ramban? What do you, Rabbi Berechya in the Midrash, teach? We ask and we listen to their answers. We discuss and we challenge. We resolve and debate. We engage in a conversation that traverses centuries and transports us to places we have never seen and milieus we have never experienced.

It is this sense of dialogue that I wanted to convey when I wrote this book. More than just an examination of philosophical or ethical ideas, this book is meant to allow readers access to original sources, as well as the classic Jewish method of learning. In each essay, I present Torah concepts, as a teacher would to her students, aiming to provoke, elicit questions, and work out life lessons together.

We should know that the Torah cannot be accessed without the proper tools. The tool that allows us to learn the philosophy of Judaism is the Midrash. Written as parable and riddle, the Midrash might seem like nothing more than a collection of simple stories. In reality, Midrash is the concrete expression of abstract ideas, using story-form to veil deep truths (Luzatto, *Maamar al HaAggados*). In these essays, I rely heavily on Midrash, in addition to traditional commentators.

These essays grew out of classes I gave in She'arim College of Jewish Studies for Women, a seminary for adult women in Jerusalem. Our students include the very advanced and the beginner. They come to Jerusalem from a variety of backgrounds, for a short or a long stay, to explore the beauty and depth of Torah. They come searching for answers to life's complexities. Together we probe the texts, question the meaning, and search for answers. Together we dig for water from the well of Torah.

Chosenness

Laughter Is Serious Business

Life is funny — or is it sad? Sometimes it's hard to tell. But whichever way it is, laughter always helps. And we Jews know a great deal about laughter. We make Jewish jokes, we make gentile jokes, we laugh at the crazy life we live, we laugh at each other, we laugh at ourselves. In short, we're always laughing. Perhaps this is because we're a nation that was born in laughter: The first Jewish child was named "Yitzchak," which means "he will laugh."

Avraham and Sarah Laugh

> Avraham threw himself upon his face and laughed; and he thought, "Shall a child be born to a one-hundred-year-old man? And shall Sarah, a ninety-year-old woman, give birth?" And Avraham said to God, "If only Yishmael might live before You!"
>
> God said, "Nonetheless, your wife Sarah will bear you a son and you shall call his name Yitzchak; and I will fulfill My covenant with him as an everlasting covenant for his offspring after him."
>
> (*Bereishis* 17:17–19)

God told Avraham he would have a child, and Avraham's reaction was to fall on his face. Falling on one's face is a sign of awe, of prayer. But, as he fell on his face, he also laughed. God then commanded that the child to be born be called Yitzchak, "he will laugh," as if to affirm Avraham's laughter.

Three days later, Sarah received the good news:

> He [an angel] said, "I will surely return to you at this time next

year, and behold Sarah, your wife, will have a son."

Now Sarah was listening at the entrance of the tent, which was behind him. Avraham and Sarah were old, well on in years; the manner of women had ceased to be with Sarah. And Sarah laughed within herself, saying, "After I have withered shall I again have delicate skin? And my husband is old!"

Then God said to Avraham, "Why is it that Sarah laughed, saying: 'Shall I in truth bear a child, though I have aged?' — Is anything beyond God? I will return to you at this time next year and Sarah will have a son."

Sarah denied it, saying, "I did not laugh," for she was frightened.

But he said, "No, you laughed indeed."

(Bereishis 18:10–15)

Rashi explains that "Sarah laughed within herself" means she looked inside herself and said, "Is it possible that these insides shall bear a child; that these breasts that have withered shall yield milk?" In other words, Sarah laughed at her insides, at the absurdity of the situation. She had long ago lost "the manner of women" (menstruation), smooth skin, and youthfulness. Could it be that she, who was now old, would give birth? And not only that, but her husband was old as well!

God (or an angel of God) asked Avraham why Sarah laughed, saying she was too old. God left out the words "and my husband is old" in the interests of marital harmony, but Sarah was taken to task for laughing; after all, is anything too wondrous for God? At this point, Sarah denied laughing, but after God said, "You did laugh," Sarah was silent.

This episode is very puzzling. Avraham and Sarah each received the happy news that they would have a child. They had a seemingly identical reaction. Avraham laughed, thinking, *Shall a child be born to a one-hundred-year-old man? And shall Sarah, a ninety-year-old woman, give birth?* and Sarah "laughed within herself, saying, 'After I have withered shall I again have delicate skin? And my husband is old!' " Yet Sarah was reprimanded for laughing while Avraham was not.

Rashi explains:

Avraham believed and rejoiced, but Sarah did not believe and sneered. Therefore, the Holy One, blessed be He, was angry with Sarah, but He was not angry with Avraham.

The reactions of Sarah and Avraham, then, were different, and the reaction of God to their laughter is also different. Sarah and Avraham both laughed, but Avraham's laughter was combined with awe. His laughter was not "I don't believe it," but rather "I do believe it!" For this reason, he fell on his face. Sarah, on the other hand, looked inside and laughed. Clearly she was thinking, *This is absurd. I'm not built for this anymore.*

The People Laugh

God had remembered Sarah as He had said; and God did for Sarah as He had spoken. Sarah conceived and bore a son unto Avraham in his old age, at the appointed time that God had spoken. Avraham called the name of his son who was born to him, whom Sarah had borne him, Yitzchak. Avraham circumcised his son Yitzchak at the age of eight days as God had commanded him.

And Avraham was one hundred years old when his son Yitzchak was born to him. Sarah said, "God has made laughter for me; whoever hears will laugh (*yitzachak*) at/with me." And she said, "Who is the One who said to Avraham, 'Sarah would nurse children'? For I have borne a son in his old age!"

The child grew and was weaned. Avraham made a great feast on the day Yitzchak was weaned.

(*Bereishis* 21:1–8)

Upon being rebuked by God for her laughter, Sarah denied laughing because she had already repented for it. Yet God insisted that she did laugh because her repentance was motivated by fear and awe of God, which, although sincere, was not complete repentance. Later, after Yitzchak was born and she held him in her arms and nursed him, she declared, "God has made laughter of me." This time Sarah's repentance was the repentance of love; she felt pure happiness and joy, with absolutely no irony. Therefore, her repentance was completed (*Sefas Emes*).

Sarah next stated that "whoever hears will laugh at me." This sounds like the laughter of the absurd again — "Sarah's nursing a baby?! Avraham has had a child at the age of one hundred?!" But Rashi says Sarah meant, "They will be happy for me." All the barren women in the world were remembered along with Sarah. Sick people were healed on that day, and prayers were answered. So there was a great deal of laughter in the world, the laughter of happiness.

However, when Sarah joyously proclaimed, "Whoever hears will laugh at/with me," she used a strange grammatical form to describe that laughter: *yitzachak*. This word combines two conjugation forms: *kal* and *pi'el*. *Yitzchak* means "will laugh;" "*yitzachek*" means "will mock." The word that Sarah used is a combination — "will laugh/will mock" (Rav Shimshon Refael Hirsch). The usage of this word implies that Sarah didn't know if those who heard of her late-in-life baby would laugh or mock. Furthermore, Yitzchak's name is in the future tense, as if the laughter had not yet begun but was yet to happen. We will discover why.

Yishmael and Yitzchak Laugh

The Hebrew word *mitzachek* comes from the root word *tzechok*, "laughter," but *mitzachek* connotes a specific type of laughter: it means mocking. Mocking implies that the object of the mocking is not to be taken seriously because it is inferior. There are two ways to mock:

> Sarah saw the son of Hagar, the Egyptian, whom she had born to Avraham, mocking (*mitzachek*).
>
> (*Bereishis* 21:9)

Rashi explains that Yishmael mocked the world, engaging in idol worship, forbidden relations, and murder. The laughter of Yishmael was the laughter of disdain.

Compare that same word, *mitzachek*, to:

> And it came to pass, as his days there lengthened, that Avimelech, king of the Philistines, gazed down through the window and saw — behold! Yitzchak was jesting (*mitzachek*) with his wife Rivkah.
>
> (*Bereishis* 26:8)

The word *jesting* in Hebrew is *mitzachek* — Yitzchak laughed with his wife, Rivkah, and, astonishingly, this is the same word used to describe Yishmael's mocking — the word that means promiscuity, murder, and idol worship!

Sarah and Avraham both laughed, but their laughter was not the same. Avraham's two sons, Yitzchak and Yishmael, both laughed, and their laughter was also different. To understand, we must examine the meaning of laughter.

Why Is Everyone Laughing?

Normally, when we think of laughter, we think of joy. The word for *joy* in Hebrew, however, isn't *tzechok*, laughter, it's *simchah*. In general, *simchah* has to do with a mitzvah or with doing the right thing. A person who does the right thing feels joyous; a person who does a mitzvah feels happy. What, then, is *tzechok* — laughter?

Rav Hirsch explains the inner meaning of the word *tzechok*. *Tzechok* is always ironic laughter, laughter that brings with it a certain amount of denial. "Come on — that's absurd, it doesn't fit." When Sarah laughed after hearing the news that she would bear a child, she laughed because the situation was so illogical: "I'm going to have a baby? Look at me! I'm old, my breasts are withered, the way of women has long since ceased from me!" She laughed at the incongruity of it.

Tzechok is the laughter we laugh when something strikes us as ridiculous. A ninety-year-old woman and a one-hundred-year-old man who have been married for many decades without issue — to think that they can have a baby is laughable.

In addition, was it not absurd for Sarah and Avraham to expect that their child, Yitzchak, was going to change the world? The child was born to elderly parents — would they have enough time to raise him? Perhaps the child would be orphaned in his youth. And, if not, how much patience would they have? How much energy? This was all against nature! And not only was the child's very existence against nature, but he was also going to change the world? Supported by whom? He was all alone! So we laugh, *tzechok*. Yitzchak was named "he will laugh" because his very existence was based on an absurdity.

Yitzchak was the only patriarch who was given his birth name by God. Avraham was given the name *Avram,* and God later changed it to "Avraham." Yaakov was given the name *Yaakov,* and God gave him the additional name of "Yisrael" (after he struggled with an angel). Only Yitzchak was given his name even before he was born, and it was never changed. This is because his name foretells a crucial element of the destiny of the Jewish people.

According to nature, there was no way for the child Yitzchak, the ancestor of the Jewish people, to be born. Nature would dictate that a ninety-year-old woman does not have babies. Nature would dictate that there was no way this child's descendants could survive as a people, scattered as they were among the nations of the world. "All of the expectation, hopes, and history of the Jewish people, its whole life and lifestyle, is based on laughable pretension" (Rav Hirsch).

It's illogical that a minute percentage of the world population has always impacted the world in a major way. Our beginning was illogical and our history continues to be illogical. Yet God desired to make the unpredictable the reality.

> He [God] took him [Avraham] outside and said, "Gaze, now, toward the Heavens, and count the stars if you are able to count them!" And He said to him, "So shall your offspring be!"
>
> *(Bereishis* 15:5)

> According to the plain meaning [of the verse], He brought him forth outside of his tent to see the stars. But according to the Midrash [God] said to him, "Go forth from your astrological speculation. For you have seen by the planets that you are not destined to raise a son. Avram has no son, but Avraham will have a son. Likewise, Sarai will not give birth, but Sarah will give birth. I shall call you [by] another name and [your] destiny will be changed." Another interpretation is, He brought him forth from the hollow space of the world and elevated him above the stars, and this is the connotation of "looking" from above downward.
>
> *(Rashi, Bereishis* 15:5)

God took Avraham outside, pointed to the stars, and said, "You see, the number of stars is uncountable, and that's how numerous the Jewish people will be." Rashi is puzzled by the word *outside*, because if God was showing Avraham the stars, they were obviously outside. Why include the word *outside* in the verse? It teaches that God instructed Avraham to leave his astrology, to go "outside," because his destiny would be outside of *mazal* — outside of constellations, outside of nature. God relates to the Jewish people in a fashion that is beyond nature and into the miraculous.

Rashi then asks another question: The Hebrew word *habet* (which signifies looking) implies focusing on a pivotal item within a broader picture (Malbim). Rashi explains that the word *habet* was used because God literally took Avraham outside the world, into outer space. He lifted Avraham higher than the stars and said, "Gaze" — see the world and the Jewish people within that world. "Avraham, you are not part of this world, you are above the stars, in a different universe."

God told Avraham to look at the stars: "So shall your offspring be." The Jewish people do not answer to the demands of nature, they answer only to God. If we imagine ourselves to be within natural circumstances, we will find our lives laughable. This has been the case throughout our history. Only sixty years ago, it would have been logical to think, *Okay, a few religious people survived the Holocaust, but surely they will soon die out.* Instead, though, today we have a proliferation of yeshivos, of returnees, and of Jewish life and institutions.

We, however, are not the only ones laughing. The nations of the world laugh, too; they look at the Jews, are fascinated by them, and laugh.

Some time ago, I had the pleasure of hearing that a woman I knew, who had been married for twenty-one years, had had her first baby. I was thrilled and I laughed. This was the pleasure that the world took when they saw Sarah give birth.

But, at the same time, when the people saw Sarah with her infant, there was a bit of mocking. "The pretension of this woman, thinking her child is going to change the world. The pretension of this man, with his ideology, his monotheism. Does he think anyone is going to embrace that? Does he think that Yitzchak is actually going to continue to promote this stuff?'

People were laughing at the boldness of Sarah and Avraham. So while there was laughter *for* Sarah, there was also laughter *at* Sarah. This explains

Sarah's statement, "Whoever hears will laugh (*yetzachak*) — their laughter will be happy laughter with me and mocking laughter at me." This type of laughter has continued throughout our history. On the one hand, people laugh with us and say, "Wow, so many Jews have achieved greatness!" Yet, at the same time, there is a mocking: "Who do they think they are?"

Every issue of the major weekly magazine *Newsweek* contains a story about Jews — about the outreach movement, about a "settler" or Jewish "fanatic," or about Israel and the peace plans. Interestingly, though, the millennium issue of *Newsweek* showed a pie chart of world religions, including Christianity, Hinduism, Islam, and atheism. Judaism didn't even get a slice of the pie; it was included in the percent listed as "other." The Jewish people are actually only .5 percent of the world population. Why is there so much attention showered on this very small group of people? It's absurd, but the world continues to laugh with us and at us.

We Will Laugh

Another word for laughter that is related to *tzechok* is *sechok* (the letter *tzaddi* in Hebrew is sometimes interchangeable with the letter *sin*).

> A song of ascents. When God brought back the captivity of Zion, we were like dreamers. Then our mouth will be filled with laughter (*sechok*) and our tongue with glad song. Then will they declare among the nations, "God has done greatly with these." God has done greatly with us, we were gladdened.
>
> (*Tehillim* 126:1–3)

Rav Hirsch explains that while *tzechok* implies irony, *sechok* is a gentle laughter. There is no mockery, only joy. It's the laughter we laugh when the absurd actually happens. When the hopes we have nourished based on God's promises become reality, our mouths are filled with laughter.

Notice that here again appears a grammatical puzzle. "Az [then] *yimalei* [will be filled]" mixes past and future. In the Hebrew language *az*, "then," is a past-tense word. Then something happened. *Yimalei* is a future-tense word. "Then," past tense, our mouths "will be filled" with laughter, future tense. The Malbim explains that if a person truly believes in a dream, in this case in the dream that the Jewish people will survive and Mashiach will come, life is always *az* — as if it's already happened. He therefore describes the dream for the future in the past tense. The potential is as real as reality that has already occurred.

This is exactly how the Jew lives, knowing that the future will be filled with *sechok*. We can laugh before it happens, because we know it will happen. Even in times of sorrow we believe in the future of *sechok*. Even when a situation is very bad, it isn't the end — the end is coming and it's going to be great. We can laugh at the failures and hardships along the way because we know that the bad things are temporary. This is the laughter of Yitzchak.

Today we laugh the laughter of *tzechok*, the laughter of irony, because it alludes to that which is missing or makes no sense, and presently there is much that makes no sense. Our future, however, promises unlimited laughter, and only the gentle laughter, the *sechok*, will fill our mouths. Until that time, we can never fully laugh (*Berachos* 31a).

Nevertheless, we already celebrate this future every Friday night when we sing "A Woman of Valor" —

> Strength and dignity are her clothing; and she laughs (*sechok*) at the time to come.
>
> (*Mishlei* 31:25)

What is the strength and dignity in which the woman of valor is clothed? Clothed in mitzvos and Torah, she is laughing the gentle laughter of the time to come. One who has lived in this world clothed in mitzvos has the right to laugh fully, for the future world is assured her.

> It is written, "Strength and dignity are her clothing, and she laughs at the time to come" (*Mishlei* 31:25). The entire reward of the righteous is kept ready for them for the Hereafter, and the Holy One, blessed be He, shows them while yet in this world the reward He will give them in the future; their souls are then satisfied and they fall asleep. Rabbi Elazar said: This may be compared to a banquet arranged by a king, who invited the guests and showed them what they would eat and drink, whereby their souls were satisfied and they fell asleep [happily]. So does God show the righteous while yet in this world the

reward which He is to give them in the future; and thus they fall asleep with satisfied souls.... Thus when the righteous are about to depart [i.e., die], God shows them their reward.

(*Bereishis Rabbah* 62:2)

How Seriously Do We Take the World?

Laughter (*tzechok*) implies that we don't take the world too seriously. Life is full of absurdities, ironies, and incongruities. But there are two ways in which to laugh at the world, one represented by Yitzchak and the other by Yishmael.

What was the laughter of Yishmael? "No need to take the world seriously. The world is absurd, it doesn't make sense, it's all a big joke. Everything is meaningless, so let's mock it. Take what you can, enjoy what you have, eat, drink, and be merry, because tomorrow you die." Yishmael laughed at the world because he disassociated from it. His laughter was not just the laughter of absurdity or incongruity; it was a mocking of life itself, the laughter of debauchery, idolatry, and murder.

Our Rabbis explain that when the Torah says Yishmael mocked, Yitzchak was the object: "Who do you think you are, Yitzchak? Do you really think that God cares about what people do? Do you really think you're going to build a nation on the basis of such nonsense?" Yishmael mocked Yitzchak, mocked Torah, and mocked the future and the idea of a God-oriented society.

Yishmael's mocking led to idol worship, murder, and promiscuity. A productive society needs three things: (1) a God-given morality, (2) respect for human life, and (3) a healthy family unit. Without morality, there is no order. Without respect for human life, anyone who gets in one's way is simply eliminated, and humanity would extinguish itself. And finally, without a healthy family unit we would become dysfunctional. Yishmael pushed away these boundaries, completely deriding his father's ideals.

The Sefas Emes explains that Yishmael laughed because the most serious sins in this world were silly in his eyes. Yishmael believed that what we see is all there is, and he felt contempt for the absurdities and illogic of the world. Hence he acted selfishly, partaking of any pleasure he wished, permissible or not.

Yitzchak was equally aware of the absurdities, and he too laughed, but his laughter was defined by the knowledge of a different reality. Yitzchak saw this world as merely the shadow of a future world.

Yitzchak's laughter at this world was defined by his experience of the *akeidah* (the binding). Yitzchak was bound at the altar, and his father prepared to kill him. The Midrash (*Yalkut Shimoni, Bereishis* 22:101) says that Yitzchak actually died and came back to life. As the knife reached his neck, Yitzchak's soul departed. When the voice was heard, "Do not send forth your hand to the lad," his soul returned. Whether he died literally or metaphorically, clearly Yitzchak witnessed something beyond the parameters of the physical world as we know it. From then on, although he ate and drank and slept in this world, his focus was always on another world, the future world. As God had promised Avraham, Yitzchak was beyond this universe.

Yitzchak, like Yishmael, was aware that this world doesn't really make sense. Bad things happen to good people, and good things happen to bad people. It's absurd! But Yitzchak knew that human beings are not able to see the whole picture — we see only a tiny ray of the Godliness that exists in this world, while the rest is concealed.

Yitzchak, who also laughed at this world, was the counterpoint to Yishmael. Yitzchak laughed with his wife (Yitzchak and Rivkah are the only patriarch and matriarch whom we actually see laughing with each other!). Yishmael, on the other hand, laughed with other men's wives (*Baal HaTurim*). To Yitzchak, the *yetzer hara* (the pull to do evil) was laughable. Because his vision of the future world was so clear, the pleasures of the physical world had no attraction for him — only the spiritual aspect of this world was important to him. Hence, laughing with his wife is an allusion to the spiritual context of their marriage.

The defining quality of Yitzchak was self-control and awe (*pachad, yirah*). Only he who experiences this fear and awe of God can be happy in this world because he has no fear of anyone or anything else. Yitzchak's face was always illuminated by joy — he was unaffected by the attractions and temptations of this world and was therefore completely free from being brought low by them. Indeed, the truly righteous are always happier than evil people.

He Who Laughs

Tzachak means "he laughed," but there is a similar word, *tza'ak*, "he cried." In Hebrew, the first and last letters are the same, but the middle letter is different. Crying out and laughter are actually the same thing because both are caused by noticing or feeling contrasts, the pairing of incompatible objects. Depending on how you look at it, incompatibility can produce different responses. If a person slips on a banana peel, he will cry out. If you see this happen, and you identify with the man, you will also cry out. If, however, you objectify him and you have no shared reaction to the situation, you will laugh at the ridiculousness of the situation. The more you identify with him, the more you experience *tza'ak*, crying, rather than *tzachak*, laughing (Rav Hirsch).

As another example, someone has a seashell and he is trying to empty the sea of water with it. This person has unrealistic hopes, desires, or plans. If you don't identify with the person, you'll think, *What an idiot!* and you'll laugh. But if you feel for the person, perhaps because you have unfulfilled dreams of your own, you'll cry.

Sometimes we don't know whether to laugh or cry. Sometimes we identify but at the same time stand outside. Sometimes we look at something subjectively and objectively at the same time. We find ourselves laughing, but we end up crying, or we find ourselves crying, but end up laughing. Both come from the same sense of, "This doesn't fit. It's absurd."

> This was the case of Rabbi Yosef the son of Rabbi Yehoshua ben Levi, who became ill and fell into a trance. When he recovered, his father asked him, "What did you see?"
>
> "I saw a topsy-turvy world," he replied, "the upper class underneath and the lower on top."
>
> "My son," he observed, "you saw a clear world. And how are we situated there?"
>
> "Just as we are here, so are we there. And I heard them saying, 'Happy is he who comes hither with his learning in his hand.' And I also heard them saying, 'Those martyred by the state, no man can stand within their border.'"
>
> (*Pesachim* 50a)

Rabbi Yosef, the son of Rabbi Yehoshua ben Levi, once experienced the future world. There, everything appeared to be upside down. The people who sought and gained prestige, honor, money, and power in this world were on the lower level of society in the other world. The poor and the miserable and the ones who sacrificed to learn Torah were on top. Those who died for the sanctification of God's Name, *al kiddush Hashem*, weren't merely unlucky victims who happened to get on the wrong bus or stop at the wrong cafe, for "no man can stand within their barrier" — they were spiritual giants. "An upside-down world," says the son. "No," says the father, "you saw a clear world. It is we who see the world upside down."

God has promised us that a time will come when we will no longer dwell in an upside-down world. For thousands of years we have hung on to our belief and faith in the future reality, even when this belief seemed to be the height of absurdity. Sometimes, God's miracles for us are so real that our trust in Him permeates our very beings, and the future is indeed our present reality. More often, this tenacity is difficult, and we laugh at ourselves for it, nevertheless knowing that God is sure to keep His promise.

Yitzchak ("he will laugh") was given a name in the future tense because everything he did in this world was defined by the reality of the next world. He was able to laugh the laughter of the absurd, but he understood that the world will ultimately have no absurdities. Everything that presently makes no sense *will* make sense. When that world is revealed to us, we will really laugh. We will laugh at the contrast between our new vision and the absurdity of our mistaken understanding. What we thought was one thing is really quite different. Our laughter will be the laughter of *sechok*, gentle laughter. "Then laughter will fill our mouths" because the laughter will be the laughter of "Wow — that's what it was? That's funny. I thought all the suffering was terrible, but it was necessary for reaching this exquisite goodness!"

Laughter Is a Serious Business

The Arizal taught that Yom Kippur (known in the Torah as "Yom Kippurim") is like Purim. Both holidays have in common an essential element, which is the rebirth and renewal of our relationship with God. On Yom

Kippur we experience this renewal by withdrawal from the physical world. On Purim we do it by entering into the physical world. The two holidays are flip sides of the same coin.

On Yom Kippur we look at the world today and we cry, realizing that we haven't accomplished so much of what God set out for us to do. We failed at much of what we meant to do. We cry because whereas we felt strong and powerful, we realize that we are actually weak and vulnerable. How absurd is our assumption that we are in charge!

On Purim, we look at the world and laugh. One day we're the weak and the powerless who are to be destroyed by Haman, but the next day Haman is the one who is destroyed! The world is absurd because what we think is going to happen and what actually happens can be so different, even opposites. When the world appears to be harsh and our enemies appear to be insurmountable, we feel small and vulnerable, but this is not the reality. The reality is that God is running the world, albeit in a veiled manner, and we are not alone. We emerge victorious and we laugh, because who would have thought it possible? We seem to stand outside of our own destiny, mere observers of our own redemption!

We have laughed many laughters throughout our stormy history, the laughter of irony, the laughter of the absurd, the laughter of incongruity, and the laughter of joy. These different laughters have helped relieve the days of tragedy and sadness and pain. When our history reaches its conclusion and the world becomes a dwelling place for God, He will be revealed to us without a curtain or veil, and we will laugh just one laughter, the laughter of rejoicing. Everything will be understood, everything will be clear, everything will be seen as a manifestation of Divine goodness and kindness and harmony, and we will all laugh together.

Building the Nation

The Mystery of the Lost Souls

And Avram took Sarai, his wife, and Lot, his brother's son, and all their possessions that they had gathered, and the souls that they had gotten in Charan; and they went forth to go to the land of Canaan; and to the land of Canaan they came.

(Bereishis 12:5)

"That they had made in Charan" — [those are] the souls which he had brought beneath the sheltering wings of the Shechinah. Avraham converted the men and Sarah converted the women and the Scripture accounts it unto them as if they made them.

(Rashi, Bereishis 12:5)

The first Jews were Avraham and Sarah, whose strength and devotion to the idea of monotheism was transmitted to their children, their servants, and their guests. Although Avraham and Sarah had many converts, students, and disciples, only their descendants held fast to these beliefs and went on to become the Jewish nation. To be more accurate, only some of their descendants became the Jewish nation. What happened to the people who had accepted Avraham's teachings to the extent that it was as if their very souls were "made" by Avraham and Sarah? And why is it that only the descendants born to the family of Yaakov become the Jewish people? Yishmael was the son of Avraham, and Eisav descended from both Avraham and Sarah, yet they and their families never became Jewish. What happened?

Bris Milah

Avraham discovered that there is one God who judges the world justly, and he did not keep this wisdom to himself. Rather, he shared it with as many people as possible:

> For I know him, that he will command his children and his household after him, and they shall keep the way of the Lord, to do righteousness and judgment; that the Lord may bring upon Avraham that which He has spoken of him.
>
> *(Bereishis* 18:19)

God chose Avraham to be the founder of the Jewish people. Avraham and Sarah brought new souls under the wings of Heaven, and the ideas of monotheism, kindness, and justice were becoming household concepts when God commanded Avraham to circumcise himself:

> This is My covenant, which you shall keep between Me and you and your descendants after you: Every male among you shall be circumcised.
>
> *(Bereishis* 17:10)

This presented a difficulty. Until this point, people were interested in Avraham's teachings. People came to him, spoke to him, and participated in discussions with him. Circumcision, he feared, might scare people away, and he expressed this fear to God:

> Said he [Avraham]: "Before I circumcised myself, people came and joined me [in my new faith]. Will they come and join me when I am circumcised?"
>
> "Avraham," said God to him, "let it suffice you that I am your God; let it suffice you that I am your Patron, and not only for you alone, but it is sufficient for My world that I am its God and its Patron."
>
> *(Bereishis Rabbah* 46:3)

Avraham was worried that people would no longer come to him when they heard that his faith required circumcision. God responded, "Don't worry; it's enough for you that I'm your God." Avraham's fears, however, were justified, because in the end, when the Jewish people as a nation went down to Egypt, there were only seventy people, all of the family of Yaakov. Not one of them were from the group Avraham had "brought beneath the sheltering wings of the Shechinah." Clearly, it was the circumcision that scared everyone away, but why?

Who's a Jew?

After the *akeidah*, Avraham sent his servant, Eliezer, to find a suitable wife for Yitzchak. Not only was Eliezer one of the souls that Avraham had "made," but he was also the elder of his household and ruled over everything that Avraham had. Avraham trusted him so much that he sent him on the mission of choosing the right wife for Yitzchak.

Eliezer agreed to do this job, but he expressed a concern:

> The servant said to him: "Perhaps (*ulai*) the woman shall not wish to follow me to this land...."
>
> (*Bereishis* 24:5)

Explains Rashi: Although the word in the text is "*ulai*" (perhaps), the spelling of the word is aberrant; it is spelled "*eilai*" (to me). This unusual spelling hints that Eliezer wanted Yitzchak to marry his own daughter. Avraham, however, was firm that Yitzchak could not marry into Eliezer's family.

Eliezer was the devoted servant of Avraham and his chief disciple, yet his daughter didn't qualify. Who did? A girl from Avraham's own country, a place of idol worshipers! Logically, it would seem that Avraham should marry his son to the daughter of his disciple rather than to the daughter of idol worshipers. After all, Eliezer's daughter was a member of his household, and therefore brought up in a moral and ethical environment, whereas Rivkah, the girl soon to be chosen for Yitzchak, was not. Avraham, however, knew that there was something intrinsic that was necessary for the creation of the Jewish nation, and the daughter of Eliezer didn't have it — but Rivkah did.

One might argue that Eliezer wasn't related to Avraham and Rivkah was, so she qualified, if not logically, then at least by lineage. However, Avraham had other relatives, closer to him than Rivkah, who didn't qualify as founders of the Jewish people: his son Yishmael and his grandson Eisav.

Yishmael, like Eliezer's daughter, was raised in the same environment as Yitzchak. In addition, Avraham loved Yishmael, spent time with him, and taught him the concepts of monotheism and hospitality. Yishmael was even circumcised! Yet the Torah is clear that Yishmael could not be the father of the Jewish people.

> Avraham said to God, "If only Yishmael might live before You!"
>
> God said, "Sarah, your wife, shall bear you a son indeed, and you shall call his name Yitzchak, and I will fulfill My covenant with him as an everlasting covenant for his offspring after him. And as for Yishmael I have heard you: Behold I have blessed him and will make him fruitful and will multiply him exceedingly, but My covenant I will establish with Yitzchak."
>
> (*Bereishis* 17:18–21)

One could argue that Yishmael wasn't worthy to be the father of the Jewish people because, although his father was Avraham, his mother was Hagar, and the positive influence of one parent was not enough to offset the negative influence of the other parent. However, Hagar, although not perfect, was righteous and she, like Eliezer, was a member of Avraham's household. In fact, Avraham remarried her after Sarah's death.

Even more puzzling is the fact that Eisav didn't qualify as a father of the Jewish people. Eisav had two Jewish parents — the same parents as Yaakov — and was raised in a righteous and pure environment. This time we can find no lineage difficulties whatsoever, so why was Eisav not worthy?

We can conclude that there was something about Eliezer's daughter, Yishmael, and Eisav that precluded them from being patriarchs/matriarchs of the Jewish people, and it wasn't their upbringing. All three had righteous parents, and Yishmael and Eisav were blood relatives of the patriarchs. In order to understand what happened to the disciples of Avraham and Sarah, and what prevented Eliezer's daughter, Yishmael, and Eisav from qualifying as our forefathers, we must examine the pillars upon which the Jewish people was founded.

The Heavenly Chariot

"And God went up from upon Avraham" (*Bereishis* 17:22) —
Reish Lakish said: The patriarchs are [God's] Heavenly Chariot. Thus it is written, "And God went up from upon Avraham;"
again, "And God went up from upon him [Yaakov]" (ibid.
35:13); further, "And, behold, the Lord stood upon him
[Yaakov]" (ibid. 28:13).

(Bereishis Rabbah 47:5)

What does the Midrash mean by saying that God "went up from upon"
Avraham? Reish Lakish explains that this is a reference to the Heavenly Chariot described by the Prophet Yechezkel. God's "vehicle," i.e., something
which He rides upon like a chariot, was composed of His holy ones, Avraham,
Yitzchak, and Yaakov. God is "able" to "ride" on the patriarchs because they
dedicated their entire lives to serving Him. Everything they did was for Him:
every thought was of God; every word they spoke was for God; and when they
acted, it was for God. Avraham, Yitzchak, and Yaakov cleaved to God so completely that their entire souls were devoted to Him, and in consequence their
souls became a vehicle through which God is brought down into this world.

Why does God require *three* souls for His chariot? Because each of the patriarchs developed a different character attribute (*middah*), or "wheel" of the
chariot. Avraham exemplified the character trait of *chesed* (kindness),
Yitzchak exemplified the character trait of *gevurah* (strength), and Yaakov exemplified the character trait of *emes* (truth).

The quality of *chesed* is also known as *ahavah* (love). *Chesed* is the act of
reaching from within to give to another. In interpersonal relationships, *chesed*
includes the giving of time, money, energy, and empathy. In our relationship
with God, it is expressed in the form of positive mitzvos (Ramban, *Shemos*
20:8), as if to say, "What can I give You, God? What can I do for You?" In this
mode of giving, our relationship with God is that of child to parent, i.e., He is
our Father.

When we say that Avraham "developed" the quality of *chesed*, we do not
merely mean that he became a giving person. What we mean is that Avraham
rooted the quality of *chesed* in his genetic makeup. In modern medicine, it is

possible for scientists to genetically alter DNA so that a parent can pass on to his child a characteristic that he did not originally possess, in such a way that future generations will inherit that characteristic as well. So too did Avraham develop the quality of *chesed* by "genetically" altering his soul, ensuring that all of his children and children's children would inherit the quality of *chesed*.

Yitzchak also developed a quality that all of his children inherited. He, too, "genetically" altered his soul to create in himself the spiritual DNA of *gevurah*.

Gevurah, the quality of self-control and inner strength, is a reflection of our *yirah*, awe of God. It is defined by holding back and self-nullification to serve God. It is a turning inward toward introspection and self-examination. In the mode of *gevurah*, a person holds back from outward movement and from doing any harm to another. In interpersonal relationships, this will express itself as "I won't do anything that will hurt you — I won't steal, I won't talk about you, I won't lie to you." By definition, *gevurah* will create distance, because it is a complete self-containment.

In our relationship with God, it is expressed in the form of negative mitzvos (Ramban, *Shemos* 20:8), as if to say, "God, I am in awe of you, and therefore I will do nothing to upset You, betray You, or anger You." In this mode of self-control, our relationship with God is that of servant to King. The servant is in awe of the King and will do nothing to arouse his ire.

Chesed and *gevurah* allow us to give expression to the entire Torah: both the positive and negative commandments. However, each one unbridled has the potential to become harmful and even destructive. It is possible, for example, to give in such a way that the giving is perverted. Uncontrolled *chesed* (*chesed detumah*) would be giving to the wrong person (for example, giving a murderer refuge), giving a person the wrong thing (for example, giving drugs to an addict), or giving in the wrong way (for example, giving in order to control another person).

The most obvious example of perverted *chesed* is engaging in forbidden sexual relationships. Intimacy should be an expression of the most giving relationship, which is marriage. In marriage, the result of intimacy is the creation of a home and family; it's about giving. In forbidden relationships, on the other hand, the sexual relationship is about self-gratification and selfish pleasure.

Likewise, it is possible for *gevurah* to become perverted (*"gevurah detumah"*). Too much self-control or introspection can result in a holding back and turning inward to the point where we see the existence of other people as an intrusion or obstacle. When the inward-focus is too intense, we become selfish, critical, and even cruel. Our Sages teach that the ultimate extreme of perverted *gevurah* is murder, the act that rids us of the person we've come to view as an intruder or obstacle.

The worst kind of *chesed* is self-directed *chesed* with no limits. (Of course, we should be kind to ourselves, but in a balanced way.) The worst kind of *gevurah* is *gevurah* towards others. These excesses express themselves in self-indulgence and selfishness. On the other hand, the best kind of *chesed* is kindness toward others, and the best kind of *gevurah* is the self-control we use on ourselves to avoid hurting someone else.

How can we utilize these qualities to their maximum without risking perverting them to negative usage? The answer is *emes*, truth. *Emes* is the balance between *chesed* and *gevurah*. *Emes* means reaching out when *chesed* is required and holding back when *gevurah* is needed. It is doing the appropriate thing at the appropriate time in the appropriate way. *Chesed* and *gevurah* balance each other out — when *chesed* threatens to become perverted, *gevurah* will restrain and limit it. When *gevurah* threatens to become too self-absorbed or critical, *chesed* will pull it out and demand giving.

Thus, the quality of acting in a balanced and appropriate way is *emes*, the truth contained in the Torah. *Toras Emes*, the Torah of Truth, defines for us when to give and when to hold back, when to move outward and when to focus inward. This quality of *emes* is the quality defined and developed by Yaakov, so much so that it became part of his genetic makeup and has been passed down to his descendants. The idea of using *emes* was expressed by the Prophet Michah:

> He has told you, man, what is good; and what does the Lord require of you but do justly and to love *chesed* and to walk humbly with your God.
>
> *(Michah 6:8)*

Walking humbly with God requires us to do *chesed* when that is appropriate and to act in the mode of *gevurah* ("to do justly") when that is called for. It is defining ourselves by the Torah, by the *emes*.

HaRav Chaim Goldvicht, *zt"l*, the founder and *rosh yeshivah* of Yeshivat Kerem beYavneh, told the following story: The Yom Kippur War left many young Israeli boys dead, and a high percentage of the deceased were *hesder* boys, soldiers who combined army service with yeshivah studies. Shortly after the war, Rav Goldvicht was asked to eulogize at the funeral of one of his students. How does one bury a student? With a heavy heart, Rav Goldvicht arrived at the cemetery, where he saw nineteen-year-old boys crying bitter tears as they watched their study partner, roommate, and friend being lowered into the ground.

That very same night was the wedding of another boy in the yeshivah, and again, the *rosh yeshivah*, Rav Goldvicht, was asked to officiate at the ceremony. He rode from the cemetery to the wedding hall, and as he pulled up, he asked himself how he would manage to rejoice at this festive occasion when his heart was crying. He got out of the car, walked into the hall, and saw an astonishing sight. There sat the groom, surrounded by his friends, who were dancing and singing with open hearts and genuine joy. Rav Goldvicht saw, to his amazement, that they were the same boys who had been crying bitter tears just a short while before at the funeral!

How did they do that? How did they go from the despair of the funeral to the elation of the wedding? By walking humbly with God. The Torah tells us how to behave in every situation — when to speak and when to be silent, when to give and when to hold back, when to laugh and when to cry. And we define ourselves by these rules of behavior. It would not be appropriate to be despondent at a wedding, for it is a mitzvah to rejoice and to bring joy to the bride and groom. These young boys defined themselves by the Torah and were able to behave accordingly.

Each of us is born with a personality and with character traits of our own, including a propensity for either *gevurah* or *chesed*. Some people are naturally more dominated by a desire to reach out and to give. For others, it feels more natural to hold back, to engage in introspection (*Michtav MeEliyahu*). *Emes*, however, is achieved only through the intellectual domination over the emotions. *Emes* requires a person to observe, think, analyze, and decide to act in one mode or the other as opposed to reacting to a situation based on one's feelings or emotions. The development of a perfect balance between *gevurah* and *chesed*, *emes*, requires a lifetime of effort.

According to Rav Dessler, each individual must first determine which is his dominant trait. Then he must perfect that *middah*. After perfecting the dominant *middah*, he must develop his recessive trait. In this way, he will reach the state of *tiferes*, glory — a balanced and truthful personality (which is *emes*) — so that he can use the proper character trait, which is now in a refined state, in every situation. In this way, a person is able to conduct himself in accordance with God's will at all times.

One's recessive character trait will never become as strong as his dominant trait. A person who by nature is defined as *chesed*, even after he has labored to develop *gevurah*, will always be predominately outward. Nevertheless, he must develop *gevurah* to the extent possible, because otherwise his *chesed* can become dangerous.

The classic illustration of the need to develop one's recessive character trait is demonstrated by a crucial event in the life of King Shaul. Shaul was commanded to make a war against Amalek and destroy man, woman, and child, because Amalek contained the seeds of God denial, cruelty, and evil. As commanded, Shaul waged the war and was victorious. However, in the aftermath of that war, he had mercy on the king of Amalek and spared his life. This *chesed* to Amalek was misplaced, and generations later the evil Haman descended from Amalek and sought to destroy man, woman, and child of the Jewish people. Although Shaul wished to be kind, he should have balanced his *chesed* with *gevurah* in order to act appropriately and with *emes*.

Each of the *avos* perfected his principal character trait. Avraham perfected *chesed*, and Yitzchak perfected *gevurah*. Then each turned to his secondary trait, i.e., Avraham to *gevurah* and Yitzchak to *chesed*. Yaakov perfected *emes* and *tiferes*, but then had to learn to apply truth and balance in a world of deceit and cruelty (i.e., the house of Lavan). The Torah introduces each of our fathers after he has perfected his dominant quality and reveals the tests he had to undergo to develop his secondary trait (*Michtav MeEliyahu*).

Avraham

Even while still in Charan, his birthplace, Avraham brought hundreds of people under the canopy of monotheism, through outreach and constant giving. The *chesed* of Avraham is reflected in the words *lech lecha* — go. Avraham was always going outside of himself to bestow goodness on others. His tent was open, guests were always welcome in his home, and the orchards that he planted were used to provide shade and feed others. In his relationship with God, he was always reaching out, building altars, and calling out in God's name.

Our Sages teach us that Avraham underwent ten tests in his lifetime. Each of these tests was to teach him how to operate in the mode of *gevurah* (*Michtav MeEliyahu*). Avraham was told to leave his father and his homeland, that is, to withhold his love for his parents and to leave them in their old age. He was commanded to fight a war, circumcise his household, and send his son Yishmael away. All of these tests required that he restrain his love in order to serve God. In the final test, Avraham was asked to sacrifice his beloved son Yitzchak, despite his deep attachment to Yitzchak and despite his belief that the spiritual future of mankind rested on this son.

> Take your son, your only son, the one that you *love*, Yitzchak...and bring him as a sacrifice....
>
> (*Bereishis* 22:2)

On the one hand, one of the conditions of this offering was that Avraham had to be in the mode of love even as he sacrificed his son (*Sefas Emes*). On the other hand, the sacrifice itself was be an expression of his awe, *yirah*, of God.

> He said, "Lay not your hand upon the lad, nor do anything to him; for now I know that you are God-fearing (*yirei Elokim*), seeing that you did not withhold your son, your only son, from me."
>
> (*Bereishis* 22:12)

Being in both modes simultaneously, Avraham has reached the pinnacle of his spiritual growth. His love of God and his fear of God were complete.

Why, then, do we attribute only the quality of *chesed* to Avraham, and not that of *gevurah*? Because although Avraham developed this *gevurah* for his own use, so that he could serve God in a balanced way, he did not root it into the genetic character of the Jewish people. That was the role of Yitzchak.

Yitzchak

We first meet Yitzchak as an individual at the *akeidah*, the binding. Yitzchak's willingness to climb on the altar, let his hands and legs be tied, and give up his life, demonstrated his self-control and willingness to hold back even his desire for life in order to serve God. Yitzchak's total negation of self, overcoming his own needs to the point that his life was of secondary value to his service of God, is what defined him. The quality of *gevurah* was Yitzchak's dominant trait and the one he perfected and "genetically" passed on to his descendants (*Michtav MeEliyahu*).

At the *akeidah*, the Midrash tells us, the angels cried and their tears fell into Yitzchak's eyes.

> When Yitzchak was bound on the altar and his father desired to slaughter him, the Heavens opened and the angels were crying. Their tears fell into his eyes, and therefore his eyes were dim.
>
> (*Rashi* on *Bereishis* 27:1, quoting *Midrash Rabbah* 65)

From the time of the *akeidah*, Yitzchak was blind. Eyes are for seeing the outside world, and Yitzchak's vision focused inward. This blindness is a metaphor for his total withdrawal from the world and his deep connection to the spiritual, to God.

Just as Avraham was described by the word "go" (*lech lecha*) because of his extroverted *middah* of *chesed*, so Yitzchak was defined by the word "sit" (*vayeishev*) because of his quality of *gevurah*, self-restraint. Yitzchak reacted to the events that occurred around him, but he didn't initiate them. For example, Yitzchak did not seek out a wife, as his son Yaakov would later do, but was brought a wife through the mediation of his father's student, Eliezer.

Although Yitzchak prayed for his wife to conceive, he did not build an altar or call out to God as his father Avraham did. Yitzchak's life was riddled with difficulties: famine, the danger of his wife being taken by Avimelech, the jealousy of the Philistines, the stopping up of the wells, his eviction from the land of the Philistines, and the fights over the wells. Yet despite this, his responses were always measured and did not include building altars where he could call out to God. Yitzchak reacted to his troubles with supreme self-control, as one would expect of the master of *gevurah*.

Nonetheless, Yitzchak was required to develop *chesed*. This he accomplished through the digging of wells.

> Yitzchak dug again the wells of water, which they had dug in the days of Avraham, his father, for the Philistines had stopped them up after the death of Avraham; and he called their names after the names by which his father had called them.
>
> (*Bereishis* 26:18)

The Torah tells us that Yitzchak continued to call the wells by the names his father, Avraham, had given them. A well represents *chesed* because it is literally a source of physical life-giving nourishment, and, metaphorically, also represents spiritual nourishment (*Sefas Emes*).

Avraham, *chesed*, had dug these wells in order to reveal the spiritual wealth buried beneath physicality. Travelers would stop at Avraham's wells for refreshment, and when giving them water Avraham would teach them about monotheism. Avraham would explain who God is and what He expects from us. In short, Avraham dug wells in order to give over the life waters, Torah.

After Avraham passed away, the pagan Philistines plugged up his wells of spirituality. Yitzchak, his son, reopened them, giving them the same names. Afterwards, Yitzchak went to Beer Sheva, where Avraham had dwelled, and at this point, God appeared to him:

> Hashem appeared to him that night and said, "I am the God of your father Avraham. Fear not, for I am with you; I will bless you and make your offspring numerous for the sake of Avraham your father."
>
> He built there an altar and he called God by name, and there he pitched his tent; there Yitzchak's servants dug a well.
>
> (*Bereishis* 26:24–25)

As Yitzchak redug his father's wells, he developed his own *chesed*, his ability to reach out. Only after he had done this and received God's blessing did he venture to Beer Sheva, the place representing Avraham's great *chesed* (*Michtav MeEliyahu*):

> He dug another well, and for that they strove not, and he called the name of it Rechovos; and he said, "For now the Lord has

made room for us, and we shall be fruitful in the land." And he went up from there to Beer Sheva.

(Bereishis 26:22–23)

After developing his recessive trait, *chesed*, and receiving God's blessing, Yitzchak finally built an altar and called out in the name of God.

Yitzchak continued to work on his trait of *chesed* until he reached old age, when he sought to bless his sons:

> It came to pass, when Yitzchak had become old, and his eyes dimmed from seeing, that he summoned Eisav, and said to him... "Make me delicacies such as I love and bring it to me and I will eat, so that my soul may bless you before I die."

(Bereishis 27:1–4)

The pinnacle of Avraham's self-development of *gevurah* was the *akeidah*. Rav Dessler says that the ultimate *chesed* for Yitzchak was giving the blessing to Eisav. A blessing is a mechanism to open something up for another person, and Yitzchak understood that whereas Yaakov didn't need the blessing because he could open up spiritual gates himself, Eisav did need the blessing.

Avraham could never reach the *gevurah* plateau of Yitzchak, and Yitzchak could never reach the *chesed* plateau of Avraham. Each perfected himself according to the strength God gave him, and this is what the Jewish people have done throughout our history. Externally, Avraham and Yitzchak looked the same, for each was obligated to serve God in both aspects, to give when appropriate and to hold back when appropriate.

Yaakov

As his fathers before him defined themselves by a spiritual quality and rooted that quality into the spiritual makeup of the Jewish people, so, too, did Yaakov. *Emes*, the ability to act with a completely suitable balance between *chesed* and *gevurah*, is the quality passed down to us by Yaakov.

After Yaakov received his father's blessing, he left home to find a wife. On his way, he stopped, gathered stones, and fell asleep:

> He lighted on a certain place and tarried there all night because

the sun was set; and he took of the stones of that place and put them under his head, and he lay down in that place to sleep.

(Bereishis 28:11)

When he awoke, there was only one stone:

Yaakov rose early in the morning, took the stone that he had put under his head, set it up for a pillar, and poured oil on the top of it.

(Bereishis 28:18)

Apparently the stones became one stone. The Midrash explains:

Rabbi Nechemyah said: He took three stones, saying: "The Holy One, blessed be He, united His name with Avraham; with Yitzchak too He united His name. If these three stones become joined, then I am assured that God's name will be united with me, too." And when they did thus join, he knew that God would unite His name with him.

The Rabbis said: [He took] the least number that "stones" can connote, that is, two, saying: "From Avraham there came forth Yishmael and the children of Keturah; from Yitzchak there came forth Eisav. As for me, if these two stones join, I will be assured that nothing worthless will come forth from me."

(Bereishis Rabbah 68:11)

What the Midrash is teaching is that Yaakov understood that the "stone" of Avraham, *chesed*, if not united with the stone of Yitzchak, *gevurah*, will yield waste, *chesed* that is not tempered. Yishmael inherited Avraham's great quality of *chesed* but did not limit it with *gevurah*, and so it became perverted. He engaged in promiscuity, which is *chesed* with no proper limitations.

Likewise, the "stone" of Yitzchak's *gevurah* was inherited by Eisav, but was not limited by *chesed*. Eisav was a murderer, as were his descendants, the chiefs of Edom and the Roman Empire. Yaakov understood that only by uniting these two "stones" of *chesed* and *gevurah* would no waste come of him *(Michtav MeEliyahu)*. His mission as he left Israel to go to Charan was to develop his own quality, *emes*, the balance of *chesed* and *gevurah*, thereby creating his own "stone."

Yaakov had twelve sons, all of whom were worthy of being the tribes of God.

As it says, "God chose His nation; Yaakov is the portion (*chevel*) of His inheritance" (*Devarim* 32:9). [The word *chevel*, portion, also means "rope," and the *midrash* explains the verse with this usage of the word.] Just as this rope is [made of] three strands, so Yaakov was the third of the patriarchs and received the reward of all of them. When Avraham was born, what does it say? "A brother is born for adversity" (*Mishlei* 17:18). When Yitzchak was born, what does it say? "Two are better than one" (*Koheles* 4:9). When Yaakov was born, what does it say? "The three-stranded rope will not quickly be broken" (*Koheles* 4:12).

(Sifrei, HaAazinu)

Both the *chesed* of Avraham and the *gevurah* of Yitzchak had the strength to fight adversity, and the combination of the two was even stronger. But once Yaakov developed the three-stranded rope of *emes*, its strength is unbreakable.

This strength is the strength of Torah. Yaakov is called "a simple man dwelling in tents" (*Bereishis* 25:27). Rashi explains that these are the tents of Shem and Ever, who were great scholars devoted to learning Torah. Yaakov learned Torah for fourteen years with those spiritual giants. And his devotion to and integration of Torah taught him how to combine the two qualities of his father and grandfather. The Torah is a prescription for life — it tells us what is fitting in every situation. It teaches us when to cry and when to laugh, when to build and when to destroy, when to give and when to withhold.

Combo Platter

As we have seen, each person is born with a propensity toward either *chesed* or *gevurah*. Only *emes* is an acquired character trait, expressed by intellectual domination over emotion.

Each person must first develop and perfect his qualities of *chesed* and *gevurah* in order to be a balanced person, after which he learns, through the study of Torah, to act with *emes*. Externally, each of us looks the same, i.e., we keep the same mitzvos, both positive and negative, but each person learns to give or restrain in appropriate measure as the situations he faces require.

However, since each individual will always be dominant in one trait or the other, the underlying motivation of our actions will be different. For instance, when a person who is predominantly dominated by *chesed* is required to discipline his child, he will do so because that is the greatest gift he can give his child. He will externally present himself in the mode of *gevurah*, but internally he will be motivated by *chesed*. This is called *"gevurah bechesed,"* the *chesed* inside of *gevurah*.

Conversely, a person who is predominantly motivated by *gevurah* will sometimes have to act in the mode of *chesed*. For example, a person whose natural inclination might be to remain silent will speak words of consolation to a mourner, overcoming his inclination to hold back in order to offer words of comfort. This is called *"chesed begevurah."*

Most situations in life require both *chesed* and *gevurah* in some proportion. There are mixed nuances in every action we take. Although we love our children, we must use discipline. In rehabilitating a patient, the therapist must be firm but encouraging.

The Matriarchs

Each of the patriarchs married a partner who had the complementary dominant quality to his own (*Zohar*). In this way, they achieved a perfect balance. Our matriarch Sarah, married to Avraham, had the dominant quality of *gevurah*. It is she who saw the evil effects of Yishmael and demanded that he be sent away. Although Avraham did not want to listen to Sarah, God knew that for the Jewish people to survive Yishmael had to be sent away, an act of *gevurah*. Sarah had also perfected her recessive quality, the character trait of *chesed*: she was an equal to Avraham in converting people to the monotheistic idea. "Avraham converted the men, and Sarah converted the women" (*Rashi, Bereishis* 12:5). Just as Avraham developed *"gevurah bechesed,"* Sarah developed *"chesed begevurah."*

Rivkah was defined by *chesed*. The Torah introduces her at a well, running to give water to a stranger (Avraham's servant, Eliezer) and even to his camels. Her primary trait of *chesed* was the counterpoint for Yitzchak's *gevurah*. Rivkah, too, perfected her secondary quality, the character trait of *gevurah*: when Eliezer wanted to take her away to become Yitzchak's wife, her family asked, "Do you want to go?" She replied, *"Eileich —* I am going." Rashi asks why didn't she simply say "yes," and explains that "*eileich*" means "I am going, whether you want me to or not." This is *gevurah*.

Rivkah also acted with *gevurah* when she received the prophecy about her two sons, Eisav and Yaakov, and withheld it from Yitzchak. She acted with *gevurah* when she tricked Yitzchak about the birthright. Why was Rivkah's *gevurah* mixed with secrecy? Although she practiced *gevurah* whenever it was necessary for the sake of the Jewish people, *chesed* was her dominant, outward trait, while *gevurah*, her recessive trait, was practiced less obviously.

Yaakov, who was both *chesed* and *gevurah*, had two wives, Rachel and Leah. Each wife was complementary to one of his character traits. "Leah's eyes were tender" (*Bereishis* 28:17) — reminiscent of Yitzchak's blind eyes, i.e., inwardness and *gevurah*, and "Rachel was beautiful in appearance" (ibid.), i.e., outwardness and *chesed*. Leah, who had weak eyes, was introspective and internal; she was beauty undiscovered and hidden. Rachel, who was outwardly beautiful, exemplifies the extroverted quality of giving.

The Torah illustrates the two sisters practicing their primary qualities. Rachel, *chesed*, gave her husband to her sister, thereby providing her sister with children and a Jewish home, the ultimate *chesed*. Leah demonstrated *gevurah* when she traded the mandrakes for a night with Yaakov:

> Then Rachel said to Leah, "Please give me of your son's mandrakes..." Rachel said, "Therefore he shall lie with you tonight in return for your son's mandrakes."
>
> When Yaakov came out of the field in the evening, Leah went out to meet him and said, "You must lie with me for I have hired you with my son's mandrakes." So he lay with her that night.
>
> (*Bereishis* 30:15–16)

Leah overcame a woman's natural modesty to go to the field and bring her husband to her tent. Her goal was not her own pleasure but the birth of another tribe in Israel. And toward that goal, she would be audacious, holding back modesty and exercising *gevurah*.

To Be a Jew

We can now answer the original question: Why is it that the souls that Avraham and Sarah "made" were not part of the Jewish people who went down to Egypt, why was Eliezer's daughter unfit to marry Yitzchak, and why did the families of Yishmael and Eisav not become Jewish?

The souls that Avraham and Sarah "made" accepted the idea of one God, but they accepted God as only as the Father, the loving One. They did not accept the idea that serving God also requires self-denial, *gevurah*, and hence circumcision was repugnant to them. Avraham was aware of this and spoke of his concern to God. As we saw, God replied that it was enough that Avraham was in the world. This is because those who were to become the Jewish people were required to exercise *gevurah* as well as *chesed*. When the people heard of Yitzchak and the *akeidah*, the total giving over, self-denial, and self-sacrifice required of the Jewish people, they could not accept it. *Gevurah* was beyond them.

Why couldn't Eliezer's daughter marry Yitzchak? Eliezer was a Canaanite, a member of a nation known for their loose morals. Part of the genetic makeup of the Canaanites was *chesed detumah*, unbridled giving in the form of promiscuity. Eliezer's daughter was defined by *chesed detumah* and could not serve as the partner of Yitzchak. Although Yitzchak needed a wife whose primary quality was *chesed*, the *chesed* had to be limited by appropriate *gevurah*, which Eliezer's daughter did not have.

Yishmael learned *chesed* from his father Avraham, and Eisav inherited the *gevurah* of his father Yitzchak, but both of them failed to develop the complementary quality. As we learned before, Yishmael's *chesed* was expressed in promiscuity, and Eisav used his *gevurah* to become a murderer. Therefore, neither of them could be the spiritual progenitor of the Jewish people.

Yishmael took a step in the right direction and attained a measure of *gevurah* and self-control: he allowed himself to be circumcised. However, he believed that this was the deepest level of self-sacrifice, and that no further self-development was required.

> Yishmael said to him [Yitzchak]: "I am more beloved than you, since I was circumcised at the age of thirteen, but you were circumcised as a baby and could not refuse."

Yitzchak retorted: "All that you lent to the Holy One, blessed be He, was three drops of blood. But I am now thirty-seven years old, yet if God desired that I be slaughtered, I would not refuse."

(*Bereishis Rabbah* 55:5)

Although Yishmael accepted *gevurah*, it was in a measured way. In contrast, Yitzchak had so much *gevurah*, albeit tempered with *chesed*, that he was willing to give up everything for God, even his life. This willingness to sacrifice everything, even when one has no intellectual understanding of why the self-sacrifice is required (clearly the *akeidah* was beyond human logic), is fundamental to the Jewish people.

Like Yishmael, Eisav inherited his father's primary character trait, Yitzchak's *gevurah*. But he had none of the *chesed* of his grandfather, Avraham. Yaakov, on the other hand, inherited *gevurah* from Yitzchak, but, in addition, he studied "in the tents" with Avraham and learned *chesed*.

Yitzchak's *gevurah* was focused inward; it was self-control and not control of others, and it was tempered with *chesed*. In sharp contrast, Eisav committed murder, which is the denial of the existence of another person. He maintained his ego at the expense and worth of other human beings. Eisav became Rome, a nation of unbridled *gevurah*.

The Twelve Tribes of Israel and, through them, the entire Jewish people descended from one man, Yaakov, who was a balance between *gevurah* and *chesed*. God gave Yaakov a number of tests and difficulties to ensure that he not only had perfected *emes*, but he also knew how to use it well. Because of this, he was able to bear the twelve tribes of Israel.

"He took of the stones of the place" (*Bereishis* 28:11). Rabbi Yehudah said: He took twelve stones, saying, "The Holy One, blessed be He, has decreed that twelve tribes should spring forth. Neither Avraham nor Yitzchak has produced them. If these twelve stones cleave to one another, then I know that I will produce the twelve tribes." When the twelve stones united, he knew that he was to produce the twelve tribes.

(*Bereshis Rabbah* 68:11)

Yaakov placed stones beneath his head when he went to sleep on his way to

Charan. When he woke up the next morning, he "took the stone [singular] that he had placed around his head..." (*Bereishis* 28:18). The Midrash explains that there were twelve stones and they united into one. This, a different version of the Midrash we saw before, contains within it the same fundamental idea that only through the complete unity of the qualities of *chesed* and *gevurah* and *emes* would the twelve tribes, the tribes of God, be born.

Without the preparation of his fathers Avraham and Yitzchak, Yaakov couldn't have achieved what he did, but through his own efforts, he was able to synthesize *chesed* and *gevurah* with *emes*, and incorporate this quality into his genetic makeup. Each of his twelve sons inherited the quality of *emes*. Each tribe was different than the next, but each carried an essential part of *emes*, so that the totality of all of the twelve tribes is the totality of *emes*.

Our patriarchs not only developed and perfected the character traits necessary for the foundation of the Jewish people, but they internalized the qualities of kindness, self-sacrifice, and truth so profoundly that these qualities became part of their genetic makeup and have been transmitted to their descendants ever since. Even thousands of years later, every Jew has the capacity to suppress his own desires and sacrifice his possessions, his ego, or even his very life, for his people and his God — even when such sacrifices go beyond intellect and logic. In some people, this capacity is deeply hidden and dormant, but there have been many cases throughout Jewish history where Jews submitted to torture or gave up their lives rather than renounce Judaism and God. From where does the Jew get such incredible spiritual strength? This nobility is his inheritance.

Klal Yisrael was built on the three patriarchs, Avraham, Yitzchak, and Yaakov, because they devoted their lives to developing the character traits required by God of His chosen people: kindness, strength, and truth. Our Rabbis teach that the world stands on three things — Torah, prayer, and acts of kindness (*Pirkei Avos* 1:2). Torah is truth, the quality developed by Yaakov. Prayer is introspection, the quality of Yitzchak. Acts of kindness is *chesed*, Avraham's spiritual gift to his children. Therefore, not only do the Jewish people stand on the foundations built for us by our patriarchs, but so, too, does the entire world.

Shame: A Jewish Approach

Just as every individual was given certain personality traits that are part of his genetic makeup, so too, were nations. Kindness, mercy, and shame characterize every Jew and are part of his essence. The quality of shame is so defining that the Talmud teaches that if you see a Jew without it, you might wonder if he is really Jewish! It stands to reason, then, that these qualities are not only part of our national identity, but are tools of our trade, things that we need to observe the Torah in its fullest sense.

We learn about shame from Adam and Chavah, the first people created, the first ones to sin and feel shame. Created in the image of God, Adam and Chavah were placed in the Garden of Eden and given everything necessary for their physical and spiritual sustenance. They could eat of any of the fruits of the tree, save the Tree of Knowledge, and their role in the world was to develop their spirituality, to serve their Master without any distractions resulting from the need to earn their daily bread.

They were created naked and remained so. Their bodies were to them the mechanism through which they would act in accordance with the Torah and they were innocent in their nakedness:

> And they were both naked, the man and his wife, and were not ashamed.
>
> *(Bereishis 2:25)*

Adam and Chavah were not ashamed of any part of the body. Arms and legs, nose and eyes, were all to be used for service of God. As the eyes were made to see the beauty and the bounty of the Garden, the nose to smell the sweet fragrance of flowers and trees, male and female organs were made for intimacy and procreation. There was no embarrassment because it was clear that these were tools for divine service.

Yet after they sinned, after they ate of the fruit of the Tree of Knowledge, something shifted. They became aware of their nakedness and became ashamed of it:

> The eyes of both of them were opened, and they knew that they were naked. They sewed together fig leaves and made themselves aprons. They heard the voice of the Lord God walking in the garden in the cool of the day. And the man and his wife hid themselves from the presence of the Lord God amongst the trees of the garden.
>
> (Bereishis 3:3–8)

Whereas previously, Adam and Chavah had been innocent and pure in their thoughts, they suddenly become aware of their bodies and felt shame. Clearly, there was a spiritual shift, and, as a result of this newfound sense of shame, they covered themselves and hid from God.

What happened? Why did shame (*bushah*) now enter their being? Why was eating the forbidden fruit the catalyst for this particular spiritual shift?

We see a similar shame enter the hearts of Yosef's brothers when he confronts them with his true identity in Egypt. Many years previous to this confrontation, Yosef's brothers had plotted against him. They thought to kill him, but then revised their plan and sold him into slavery. Yosef's brothers went home and presented their father, Yaakov, with Yosef's bloody clothes, allowing him to assume Yosef was dead. This charade continued for twenty-two years, until the brothers went to Egypt to buy grain during a terrible famine.

Meanwhile, Yosef had risen from slavery to power and become the viceroy of the entire Egyptian nation. When his brothers stood before him to buy grain, Yosef recognized them. After testing their loyalty to each other, he finally revealed himself to them:

> Yosef said to his brothers: "I am Yosef. Is my father still alive?" And his brothers could not answer him for they were shocked (*nivhalu*) at his presence.
>
> (Bereishis 45:3)

Rashi explains that the shock they felt was not surprise, not fear, but shame (*bushah*), "They were shocked — because of shame."

All of the years since the time they had planned to kill Yosef and had sold him into slavery, they were not ashamed. Watching their father cry daily for twenty-two years over the loss of his son, they were not ashamed. Suddenly, Yosef revealed his identity to them with the simple words "I am Yosef," and they are deeply ashamed and frightened.

Where did their confidence in their actions disappear to? Why did they shift from a state of surety to one of shame?

The Midrash makes a connection between the shame of the brothers when confronted by Yosef to our shame when we will stand before God, in the final days:

> "And he raised his voice and wept and his brothers were not able to answer him" (*Bereishis* 45:3). Abba Kohen Bardla said: Woe to us on the Day of Judgment! Woe to us on the Day of Rebuke! Bilam, the wisest man of the gentile nations, was not able to stand before the rebuke of his donkey, as it is written, " 'Was I ever in the habit to do this to you?' and he said, 'No,' " (*Bemidbar* 22:30). Yosef was the youngest of the tribes and they were not able to stand before his rebuke, as it is written, "And his brothers could not answer him for they were shocked at his presence."
>
> When the Holy One, blessed be He, will come and rebuke each individual according to what he is, as it says, "I will rebuke you and display [your deeds] before your eyes" (*Tehillim* 50:21), how much more so [will we not be able to stand before His rebuke]!
>
> (*Bereishis Rabbah* 93:3)

Just as the brothers, the tribes of God, felt shame while standing in front of Yosef, we will feel shame when we will stand before God on the Day of Judgment. Still, Yosef never rebuked them, nor did he ever confront them with the hatred they displayed. He merely said a few words: "I am Yosef." Why do our Rabbis call this "rebuke"?

And why does the Midrash include Bilam in the equation? Bilam was the prophet of the nations of the world and he was asked by them to curse the Jewish people. God came to him in a vision, but Bilam decided to ignore God and carry out his mission. God became angry and sent an angel to stand in the way. Bilam did not see the angel, not wanting to heed the instructions of God, but his donkey did see the angel and stopped. Bilam was so angered that he struck her with his staff. God opened the mouth of the donkey and she said, "Was I ever in the habit to do this to you?" Despite the miraculous nature of a talking donkey, Bilam again chose to ignore the rebuke and went on his way to curse the Jewish people.

Bilam was rebuked, yet he ignored the rebuke. Why do the Rabbis connect Bilam's refusal to heed rebuke, Yosef's brothers' shame when he revealed himself to them, and the Jews on the final Day of Judgment?

On Yom Kippur, we stand before the Holy One, blessed be He, and we are constantly reminded of our state of shame:

> My God, before I was formed I was unworthy, and now that I have been formed, it is as if I have not been formed. I am dust in my life and will surely be so in my death. Behold — before You, I am like a vessel filled with shame and humiliation. May it be Your will, Hashem, my God and the God of my forefathers, that I not sin again. And what I have sinned before You, may You cleanse with Your abundant mercy, but not through suffering or serious illness.
>
> (*Amidah* of Yom Kippur)

> Do not enter into judgment with us, for no living being can justify itself before You. What can we say before You, Hashem, our God? What can we declare and what justification can we offer? Our God, we are ashamed of our deeds and humiliated to lift our faces to You, our God.
>
> (*Ma'ariv* for Yom Kippur)

These prayers precede the *vidui*, confession, of Yom Kippur, because shame is a spiritual state, a place on the line of proximity to God. As we stand before our Creator to measure our lives, we feel shame.

What Is Shame?

Rav Shimshon Refael Hirsch explains that shame is the feeling of a person who has fallen short of his own expectations. When a person has not acted in the manner he expects of himself, he feels ashamed. Each of us has a picture of ideal self, of who we would like to be or who we would like to become. When confronted with a version of ourself that does not look like this picture, we feel shame.

This feeling of shame is a gift from God, implanted deep in our consciousness. It prods us to an understanding that we have failed to live up to our potential. Although God created us in His image and gave us a mission to serve Him, there are times when we fail to act in the ways of greatness that He set out for us. Of course, God knew that since we are human beings, we would not always succeed in achieving this lofty goal, so He gave us a tool that would make us our own monitors and guardians.

Since we all have a picture of our ideal self, God entrusted us with the mechanism with which to judge ourselves. The consciousness of this ideal is what we call conscience. The condemning verdict when we fall short is called shame, *bushah* (Rav Shimshon Refael Hirsch on *Bereishis* 3:25).

What Is Man? A Little Lower than Angels

The modern world of psychology has made it a goal for every person to be normal. Sometimes it changes the definition of what normal is, but nevertheless, the goal doesn't change. Indeed, the objective of child-rearing and of self-development has become to raise normal, healthy children and to be okay ourselves. While these are fine goals that cannot be challenged, they remain limited and small. They confine us to a role of the standard and common. They say little about the potential for greatness that the Torah assigns us:

> What is man, that You are mindful of him, and the son of man, that You visit him? For You have made him a little lower than the angels and have crowned him with glory and honor.
>
> (*Tehillim* 8:5–6)

Our capacity as human beings goes way beyond normal. We can be great, "a little lower than angels." This is not to say that we are born that way, but rather that we have the ability to achieve something just a little less than the pure spiritual level of angels. In fact, if we serve God from free will, we have a tremendous gain over the angels, because the angels are preprogrammed to serve God, while we are not. Therefore, when we choose divine service, we are "crowned with glory and honor."

How do we achieve this? How do we move beyond "normal" to greatness? We achieve this through the intellectual domination of thought, action, and emotion. The first step is to know ourselves: our weaknesses and our strengths. Through honest evaluation of who we are, we know when we will need extra-firm safeguards and which tools we can utilize to grow. We must also know our goals as Jews. Who do we want to become within our lifetime? What qualities do we want to develop? What negative tendencies do we want to curb? What is right and what is wrong?

Shame is the mechanism that we will use in checking our conscience. How much shame we feel will correspond directly to our knowledge of right and wrong. The more we understand and become sensitive to Truth, the more *bushah*, shame, we feel at falling short of its demands. The more sensitive we are to the will of God, the bigger our conscience, the more we are embarrassed at having strayed even a "little bit" from the path of Torah. Therefore, shame is a force equal to its counterparts, intellect and knowledge (*Orchos Tzaddikim, Sha'ar Shishi, Sha'ar Bushah*).

Shame is the external revelation of an internal connection to God.

The World and Man

Although the body and soul have different pulls, one to the physical and the other to the spiritual, the Torah provides a mechanism for them to dwell in harmony. That mechanism is mitzvos.

Mitzvos enable a person to use the physical world in a way that releases the sparks of holiness within it. While the physical world may seem devoid of spirituality, this is really a facade. "The whole earth is filled with His glory" (*Tehillim* 72:19). All physicality emanates from and is continually nurtured by its spiritual source, and its core retains this spiritual identity. Torah teaches us how to release this spirituality. For instance, sometime before Sukkos, a person buys an *esrog*. The day before Sukkos, the *esrog* is nothing but a fruit, a citron with no holiness attached to it. It's just a fancy lemon. But on Sukkos day, when the person puts the citron together with the *lulav*, says a *berachah,* and waves them, he releases the holiness of the fruit. The citron is no longer an ordinary fruit but has sanctity and, as such, must be treated differently. One can no longer dispose of it in any way he wishes to but must treat it appropriately.

The more a person perfects himself, the more he is able to distinguish between the sparks of holiness in the physical world and the part of physicality that is nothing but the facade. When a refined and developed person uses the world properly, to bring God into it, he experiences pride in his spiritual achievements. Therefore, he feels no shame at his body, for he has learned how to use it properly, in the most holy way.

This is why Adam and Chavah felt no shame before they sinned. Their physical bodies were used for holy acts, for bringing God's presence into the world. There was no reason for shame.

On the other hand, if a refined person reveals within himself physicality devoid of Godliness or acts in a way that is merely about his own pleasure, he is embarrassed to stand before his Creator. His soul, which craves a connection to God, feels pulled down by his body, and he experiences shame at the lack of sanctity in his physical actions.

This is the essential part of shame that a person must internalize: Everything is imbued with the life force of God. So how could he use the energy of God in the opposite manner that He wills it to be used? (*Sefas Emes*).

God imbued a holy purpose into everything He created. He then gave it all to man to use according to its purpose. When man uses the "life" of the world for a misguided purpose, he abuses the very gift God gave him. Since the physical world was created in order for us to elevate it to its most spiritual level, using it as pure physicality countermands the will of God.

Now we understand why Adam and Chavah felt shame at their nakedness after the sin. Having disobeyed the mitzvah of God, they "tasted" their own desires. They knew what it was to allow their own physicality to reign over the moral imperative. They felt shame.

This warning signal from their internal guardian of morality was the voice of God that speaks within man. Having fallen short of their own expectations of their Divine soul, they were embarrassed.

The Lord God called to the man and said to him, "Where are you?"

He said: "I heard Your voice in the garden and I was afraid because I was naked; and I hid myself."

(*Bereishis* 3:9–10)

When God asked, "Where are you?" He was not asking for Adam's geographical location, because of course He knew Adam's physical hiding place. What God was asking was, "Where are you spiritually? You are not where you are supposed to be." Adam answered the question, "I was afraid; I know I failed." Fear of facing God and being measured by Him overpowered Adam. Shame made him feel naked, exposed to the reality of his own failure. "I was naked," Rashi explains, means that he was naked of the mitzvah, empty of holiness.

Whenever a person is caught at a mistake, he feels shame. Sometimes the reason for the shame is that others have seen him in his inappropriateness or foolishness. His honor was trampled on, and others have witnessed it. This kind of shame is the result of environmental expectations, so that changing the environment would immediately reduce the shame.

This is not the same as the shame before God that a person feels at the collapse of his spiritual building. Obviously, this embarrassment is not because he feels his devaluation as a human being striving to stand upright in God's presence. Nevertheless, shame before society has its place. Sometimes it keeps our conscience alive when we lack the connection to God.

Ulla said: Jerusalem was destroyed only because [its inhabitants] were not ashamed of each other, for it is written, "Were they ashamed when they committed abomination? No, they were not at all ashamed [therefore, they shall fall]" (*Yirmeyahu* 6:15).

(*Shabbos* 119b)

If a person sins and is embarrassed in front of his friend or neighbor, his shame is small but alive! But if he feels no embarrassment, no shame, there is no hope for his repentance.

Shame: The First Step to Reconciliation

This nation is distinguished by three characteristics: They are merciful, they feel shame, and they are benevolent.... They feel shame, as it is written, "That His fear may be before you" (*Shemos* 20:17).... Only he who cultivates these three characteristics is fit to join this nation.

(*Yevamos* 79a)

Shame is a Jewish trait. Since the Torah delineates a high standard of expectations, it would be impossible to monitor ourselves without shame. The more learned and the more integrated a Jew is, the more his shame functions to push him to *teshuvah*, repentance.

Shame is not a crippling kind of guilt or a neurosis. It is future oriented, opening up the wonderful possibility of positive change. As the first step to *teshuvah*, shame erases any guilt. At Sinai, God revealed Himself directly to the Jewish people, so that "fear of Him may be before your faces" (*Shemos* 20:17). Our Rabbis explain that this fear is *bushah*, shamefacedness.

> "That fear of Him may be before your faces." By this is meant shamefacedness — so that you should not sin. This teaches that shamefacedness leads to fear of sin. Therefore, it was said that it is a good sign if a man is shamefaced. Others say no man who experiences shame will sin easily, and he who is not shamefaced — it is certain that his ancestors were not present at Mount Sinai.
>
> (*Nedarim* 20a)

Why is shame called "shamefacedness" (*boshes panim*)? What is the connection between shame and the face? The Hebrew word for face is *panim*, which stems from the word "inside." Why is a face called *panim*, inside, when it is clearly outside? What is on a person's face is what he feels inside. If he is delighted, his face lights up. If he is depressed, his face reflects his inner emotion. Shamefacedness, *boshes panim*, is the external revelation of an internal spiritual state.

Shame leads to the fear of sin. Therefore, shame is spiritually healthy, as the Gemara calls it: "a good sign." Since revelation at Sinai forged shame into the national Jewish identity, a person who has no shame wasn't at Sinai and isn't part of the Jewish people. This is why the Gemara states, "He who is not shamefaced — it is certain that his ancestors were not present at Mount Sinai."

At Sinai, we created a relationship with God. We were given an understanding of our potential as Jews, and we were taught that everything in this world was created to serve God. At Sinai, standards were set up with the understanding that failure to achieve those standards is a "sin before God." National and individual conscience was put in place.

The opposite of *boshes panim*, shamefacedness, is *azus panim*, impudence (literally, bold-facedness). Impudence is the spiritual state of a person who has no consciousness or caring about his divine soul or aspirations for betterment. He feels no shame because he is closed to the divine part of himself. Therefore, *teshuvah* is impossible for him. He simply has no mechanism to bring him back to God.

This is why in our daily prayers, we beseech God for the strength in containing impudence:

> May it be Your will, O Lord our God, and God of our fathers, to deliver us from the impudent and from impudence, from an evil man, from evil blemish, from the evil impulse, from an evil companion, from an evil neighbor, and from the destructive Accuser, from a hard lawsuit and from a hard opponent, whether he is a son of the covenant or not a son of the covenant!
>
> (Morning prayers; from *Berachos* 17a)

We ask that God protect us from those who feel no shame, who have no conscience. And we ask that we should not become brazen ourselves. We should not be closed to the possibility of shame, because if we are we will have no mechanism for change.

A Study in Shame and Impudence: Adam and Kayin

After Adam and Chavah sinned, they had a new awareness. They saw the world in a different light:

> The eyes of them both were opened, and they knew that they were naked. They sewed together fig leaves and made themselves aprons. They heard the voice of the Lord God walking in the garden in the cool of the day. And the man and his wife hid

themselves from the presence of the Lord God amongst the trees of the garden.

The Lord God called to the man and said to him, "Where are you?"

He said, "I heard Your voice in the garden and I was afraid because I was naked; and I hid myself."

(*Bereishis* 3:7–10)

Adam and Chavah became aware of physical lust, a desire to use the physical world for a purpose other than spirituality. This was eye-opening for them. They became conscious of something that was visible that should not be so. They covered themselves with fig leaves, and then they hid, as if to "take cover" in the trees. They were not hiding from punishment, but from their own shame, their feelings of unworthiness, of standing in the presence of God, undeserving of His closeness (*Seforno*). They understood the real calling of man and their failure. They were ashamed.

Why was Adam afraid? He felt his smallness as a human being compared to the greatness of God. A person who measures his value by the value of the Infinite is imbued with awe. This is called *yiras haromemus*, awe of the exaltedness of God. Adam was in awe of his Creator, all the more so because of his own failing.

Like Adam, Kayin also sinned, but, unlike Adam, he did not hide.

Kayin talked with Hevel, his brother; and it came to pass, when they were in the field, that Kayin rose up against Hevel his brother, and slew him. The Lord said to Kayin, "Where is Hevel, your brother?"

He said, "I do not know. Am I my brother's keeper?"

(*Bereishis* 4:8–9)

When asked by God where his brother was, Kayin responded, "I do not know."

Like one who thinks he has tricked the Most High!

(*Rashi*)

Kayin was closed off to shame. He felt no remorse for the sin. In fact, he turned the accusation around, "Am I my brother's keeper?" Am I the one who is supposed to guard the world? You, God, created the world, You are the Keeper of the world.

How could Kayin repent if he did not regret? Blaming others, refusing to accept responsibility for his own failure, how could he take the opportunity to grow, to change?

God did not ask the same question of Kayin that He did of his father, Adam. He did not ask, "Where are you?" but "Where is your brother?" Adam was aware of his sin; he felt shame, covered himself, and hid. Not so Kayin — Kayin did not admit that he failed. He was unaware of his potential, uncaring of his failed capacity as a human being, so God tried to create an opening, the beginning of a consciousness. "Where is Hevel, your brother?"

Rashi explains the nature of the rhetorical questions asked by God:

> "Where are you? — He [God] knew where he was, but [He asked in order] to enter into conversation with him so that he should not be afraid to answer, [as he would be] if He should punish him suddenly.

> "Where is Hevel, your brother?" — To enter with him into words of gentleness, perhaps he would repent and say, "I killed him and I have sinned to you."

God asked these questions to enter into a dialogue with the sinner, a dialogue that would lead to real change and growth. Since each sinner was in a different spiritual place, God asked different questions, with different purposes. He would punish Adam for his sin, and there would be no need to explain why, for Adam already knew what he had done wrong. He approached him gently, so as not to frighten him; Adam's own shame had frightened him enough.

But Kayin required a different approach. He was totally unaware of his failure, and God wanted to lead him to consider his actions, to gently guide him to a state of shame. He therefore asked a question that might have led Kayin to self-examination, to introspection, and ultimately to *teshuvah*.

Why were Adam and Kayin's responses so different? Why did Adam feel remorse and Kayin not? The Sifsei Chachamim, a commentary on Rashi, speculates that Adam, created by God's "hands," was aware that he was created in the image of God, "a little lower than angels." His awareness allowed him to see his own failure. But Kayin, born of a human union, was less in tune with his own godliness and therefore less aware of his sin.

The more we understand of truth, the more shame we feel at our downfall.

Unmasking Reality: Another Level of Shamefacedness

Imagine the possibility that you live your life a certain way, filled with the surety that you are doing the right thing, building your life as you think God expects you to do. Then, in one split second of blinding clarity, you are proved wrong. Everything you thought to be moral, fair, and right is actually unethical and unjust.

Imagine you are the brothers of Yosef — for twenty-two years, you believed that your brother Yosef, a dreamer of dreams, a schemer of schemes, was planning your demise. For twenty-two years, you believed that you had judged him rightly and had sold him to avoid the loss of your own spiritual heritage. You thought your father's pain was a necessary outcome of your wholesome judgment.

And after twenty-two years, a few words change your entire perspective: "I am Yosef." These words make you realize that you were wrong, and all the pain you caused was unnecessary. Reality stares you in the face. The dreams he had dreamed came true. He is the king, and you are bowing down to him. The extra love of his father was deserved, his unique strength was validated, his yearnings were vindicated.

The world is turned upside down with the words, "I am Yosef." And you feel shame.

At the moment of revelation, the ground fell from beneath the feet of Yosef's brothers. They could not deny that they were wrong, although there was no accusation, no rebuke. Only a few words: *I am Yosef*. But those few words changed everything. The brothers recognized Yosef's unique and important place in the Jewish people's destiny, and the foundation was laid for Jewish unity.

Compare the reaction of the brothers to the reaction of Bilam. God showed Bilam a talking donkey, something that should have upset all of his philosophical ideas. Bilam believed that there is no possibility to fuse spiritual and physical, that a donkey is a donkey with no spiritual underpinnings. Then this least spiritual of animals began to talk. The Hebrew word for "donkey" is *chamor*, which means material, physical. How can one undertand a talking donkey? Could it mean that even the most physical of animals has something spiritual in it? Bilam heard the donkey, argued with her, and refused to change his worldview.

When confronted with a different reality than the one we had assumed, there are two diametrically opposed ways of reacting. When the ground falls from underneath, when our honor is trampled on by truth, we can dig in and forcefully hold on to the old way, the old belief, the old action. This is *azus panim*, brazenness. Or we could grab onto truth, change, and return to our rightful place. Only shame could bring this about (Rav Chaim Goldvicht).

The Final Unmasking

> Woe to us from the Day of Judgment! Woe to us from the Day of Rebuke!
>
> (*Bereishis Rabbah* 93:3)

Just as Yosef's brothers were ashamed when he said, "I am Yosef," so will we be ashamed when we face the Holy One, blessed be He, on the day of Judgment, and He says, "I am God." The ground will sink under us, as we see our suppositions collapse. However, the ability to feel shame and the openness to feeling shame will bring us forgiveness.

> The brazen goes to Gehinnom, but the shamefaced goes to the Garden of Eden. May it be Your will, Hashem, our God and the God of our fathers, that the Holy Temple be rebuilt, speedily in our days, and grant us our share in Your Torah.
>
> (*Pirkei Avos* 5:20)

Why do the brazen go to Gehinnom? Without shame, there is no possibility for change. But the shamefaced go to the Garden of Eden, because their internal monitor of conscience keeps them within appropriate boundaries.

What is the connection between the rebuilding of the Temple and shame-facedness? When we feel the embarrassment of our erroneous ways, we take steps towards the rebuilding of the Temple.

May it be rebuilt speedily in our days!

Initiative: The Legacy of Leah

Ask a Jew a question, and he'll answer with a question. Try to give an answer, and he'll retort with another question. To us, the questions are always more important than the answers. They keep us thinking, analyzing, and growing in Torah. Inquiry is the methodology of Jewish learning. And, surprisingly, it is something we acquired from our mother Leah.

30:14 Reuven went in the days of the wheat harvest and found mandrakes in the field and brought them to his mother Leah. Then Rachel said to Leah, "Give me, I beg of you, of your son's mandrakes."

30:15 She said to her, "Is it a small matter that you have taken my husband? Would you take away my son's mandrakes also?"
Rachel said, "Therefore he shall lie with you tonight for your son's mandrakes."

30:16 Yaakov came from the field in the evening, and Leah went out to meet him and said, "You must come in to me, for I *have hired* you with my son's mandrakes." He lay with her that night.

30:17 God heard Leah, and she conceived and bore Yaakov a fifth son.

30:18 Leah said, "God has given me my *reward*, because I have given my maid to my husband," and she called his name *Yissachar*.

30:19 Leah conceived again and bore Yaakov the sixth son.

30:20 Leah said, "God has endowed me with a good dowry; now my husband will live with me, because I have borne him six sons," and she called his name Zevulun.

30:21 Afterwards, she bore a daughter, and called her name Dinah.

30:22 God remembered Rachel, and God listened to her and opened her womb.

30:23 She conceived and bore a son; and she said, "God has taken away my reproach."

30:24 And she called his name Yosef, and said, "The Lord shall add to me another son."

(Bereishis 30:14–24)

- The above-quoted conversation between the matriarchs is puzzling. They seem to be jealous of each other, and their nonchalant bartering of Yaakov is indelicate, to put it mildly. How is it possible that our holy ancestresses spoke this way?

- Leah's audacity in going out to meet Yaakov is surprisingly out of character. Her words "come to me" appear to lack modesty or subtlety. Yet before this episode, Leah is portrayed in the Torah as a gentle, introspective person. How are we to understand her actions?

- There appears to be no indication that Leah's actions here included prayer. Why does the text tell us (in verse 17) that God "heard" Leah?

- The text uses various forms of the Hebrew word *sachar*. The first time, in verse 16, Leah declares, "I have hired you" (*sechor secharticha*). The second time, verse 17, she speaks of her child as her reward (*sechari*) for her actions. And the child himself is named Yissachar, perhaps after both her action and God's response to her. This suggests that God responded to Leah's audacity by giving her another child! Why was she rewarded, and why with this particular child?

- Our Rabbis teach us that Rachel was punished because she treated her husband lightly (*Rashi* on *Bereishis* 30:15), yet, according to Seforno, Rachel too was given a child (Yosef) as a reward for her part in the bartering described above. Which is it? If both, why?

Leah's Focus

The creation of the nation of Israel was the dream and the goal of our patriarchs and matriarchs. To do so, they not only created an ideology, but also developed spiritual traits that would make the nation suited to teach the world about monotheism. The building of the nation would require total dedication to the greater goal of bringing Torah into the world, and both our fathers and mothers were totally devoted to this cause.

The three patriarchs, Avraham, Yitzchak, and Yaakov, developed the qualities of *chesed*, *gevurah*, and *tiferes*, which became the spiritual DNA of the Jewish people (see above, "Building the Nation"). The matriarchs also developed genetic spiritual qualities, but their primary focus was to build the future generations, children who would carry the spiritual qualities developed by the patriarchs, enhance them, and build a nation upon them.

Each of the twelve tribes had a unique characteristic that was an extension or further development of one of the qualities of the patriarchs and matriarchs. For example, Reuven's quality was repentance (*teshuvah*) and Yehudah's quality was kingship (*malchus*), both qualities being applications of inherited Jewish character traits.

Interestingly, despite the fact that the matriarchs' goal was to build new generations of Jewish people, three of the four matriarchs experienced prolonged infertility. Sarah didn't have a child until she was almost ninety. Rivkah was married for twenty years before she gave birth. Rachel cried out to her husband in helplessness, "Give me children or else I will die!" (*Bereishis* 30:1). Only Leah gave birth quickly and in successive order, although according to the Midrash (*Pesikta D'Rav Kahana* 20:1), she was also originally barren. If Leah, too, was born incapable of having children, as were all of the matriarchs, how was she able to have children so easily?

> Leah was destined to marry Eisav and Rachel to [marry] Yaakov. Leah would sit at the crossroads and ask about Eisav to know his actions. [People] would say to her, "He is a bad man. He spills blood, robs travelers, and is brazen. His whole self is like a cloak of hair. He is evil and he does all the abomination of God." When she heard this, she cried and said, "Rachel, my little sister, and myself came out of one womb. Rachel will marry

the pious Yaakov and I will marry the evil Eisav." She would cry and torment herself until her eyes became soft. Therefore, it is written, "And the eyes of Leah are soft" (*Bereishis* 29:17). "God saw that Leah was hated" and that the acts of Eisav were hated before her. But when Rachel heard that she would marry Yaakov, her heart was happy and proud.

Since they both married Yaakov, God said, "The one who cried, afflicted herself, hated Eisav's doings, and prayed before Me in judgment that she wouldn't be pushed away from this pious man, she will be given children first." Therefore it says, "God saw that Leah was hated" (ibid. 29:31).

(Tanchuma, Vayeitzei 4)

Leah knew that she was fated to marry Eisav. This was not just a rumor — Eisav was indeed the person she was destined to marry, the one God had chosen for her. Leah wept because she desperately didn't want this destiny. She wept so profusely and so often that her eyes became tender.

When the Lord saw that Leah was hated (*senuah*), He opened her womb; but Rachel was barren. Leah conceived and bore a son, and she called his name Reuven, for she said, "Surely the Lord has looked upon my affliction; now my husband will love me."

She conceived again and bore a son, and said, "Because the Lord has heard that I was hated, He has therefore given me this son also," and she called his name Shimon.

She conceived again and bore a son, and said, "Now this time will my husband be joined to me, because I have borne him three sons;" therefore his name was called Levi.

She conceived again and bore a son, and she said, "Now will I praise the Lord;" therefore she called his name Yehudah, and ceased bearing.

(Bereishis 29:31–35)

God saw that Leah was hated, but who hated her? Could Yaakov have treated Leah in such a negative manner that she would feel hated? It is impossible that Yaakov would mistreat his wife (*Bava Basra* 123a). We assume that the verse is speaking in relative terms, that is to say that, compared to Rachel, she wasn't beloved (*Kli Yakar*).

The Midrash explains (based on an alternative translation of *senuah*) that "Leah was hated" means that the deeds of Eisav were hated by her. In other words, "God saw that Leah was hated" means that when God saw that Leah hated Eisav's character so much that she cried and afflicted herself and prayed that her destiny be changed, He responded by giving her children: "God saw that Leah was a hater [of evil], and therefore He gave her children."

Was Leah not audacious? Should Leah have been content with her destiny, such as it was? Should she have said, "Everything comes from Heaven," and made the best of it?

Obviously not. Her prayers were accepted and God made her a mother in Israel. He saw fit to change her destiny because of her pure intentions and prayers — so much so that He gave her more than she asked of Him. Leah conceived immediately and never suffered through a moment of infertility, although she had been born barren.

After marrying Yaakov, Leah didn't breathe a sigh of relief, settle in, and bask in her "narrow escape" from Eisav. Since her misery and tears were not about finding personal fulfillment, she continued to remain focused on the creation of the Jewish nation.

The matriarchs knew prophetically that Yaakov would father twelve tribes and that he would have four wives. This seemed to mean that each wife would have three sons. Leah gave birth to Reuven, Shimon, and Levi, and each time she named a son she included God in the name. When she gave birth to Yehudah, however, there was a change in the naming: "This time I will thank God." Leah understood that the fourth child was more than her alloted share (*Rashi, Berachos* 7b).

Leah overcame all of the decrees of nature to which she should have been subject: marriage to an evil man, infertility, and her allotted share of children. She did so through her desire to serve Hashem, and she trusted that He could change her destiny. About Leah's prayers it was said:

> Rav Huna said: Strong is prayer, for it annulled the decree [her natural destiny].

> (*Bereishis Rabbah* 71:2)

The Mandrakes

Reuven brought the mandrakes (*duda'im*) to his mother when he was four years old. Our Sages offer different opinions as to what the mandrakes were. Some say they were a medicinal fertility aid, some say they served as a spiritual aid (*segulah*) for fertility, and some say that they gave off a perfume that would attract one's husband. In any case, these mandrakes were identified no less than four times as the mandrakes of Reuven (*Bereishis* 29, verses 14, 15, and 16). Although they were Reuven's mandrakes, or perhaps now Leah's mandrakes, Rachel wanted them. Rachel wanted to borrow something from Leah — perhaps her spiritual ability to break through boundaries and to attain something beyond her destiny.

Leah also wanted something — she wanted more children! Although she had her share, Leah was anxious to build the nation (*Ohr HaChaim, Bereishis* 30:17). She knew that there were to be twelve children, but so far only eight had been born (Leah had four sons, and each of the handmaidens had two; Rachel had been married for five years and hadn't conceived). It was a very selfless ambition — a desire to bring children into the world for the honor of her creator (Seforno).

When Rachel asked Leah for the mandrakes, Leah answered, "Is it a small matter that you have taken my husband? Would you take away my son's mandrakes also?" Yaakov, perhaps because he was sensitive to the fact that Rachel's infertility was very painful to her, made his main habitation in Rachel's tent (Eliyahu Kitov). Later in our history, the same thing would happen when Chanah was barren, and her husband doted on her more than on Peninah, his second wife who had given birth to many children. Leah, therefore, asked her sister for an extra night with Yaakov.

Rachel had always given to Leah at great personal self-sacrifice. She gave Leah her place under the *chuppah* and she gave Leah the signs so that she would not be shamed. She never once withheld, never once complained. Why? Because Rachel had the same goal and the same focus as Leah: building the Jewish nation.

Rachel, understanding Leah's motivation, didn't hesitate. She gave Leah the night with Yaakov. Leah, understanding Rachel's motivation, also didn't hesitate. Leah gave the mandrakes, hoping that Rachel would have children too. Each woman was focused on creating the twelve tribes of Israel. Self-sacrifice, whether giving up a son's flowers or a night, was the foundation of the building of the nation.

Leah's Bold Behavior

"Leah went out to meet him" (*Bereishis* 30:16). This teaches that she did not [even] let him wash his feet. She said, "You must come in to me" (ibid.). Rabbi Abahu said: The Holy One, blessed be He, saw that her motive was none other than to produce tribes, therefore Scripture finds it necessary to state, "You must come in to me." Rabbi Levi observed: Come and see how acceptable was the mediation of the mandrakes, for through these mandrakes there arose two great tribes in Israel, Yissachar and Zevulun. Yissachar studied the Torah, while Zevulun went out to sea and provided Yissachar with sustenance, and so the Torah spread in Israel; thus it is written, "The mandrakes give forth fragrance" (*Shir HaShirim* 7:14).

(*Bereishis Rabbah* 72:5)

Leah's behavior was audacious.

This behavior would seem immodest, inappropriate for a matriarch of the Jewish people, yet the Midrash testifies to the righteousness of her action by saying, "Her motive was none other than to produce tribes." Indeed, so great was her deed that she was rewarded with the birth of not one, but two great tribes in Israel, each of whom were devoted to the learning of Torah.

We have seen Leah's prayers nullify decrees of destiny, yet here we see something additional. We see her actions result in a change of destiny (*Ohr HaChaim, Bereishis* 30:17). What looks immodest is actually internally and externally a modest action because her intention and focus were completely on the mitzvah of procreation and not physical pleasure — like Adam and Chavah before their sin (Seforno).

In turn, God "heard" her actions as He would a prayer. "And God heard Leah." He heard and acquiesced to her supplication.

She said, "Come to me," and he [Yaakov] slept with her that

night (*balailah hu*). Rabbi Abahu says: As if it were possible to say in [God's] contemplation. He [God] alone knew that her only thought was to establish tribes.

(*Yerushalmi, Sotah* 3:4)

The words, "*balailah hu,*" are unusual. The verse should say "*balailah hahu,*" rather than "*balaila hu,*" literally, "that night he." To whom does the pronoun "*hu*" ("he") refer? Rabbi Abahu explained that "*hu*" is God; God alone knew that Leah's intention was purely to serve Him by establishing the tribes. She was acting as His partner.

To do this, she had to gather strength that was not natural to her, qualities that were not part of her innate composition. The verse, "All the glory of the King's daughter is inside" (*Tehillim* 48:14) applies to Leah. Even so, "Leah went out" — that is, she left her nature to bring about more tribes in Israel.

This "leaving her nature" indeed describes Leah's actions and prayers from the beginning. It is as if she is able, through her tremendous desire to serve God in complete devotion, to break through whatever barriers stand in her way. Her supplications and her actions override her nature. Thus God's response to her is to override her destiny and create a new one for her.

Leah assessed the situation — four more sons were to be born in order to complete the formation of the tribes of Israel. This quality of initiative and the ability to properly apply knowledge to new situations is called "*binah*." This was the quality that Leah used to develop her plan to bring forth the rest of the twelve tribes of Israel. She wanted to give birth to more tribes because she saw that Rachel was barren and that she, too, had stopped giving birth after Yehudah. When her son Reuven brought the mandrakes, she used that gift as the means to get an extra night with Yaakov in order to bring her plan to fruition. The mandrakes served that plan.

Leah felt no shame about her boldness because shame is an embarrassment that we feel when seeking our own agenda and not God's. Had Leah's desire been rooted in her own physical pleasure, she would have felt shame. But because her desire was rooted solely in her divine service, there was no shame.

Shame is the equivalent of conscience. A person is ashamed when there is something bothering his conscience, because of something he did wrong.

Therefore, although Leah's behavior appeared to be completely immodest from the outside, from the inside it was not immodest or inappropriate. Leah's behavior was not the manifestation of her desires, but about serving God.

Winning and Losing

"Then Rachel said to Leah, 'Give me, I beg of you, of your son's mandrakes.' She said to her, 'Is it a small matter that you have taken my husband...?' " (*Bereishis* 30:14). Rabbi Shimon taught: Because she [Rachel] treated that righteous man [Yaakov] so slightingly, she was not buried together with him. Thus it says, "Therefore he shall lie with you tonight," hinting: With you will he lie in death, but not with me.

Rabbi Elazar said: Each lost [by the transaction], and each gained. Leah lost the mandrakes and gained the tribes and the birthright, while Rachel gained the mandrakes and lost the tribes and the birthright.

Rabbi Shmuel bar Nachman said: One [Leah] lost mandrakes and gained [two] tribes and the privilege of burial with him; while Rachel gained mandrakes and lost the tribes and burial with him.

(Bereishis Rabbah 72:3)

The first half of the *midrash* implies that Rachel sinned by treating the marital bed lightly, and the punishment was that she would not be buried with her husband. The second half of the *midrash* seems to have a different message: Rachel lost something yet also gained by her actions. She lost two tribes and eternal burial with Yaakov, and her gain was the mandrakes.

Yet it is hard to understand Rachel's gain, especially compared to her loss. It seems that the gain is not much, whereas the loss is highly significant.

The Midrash implies that the tribes given to Leah as a reward for the mandrakes would have been Rachel's. Therefore, either the mandrakes were so important that they were worth the two tribes Rachel lost, or Rachel foolishly gained something little and lost something big. Which is it?

Could Yissachar and Zevulun have been Rachel's children? If we can understand who Yissachar and Zevulun are, then we'll understand why it was

Leah rather than Rachel who gave birth to them. This whole episode of the mandrakes is an expression of "measure for measure" (*middah keneged middah*), of giving something and receiving the most appropriate thing back. So this is an issue of "rightfulness." Yissachar and Zevulun were born to Leah, rightfully, because of who Leah was. Therefore, since the Midrash says that Rachel lost something, it must be that in a certain way Rachel could have had these children. Yet she didn't have an essential quality or power that was required of the mother of Yissachar and Zevulun.

Yissachar and Zevulun

Rabbi Shmuel bar Nachmani, citing Rabbi Yochanan, [said]: A woman who lays claim on her husband to the [marital] obligation will have children the like of whom did not exist even in the generation of Moshe. For of the generation of Moshe it is written, "Get you from each one of your tribes, wise men and understanding, and full of knowledge" (*Devarim* 1:13), and then it follows: "So I took the heads of your tribes, wise men and full of knowledge" (ibid., 15). He could not find men of "understanding." Now, in the case of Leah, it is written in Scripture, "Leah went out to meet him, and said, 'You must come to me for I have hired you' " (*Bereishis* 30:16). Subsequently it is written, "Of the children of Yissachar, men with understanding to set the times, to know what Israel should do, two hundred chiefs, with all of their brethren following their counsel" (*Divrei HaYamim* I 12:33).

(*Eiruvin* 100:2)

Leah's actions for the sake of Heaven were rewarded with a tribe that produced wise men, men capable of understanding and full of knowledge.

Of the children of Yissachar, men with understanding [*yodei binah le'itim*] to set the times, to know what Israel should do — two hundred chiefs, with all of their brethren following their counsel.

(*Divrei HaYamim* I 12:33)

What characteristic is the text implying when it tells us that the children of Yissachar had an "understanding [*binah*] to set the times"?

Rashi defines *binah* as understanding something from something else (*Shemos* 31:3). When a person with *binah* learns something new, he understands it in his heart from things he learned previously. He puts the new information together with the information he has acquired in the past, and he has the ability to apply the old information in the new, different situation. *Binah* involves an individual's own input. Through his labor and focused drive, he is able to use his knowledge constructively. In contrast to *binah* is another kind of knowledge called *chochmah*. *Chochmah* is information and knowledge. Rashi gives an example of the difference between *chochmah* and *binah*:

> "Wise men and understanding" (*Devarim* 1:13).... What is the difference between wise men and understanding men? A wise man (*chacham*) resembles a wealthy money changer. When people bring him dinars to consider, he considers, and when they do not bring them to him, he merely sits and gazes. An understanding man (*navon*) resembles a merchant money changer. When people ring him money to consider, he considers, and when they do not bring it to him, he seeks [business] and brings money of his own.
>
> (*Rashi, Devarim* 1:11)

Chochmah is knowledge that is given to man as a free gift from God, given to us in the form of the written Torah. There is no human input or creativity here; in fact we are forbidden to add or subtract from the Torah, and if even one letter is wrong, the Torah scroll is not kosher. The written Torah is the direct transmission from the mouth of God. The Torah of Moshe is pure absorbing-from-the-source. The quintessence of *binah* is the oral Torah (the Mishnah, Gemara, and Midrash), because in learning the oral Torah, one must apply previously learned information to new situations.

The oral Torah is the application of the written Torah to human issues. It requires the use of the intellect to ask, answer, argue, and conclude, based on the principles of exegeses that God gave us. Our task is to absorb the *chochmah* and then to labor and develop an understanding of how to apply God's eternal laws to daily life, an ongoing process. When a person uses his *binah* to increase his understanding, he actually builds his inner soul (*binah* comes from the Hebrew word for "build").

The interaction between the written Torah and the oral Torah, i.e., pure knowledge versus understanding how that knowledge should be applied in the physical world, is seen most clearly in the setting of time for Rosh Chodesh, the new month. Our Sages were given the information of what Rosh Chodesh is, and then they had to apply it to each new moon. They had to decide, "Is today Rosh Chodesh or not?" This application of the theoretical to the practical was so powerful that even God accepted their decision as to the date of Rosh Chodesh!

> Rabbi Hoshea taught: If the Beis Din [Sanhedrin] below declared: "Today is Rosh HaShanah," the Holy One, blessed be He, would say to the ministering angels, "Erect the platform. Let the defense attorneys stand and the prosecutors stand, because the Beis Din below decreed: Today is Rosh HaShanah."
>
> However, if the witnesses delayed in coming, or the Beis Din decided it was going to let the [new] year pass until tomorrow, the Holy One, blessed be He, would say to the angels, "Remove the platform and remove the defense attorneys and remove the prosecutors, because the lower court declared that tomorrow is Rosh HaShanah."
>
> What is the reason for this? "Because it is a law in Israel, a judgment of the God of Yaakov" (*Tehillim* 81:5).
>
> (*Pesikta DeRav Kahana* 5:13)

The great sages who have the power "to set up the time" are called "*yodei binah le'itim*," "men of understanding to set the times." The Chanukah poem *Maoz Tzur* celebrates the establishment of a new holiday, a new time in Israel, with the following words: "*Bnei vinah yemei shemonah, kavu shir urenanim* — People of understanding set up the eight days of Chanukah."

Yodei binah le'itim refers to the power of our Sages to set up time. The two hundred chiefs are the two hundred heads of the Sanhedrin who came from the tribe of Yissachar. One of the duties of the Sanhedrin was to determine when the new month began. Once they declared Rosh Chodesh, it was clear when the holidays would fall. Thus, the Sanhedrin "set up time" for the Jewish calendar.

A disproportionate number of men from the tribe of Yissachar became

Torah sages. In the verse from *Divrei HaYamim* that we saw above, it is recorded that there were fully two hundred heads of the Sanhedrin from the tribe of Yissachar. This ability to learn and apply knowledge, *binah*, is an inheritance from our mother Leah.

The Gemara in *Eiruvin* taught us that a woman who lays a claim on her husband to have children will have a child like Yissachar, a person who knows how to learn something from something else, who knows how to apply theoretical knowledge in the practical world. This reward was given to Leah, measure for measure. What did she do to merit a child with *binah*? She initiated something new, finding the practical solution to a theoretical problem.

The reward for Leah's initiative, for her idea to overcome her modest nature in order to enlarge the family of Yaakov, was the birth of a tribe, Yissachar, whose spiritual characteristic is the power of Torah, of initiating ideas (*chiddushim*) in Torah. This is why our Rabbis promised that whoever acts as Leah did will have children as Leah did. Her *binah* was rewarded with a tribe of *yodei binah* (Rav Chaim Goldvicht, *zt"l*).

Leah was rewarded, as well, with the birth of a second tribe, Zevulun, who would "dwell at the shore of the sea and be a haven of ships" (*Bereishis* 49:13).

> From where did all this greatness come to Yissachar? From Zevulun, who engaged in trade and supported Yissachar who was devoted to the Torah; thus it is written, "Zevulun shall dwell at the shore of the sea" (*Bereishis* 49:13).
>
> (*Bereishis Rabbah* 72:5)

Yissachar and Zevulun were partners both in this world and in the World to Come. Zevulun played the crucial supporting role to Yissachar's task of learning Torah.

Claiming Inheritance

Every inheritance must be claimed and developed in order for it to really belong to the inheritor (Rav Chaim Goldvicht). When did Yissachar claim the inheritance of *binah* that he received from his mother?

In the desert, when the Jewish people were commanded to build the Tabernacle, God told the people to bring gifts for its construction. He was very specific about what was needed: gold, silver, goat's hair, etc. The people generously contributed of their own possessions to its construction. The heads of each tribe, in contrast, waited to see what the people would bring before they contributed themselves. But in the consecration of the Tabernacle, they insisted on bringing their own gifts, before everybody else.

> Rabbi Nassan said: Why did the princes decide to donate first over here [at the Tabernacle's consecration ceremony] and by the construction of the Tabernacle they weren't first to donate? They said: "The public will donate whatever they donate, and whatever they leave out, we'll fill in." When they saw that the public had filled everything in, as it says, "For the material they had was sufficient for all the work to do it, and too much" (*Shemos* 36:7), they said, "Now what can we do?" They brought the *shoham* stones and the set of stones for the vest and the breast plate. Therefore, they donated here first.
>
> (*Rashi*, *Bemidbar* 7:3)

When it came time to consecrate the Tabernacle, the princes wanted to be among the first to bring their gifts, so that they would not be left out of the celebration! The Torah records:

> They brought their offering before the Lord, six covered wagons and twelve oxen; a wagon for two of the princes, and for each one an ox; and they brought them before the Tabernacle. The Lord spoke to Moshe, saying, "Take (*kach*) it from them, that they may do the service of the Tent of Meeting; and you shall give them to the Levites, to every man according to his service."
>
> (*Bemidbar* 7:3–5)

> When the Tabernacle was constructed and there was nothing lacking, [the heads of the tribes] wondered: *What is there that we can bring?* So they went and brought wagons upon which the Tabernacle could be carried. Who gave the advice to do this? The tribe of Yissachar, who addressed them thus: "Will the Tabernacle which you have made fly in the air? Take a gift of wagons so that it may be carried on them."
>
> (*Bemidbar Rabbah* 12:16)

Moshe did not know whether to accept this gift, as it was not on the list of items that God had told Moshe. He hesitated until God said, "Take it from them."

Why did Yissachar conceive of this idea to bring wagons? And why did God declare, "Take it from them"?

The Tabernacle was a portable building, one that would be transported from place to place as the Jews wandered in the desert. Each time they traveled, the Tabernacle would be dismantled and transported to the next stop, and at each new camp it would be reassembled. But how would it be transported from place to place?

Yissachar's idea was that wagons could transport the Tabernacle.

> "They brought them before the Tabernacle" (*Bemidbar* 7:3). This teaches that they brought them and handed them to the congregation. They came and stood before the Tabernacle, but Moshe would not accept it from them until he was told by the Almighty: "Take it from them"... At that moment Moshe was afraid and thought: Is it possible that the Holy Spirit has departed from me and rested upon the princes? The Holy One, blessed be He, said to him: "Moshe! Had I commanded them [what] to bring, I would have asked you to tell them." But it was not so. It was thus (*kach*) of their own accord. The idea emanated from them. Thus their opinion tallied with that on high.
>
> (*Bemidbar Rabbah* 12:18)

Why did Moshe question God about whether to take the wagons from them? Because wagons weren't on the list given to him by God. Moshe's greatness was that he always did exactly as he was told. He never initiated anything new. Therefore, his name is synonymous with the written Torah — it is called *Toras Moshe* (the Torah of Moshe). If God told him to take x, y, and z, he took x, y, and z. The wagons were extra, so he asked God. God's answer was to take it from them.

Rav Chaim Goldvicht, *zt"l*, explained that when God said to Moshe, "Take it from them," it did not only mean that Moshe should take the wagons. It also meant that he should take the idea itself from them. It was their *chiddush* — their new idea. They looked and saw that something was needed that was not on the list, and they made a logical conclusion from the application of what they saw. This is the power of the oral Torah, the result of applying one's own *binah*.

Yissachar's idea contained within it a metaphor as well. "Now that you have the Tabernacle, who is going to carry it?" means, "Now that You brought the Torah into the world, You need someone who is willing to take the responsibility to continue to transport it. Who will carry the Torah for You?" The answer is that the people who learn the oral Torah will carry it. They will labor and study and learn how to apply it. They will question, debate, and resolve questions. They will initiate new ideas, using the tools the Torah gives them. When Yissachar initiated the idea of wagons, he expressed his ability and desire to make Torah a living reality. This is the *binah* of Yissachar, which was later manifested by the fact that two hundred heads of the Sanhedrin came from this tribe.

And this was the way in which he earned the spiritual gift of his mother Leah.

The Legacy of Leah

Leah's reward for going out was that the child who would be born from this union, Yissachar, would have *binah* — so much *binah* that his tribe could set time in such a way that it actually established a reality. But why is it that in the time of Moshe, there were no men of understanding, as described in *Eiruvin*? It's true that there were some men with *binah*, because the tribe of Yissachar, as we saw, used *binah* when they suggested bringing the wagons, but the Torah itself states that Moshe could find no men with this understanding.

Rav Chaim Goldvicht, *zt"l*, explained that *binah* wasn't needed during the time of Moshe. During the lifetime of Moshe, God gave complete clarity to the Jewish people. God revealed His will, and if there were any questions, Moshe would ask God Himself. Should I take these wagons or shouldn't I? Moshe had a question, so he went straight to the Source. When he chose the elders who would answer questions and guide the people, they, too, had no need of *binah*: when they had a question, they asked Moshe and Moshe asked God. Therefore, the quality of *binah* remained in potential only, undeveloped, as it wasn't necessary for that generation. In fact, *binah* would have been counterproductive to the real mission of the forty years in the dessert — direct transmission of Torah through Divine revelation.

When the Jewish people entered the Land of Israel, however, Moshe was no longer with them and the direct-revelation pipeline was removed. There was not as much direct communication in any event, and the vivid clarity of Moshe was gone altogether. But they still had prophets who could communicate with God.

As time passed, prophecy also waned, and the period of Wisdom began, as well as the period of the leadership of the Torah scholars. Without prophecy, revealed communication from God, scholars could nevertheless use the knowledge of Torah, the logical tools of inquiry and application of wisdom to new situations. They could use the quality of "from them."

Throughout the many generations that followed, the elders and the Sanhedrin used this quality to set time, to set laws, and to figure out how to apply the fixed Torah to the reality of life. Until our own day, this process continues. For example, one hundred years ago our rabbis had to decide whether it was permissible to see electricity on Shabbos; today they have to decide whether medical advances such as brain cell transplant is permitted, and always in strict accordance with God's commandments and the Torah.

What does it mean that Yissachar knew how to set times?

The Rabbis had the ability to determine Rosh Chodesh, which in turn determined when the holidays fell. In addition, they could set up leap years.

> "Of the children of Yissachar, men with understanding to set the times..." (*Divrei HaYamim* I 12:33). What is meant by "the times"? Rabbi Tanchuma explains it to mean the seasons, while Rabbi Yosei says it means intercalculations. "To know what Israel should do" (ibid.), i.e., to know on what day they were to celebrate the festivals.
>
> (*Bemidbar Rabbah* 13:15)

While the Gregorian calendar is based on the sun and the Moslem calendar is based on the moon, the Jewish calendar is based on the moon with the rectification of the sun. Jewish holidays must always come out in the same season, so although our primary system is a lunar calendar, there is a leap year seven times in every nineteen years to adjust the calendar to the season. (In contrast, the Moslems' holiday of Ramadan can come out at any season.)

In the early days, the Sages set up the calendar, and they decided which years were leap years. Today we use multiyear calendars that were prepared long ago by our Sages when they saw that the impending exile would be very difficult and long, and it wouldn't always be possible to set times.

What is the significance of this setting of the calendar? Each holiday has its own spiritual reality. Pesach is the "time of our redemption," Sukkos is the "the time of our joy," and so on. In other words, we were redeemed from Egypt on Pesach because the spiritual quality of the month of Nissan is redemption. The one who has the power to devise the calendar has the responsibility of setting it up to be in tune with its spiritual quality. But it works the other way as well — that is, that the one who is given the power to set up the calendar is also given the power to set up the spiritual reality.

This is illustrated in the *midrash* we saw above, which described how God waited to see when the courts declared Rosh HaShanah so that He could set up His Heavenly courtroom. In other words, God Himself followed the courts below in setting the spiritual reality of each season and holiday!

The Chanukah poem *Maoz Tzur* states that "men of understanding" established eight days of song and jubilation. The poem is celebrating the ability of the Sages to set up a spiritual reality via the setting of time (Rav Chaim Goldvicht). The establishment of the holiday of Chanukah is not just the inauguration of a new celebration, but the introduction of a new spiritual reality in time, a time of "lights."

In *Parashas Naso* we learn of the gifts brought by the princes to the consecration ceremony of the Tabernacle (*Bemidbar* 7:12–25). Each prince brought the very same thing, yet each donation is listed individually. Virtually the same words and phrases are repeated twelve times, with the only changes being the name of the prince and the day.

There are, however, some important variances.

> He who offered his offering (*hamakriv*) on the first day was Nachshon, son of Aminadav, of the tribe of Yehudah. His offering was one silver dish, the weight of which was one hundred and thirty shekels, and one silver bowl of seventy shekels, after the shekel of the Sanctuary, both of them full of fine flour mingled with oil for a meal offering; one spoon of ten shekels of

gold, full of incense; one young bullock, one ram, one lamb of the first year, for a burnt offering; one kid of the goats for a sin offering; and for a sacrifice of peace offerings, two oxen, five rams, five male goats, five lambs of the first year. This was the offering of Nachshon, the son of Aminadav.

On the second day, Nesanel, the son of Tzu'ar, prince of Yissachar, did offer (*hikriv*). He offered for his offering one silver dish, the weight of which was one hundred and thirty shekels, and one silver bowl of seventy shekels, after the shekel of the Sanctuary, both of them full of fine flour mingled with oil for a meal offering; one spoon of ten shekels of gold, full of incense; one young bullock, one ram, one lamb of the first year, for a burnt offering; one kid of the goats for a sin offering; and for a sacrifice of peace offerings, two oxen, five rams, five male goats, five lambs of the first year. This was the offering of Nesanel, the son of Tzu'ar.

On the third day, Eliav, the son of Cheilon, prince of the children of Zevulun. His offering was one silver dish, the weight of which was one hundred and thirty shekels and one silver bowl of seventy shekels, after the shekel of the sanctuary, both of them were full of fine flour mingled with oil for a meal offering; one spoon of ten shekels of gold, full of incense; one young bullock, one ram, one lamb of the first year, for a burnt offering; one kid of the goats for a sin offering; and for a sacrifice of peace offerings, two oxen, five rams, five male goats, five lambs of the first year. This was the offering of Eliav, the son of Cheilon.

(*Bemidbar* 7:12–29)

A careful reading of the text shows us that there are three different introductions to the gifts given. On the first day, Nachshon of the tribe of Yehudah is described as "the one who offered his offering" (*hamakriv*). On the second day, Nesanel of the tribe of Yissachar "offered his gifts" (*hikriv*). On the third day, as well as every day after this, there is no mention of the word *offer* in either form.

We learn that both Yehudah and Yissachar are distinguished from their brothers, and they are different from each other, as well. The key to understanding these differences is found in a Hebrew grammatical point. The Hebrew language in the Torah makes use of what's called a "reversing *vav*," a *vav* that reverses the tense of the verb. For instance, *vayomer* means "he said," even though *yomar* means "he will say," because the *vav* reverses the tense. Using the reversing *vav* is the normal style of the Tanach. However, sometimes the text uses a past-tense verb without the reversing *vav*, for example in verse 18 (*hikriv*). This usage always connotes the past perfect tense, that is to say, the distant past. In our verse, it means that the prince of Yissachar "had brought" a sacrifice, he brought before, previous to this point in time. Since the text tells us that "Yehudah brought" and that "Yissachar had brought," it is telling us that Yissachar brought first, before Yehudah.

Yet, if that were true, why not list Yissachar as the first one to bring the sacrifice? The Torah is teaching us that it was as if Yissachar had sacrificed first, even though in reality, Yehudah went first. Why? Because Yissachar advised the princes to bring the wagons.

> "On the second day Nesanel, the son of Tzu'ar, prince of Yissachar, did offer (*hikriv*)" (*Bemidbar* 7:18). Why was the expression *hikriv* used in his case? *Hikriv* makes it seem as though he was the first to present his offering. Why should this honor have been given him? Since he had the credit of having given the advice to the princes, Scripture regards him as though he was the first to present his offering. Abba Chanan says in the name of Rabbi Eliezer: As a reward for the merit of having given counsel, he was privileged to have understanding given to his tribe, as it says, "And of the children of Yissachar, men that had understanding of the times" (*Divrei HaYamim* I 12:33).
>
> (*Bemidbar Rabbah* 13:15)

Although Yissachar is given credit by the Torah for presenting the gifts first because he advised the princes to bring wagons, Yissachar could not go first in practice because the tribe that represents kingship must go first. The essence of kingship, *malchus*, is of having *yiras Hashem*, fear of God, and knowing that God is the real king. In other words, what made Yehudah a king was that he knew he was actually a servant! Once a person understands that

God is King, and therefore fears Him, he can proceed to the next step, which is learning Torah. But before a person can acquire wisdom from learning, he must have fear of Heaven, i.e., he must know that the wisdom he is learning is divine wisdom.

> The beginning of wisdom is the fear of God.
>
> (*Tehillim* 111:10)

Yehudah brings his offering first since his spiritual quality is *malchus*, the fear of God. Yissachar brings the second gift since his quality is Torah learning. The wisdom doesn't come to a person unless he has fear of God (*Nefesh HaChaim* 4:5).

Yissachar set in motion an essential energy that would be required at a future time. In the days of the revelation of God's Presence through Moshe and the prophets, the strength of Yehudah would come first. But a time would come when God would "hide His face" from us, and we would experience a lack of clarity. Then the learning of Yissachar would come first (Rav Chaim Goldvicht, *zt"l*).

As discussed above, in the time of Moshe, *chochmah* was the dominant wisdom utilized, since any question or incomprehensibility could be clarified by asking God directly. But later in history, when direct revelation ceased, there would a need for the quality of "from them" *binah* of Yissachar. The difference between wisdom and prophecy is illustrated in a parable given by the Brisker Rav.

A blind man is in a house and wants to get out. He gropes around to find the exit. He feels an opening, but it's near the ground, like a tunnel, so he says to himself, *Most places have a door that you walk through to go out. This tunnel is probably not the exit.* Next he finds an opening in the middle of the wall, but it doesn't go down to the floor. He thinks, *Normally you don't need to climb onto a chair to get through a door.* He continues searching and finds some steps which lead up to the roof. He thinks, *I could go out this way, but usually you don't go out of a house through the roof.* At this point, a seeing man enters from another room and looks around, and sees clearly that the way out of the house is the tunnel.

This is the difference, says the Brisker Rav, between relying on prophecy and direct revelation from God, and relying on the those who achieve wisdom through their own efforts, i.e., our Sages. When you can see, you don't need logic. You look around and see that the tunnel is the door. Although that's not the door you might have built, that's the door. But when you can't see, you need to feel around to find the opening. The blind man must develop his sense of touch, but in addition he develops his sense of intuition and logic, of drawing conclusions, of applying that which he knows from other situations to this new one. A blind man can do that, whereas a seeing man doesn't need to.

Another illustration of this idea is the difference between the First Temple and the Second Temple. The First Temple was based on revelation and prophecy. Constant miracles occurred there. For example, the fire on the altar was lit from Heaven, and the light from the inside of the Temple illuminated the outside world. The Second Temple had no prophecy and no miracles. Rather, the great Rabbis and Sages of the Sanhedrin (including the two hundred heads of Sanhedrin who were from the tribe of Yisschar) gave guidance to the Jewish people. They had no prophecy, but they certainly had wisdom and logic. During the period of the First Temple, we celebrated only the holidays of the Torah. During the period of the Second Temple, our Sages added two holidays: Purim and Chanukah. Purim and Chanukah came "from them."

The power of logic, *binah*, of developing new applications of the oral Torah, is what has kept us alive throughout the exile.

The Descendants of Leah

When Leah took the initiative to create new tribes in Israel, when she "went out" of her natural modesty for the sake of Heaven, she applied the power of *binah* and acquired the power for her children. They inherited this quality of being able to push boundaries and to initiate from her, and it was up to them to develop it and to earn it, as the tribe of Yisschar did.

Her descendant David expressed this quality in its most spiritual form. His very name is hinted to in the Hebrew word for mandrakes, *dudaim* (*Agra Dekalah* 141:2), and it is in his role as king of Israel that he pushed the borders of the country by initiating war, by using the power of "going out" to fight the enemies of God. For this he is nicknamed *Adino HaEtzni* (*Shmuel* II 23:8).

> He is called Adino HaEztni. When he sat and learned Torah, he was made himself as soft and pliant (*adin*) as a worm. When he

went out to war, he hardened himself like a board (*etzni*).

(*Mo'ed Katan* 16b)

When Leah "went out," she did so for the sake of Heaven. Though she pushed her boundaries, she did so only for the sake of Heaven. So too, David — though he was a warrior, he never killed because of blood lust, but solely for the sake of Heaven. This is why, says Rav Dessler, David could not build the Temple.

> God said to me, "You will not build a house for My name because you have been a man of battles and you have shed blood." And the Lord, God of Israel, chose me before all the house of my father to be king over Israel forever.
>
> (*Divrei HaYamim* I 28:3–4)

At first glance, it appears that David could not build a House of God because of his exploits as a warrior. Yet our Rabbis teach that so great was David that if he had built the Temple, it could never have been destroyed (*Yalkut Shimoni, Shmuel* II 145). Rav Dessler explains that when David went to war, it was to fight the battles of God, to banish idolatry and to bring God into this world. We can all imagine what it is to do mitzvos for the sake of Heaven, but killing is so antithetical to our way of thinking that it is hard to imagine killing for the sake of Heaven. But David did just that.

It was not because of a love of violence that David killed, or even for a personal revenge or motivation, but rather that David was capable of pushing aside his sublime sensitivity when that was required by God. David "went out" to war, as Leah "went out" to produce children — with the focus on their Creator and on His will.

There is another child of Leah that "went out" as did her mother, but she is faulted for her actions.

> "Dinah, the daughter of Leah, went out" (*Bereishis* 34:1). "Behold, everyone that uses proverbs shall use this proverb against you, saying: 'As the mother, so her daughter' " (*Yechezkel* 16:44)....
>
> (*Bereishis Rabbah* 80:1)

"And Dinah, the daughter of Leah, went out" — and not the daughter of Yaakov. The text connects her with her mother. Just as Leah is one who goes out, so is [Dinah] one who goes out. Where is this [recorded]? As it says: "And Leah went out to greet him" (*Bereishis* 30:16). Yechezkel said: " 'As the mother, so her daughter.' You are your mother's daughter" (*Yechezkel* 16:44–45).

(Tanchuma, Vayishlach 7)

The Midrash asks why Dinah is identified here as the "daughter of Leah." and not the daughter of Yaakov. And the answer is that Dinah acted as Leah when she "went out" — that she imitated her mother's actions in going out. What the Midrash is implying, then, is that the same spiritual quality that we have praised in Leah was used by Dinah to her detriment.

To understand why, let us examine the story of Dinah's going out.

Dinah, the daughter of Leah, whom she bore to Yaakov, went out to see the daughters of the land. When Shechem, the son of Chamor the Chivite, prince of the country, saw her, he took her, lay with her, and defiled her.

(Bereishis 34:1–2)

At first glance, it would be hard to fault Dinah for something that she did not initiate, yet the *midrash* above does fault her. The key to understanding Dinah's error is in the words "went out to see the daughters of the land."

To see, and to be seen. She sought to see and she was seen, as it says, "And Shechem, the son of Chamor, saw her."

(Tanchuma, Vayeitzei 7)

Why did Dinah go out? She wanted to see what was going on, to see the marketplace, the excitement of the world at large. She did not go out, as her mother did, with a vision of what needed to be done for the sake of Heaven. She went out for the sake of going out, with no higher focus other than her own pleasure. The lack of focus on her true purpose in the world, as a servant of God, was her undoing.

Because she is the daughter of Leah and she inherited her mother's quality, her life could have been so different. Indeed, the Midrash tells us that she would even have been capable of initiating great changes in Eisav and bringing him to repentance.

"He [Yaakov] rose up that night and took his two wives, and his two handmaids and his eleven children" (*Bereishis* 32:23). Where, then, was Dinah? He put her in a chest and locked her in, saying, "This wicked man [Eisav] has an aspiring eye; let him not take her away from me." Rabbi Huna said in the name of Rabbi Abba Bardela the Priest: The Holy One, blessed be He, said to him, " 'To him that is afflicted, kindness is due from his friend' (*Iyov* 6:14).... You would not give her in marriage to a circumcised person [Eisav]; behold she is now married to an uncircumcised one. You would not give her in legitimate wedlock; behold she is now taken in an illegitimate fashion." Thus it is written, "Dinah, the daughter of Leah...went out."

(*Bereishis Rabbah* 76:9)

When Yaakov came back to Israel from the house of Lavan, he brought his wives and eleven children with him, but his one daughter, Dinah, is not mentioned. The Midrash explains that Yaakov had hidden her so that his brother Eisav would not try to marry her. Who could blame him for protecting his daughter from the eyes of an evil man? Yet the Midrash does indeed fault him for not being empathetic to the affliction of Eisav. Surely Yaakov should have tried to help Eisav return to the path of God. Perhaps with Yaakov's assistance, Eisav would have merited to marry Dinah (Rav Chaim Goldvicht, *zt"l*). The Midrash states this in strong terms — "You would not give her in marriage" — to teach us that the potential to assist Eisav was so great that he could have married Dinah had Yaakov helped him.

Both Yaakov and Dinah did something wrong that resulted in the degradation of a daughter of Israel. Yaakov withheld his assistance from Eisav, and Dinah "went out" with a lack of focus on her important role as a servant of God.

Dinah inherited the spiritual gift of her mother Leah — the gift of initiative, of seeing the situation and figuring out what do to further the agenda of God, with no boundaries in that Divine service. Because of this ability, Dinah could have even brought a wicked Eisav to repent. Her mother Leah was destined to have married Eisav but prayed that she would not be forced to do so. She is not faulted for her prayer and her self-affliction, but praised and deemed worthy to marry Yaakov and even to conceive children immediately and successively. Yet Dinah and Yaakov are faulted, because the power of "going out" was even greater in Dinah than in Leah. Leah could not have saved Eisav — but Dinah could have!

Instead of using that power in a constructive way, by bringing Godliness into the world, she used it "to see and be seen." She did not aim her talent in a holy direction that could have even changed Eisav, but squandered it for her own pleasure. For this, she is faulted, as is her father who should have seen her potential and guided her to use it well.

Yet Leah is the one who is most connected with her daughter's decision to "go out to see the daughters of the land." "As the mother, so the daughter." Why?

In judging the righteous, there is a general rule that even a small sin is weighed heavily. The Torah is never shy to point out even the slightest error of our matriarchs and patriarchs. We can understand Leah's mistake better by examining several *midrashim* dealing with the Torah concept of a "sin done for the sake of Heaven."

> Ulla said: Both Tamar and Zimri committed adultery. Tamar [appeared to] commit adultery and gave birth to kings and prophets. Zimri committed adultery and on his account many tens of thousands of Israel perished.
>
> A transgression performed for the sake of Heaven (*lishmah*) is [as good as] a precept performed not for the sake of Heaven (*lo lishmah*).
>
> (*Nazir* 23b)

This Gemara introduces the idea of a transgression done for the sake of Heaven. The example given is that of Tamar who disguised herself as a prostitute in order to perform the mitzvah of levirate marriage. (This was not really adultery, but it appeared to be.) As a result of her "transgression," the Davidic kingship was established.

When a righteous person — who has insight into the Divine will, as did Tamar — performs an action for the sake of Heaven that externally appears to be a sin, that action is deemed a transgression for the sake of Heaven. (This concept of a transgression for the sake of Heaven only applies in specific circumstances.)

Rav Chaim Goldvicht, *zt"l*, explains that such a person would have to approach the "sin" with trepidation and awe, because although his focus and goal is to perform Divine service, it could appear to be *chillul Hashem*, a desecration of God's name. For instance, when Yaakov misled his father Yitzchak by pretending to be Eisav, thus acquiring the blessing of Eisav, he did so "with head bowed, compelled and crying" (*Bereishis Rabbah* 5:15). When Avraham took his beloved son Yitzchak to the altar to be sacrificed, his love and fear of God was the focus of his attention, but he was aware that it externally appeared to be a sin (*Michtav MeEliyahu*).

> "Yitzchak spoke to Avraham, his father, and said, 'My father?' "
> (*Bereishis* 22:7). Samael [a wicked angel] went to the Patriarch
> Avraham and upbraided him, saying, "What does this mean, old
> man! Have you lost your wits? You go to slay a son granted to
> you at the age of a hundred?!"
> "Even this I do," replied he [Avraham].
> [Samael] responded, "If He sets for you an even greater
> test, can you stand it?"
> Said he [Avraham], "As it is written, 'If a thing be put to you
> as a trial, will you be wearied?' (*Iyov* 4:2)."
> "Even more than this," he replied. "Tomorrow He will say
> to you, 'You are a murderer and are guilty.' "
> "Still am I content," he rejoined.
>
> (*Bereishis Rabbah* 56:4)

When Rus came to the threshing floor of Boaz in the dark of night, she was clear that this was a necessary act to perform the mitzvah of levirate marriage and not to pursue her own desires. Boaz testified to her intention and focus:

> Blessed be you of the Lord, my daughter, for you have shown
> more loyalty in the latter end than at the beginning, inasmuch as
> you did not follow the young men, whether poor or rich.
>
> (*Rus* 3:10)

Yet Boaz trembled to see her, fearful that her intentions be misunderstood:

> And it came to pass at midnight that the man was startled.... He said,
> "Let it not be known that a woman came into the threshing floor."
>
> (*Rus* 3:8, 14)

When Leah went out to the field to claim her husband, she did not appear to the observer to tremble at her actions. The trepidation that her act might be misunderstood was missing, and this was the slight error that she made. Her daughter Dinah, therefore, inherited her quality of overcoming boundaries without fully absorbing the focus of acting for the sake of Heaven. Hence, when Dinah used this quality "to see the daughters of the land," she does not hear her mother's voice within her warning her not to do this act. For this, Leah is criticized (Rav Chaim Goldvicht, *zt"l*).

Reuven, too, had Leah's ability to intuit and initiate change. In fact, Reuven was the very child who started the process by bringing his mother the mandrakes. They were indeed "his" mandrakes. The text tells us many times that these mandrakes belong to him.

> Reuven went in the days of the wheat harvest and found mandrakes in the field and brought them to his mother Leah. Then Rachel said to Leah, "Give me, I beg of you, of *your son's mandrakes*."
>
> And she said to her, "Is it a small matter that you have taken my husband? Would you take away *my son's mandrakes* also?" Rachel said, "Therefore he shall lie with you tonight for *your son's mandrakes*."
>
> Yaakov came from the field in the evening, and Leah went out to meet him and said, "You must come in to me, for I have hired you with *my son's mandrakes*." He lay with her that night.

Perhaps the mandrakes represent the power of *chiddush*, of initiating a new idea, using the power of *binah*. These mandrakes, this quality of *chiddush*, belonged to Reuven, but he, too, used it improperly.

> When Rachel died, Yaakov took his bed, which was found regularly in Rachel's tent rather than in the other tents, and placed it in the tent of Bilhah [Rachel's handmaiden]. When Reuven saw this he claimed his mother's insult...and moved the bed [to his mother's tent].
>
> (*Rashi, Bereishis* 35:22)

He reasoned that while Rachel was alive, she was the *akeres habayis*, the foundation of the home, and therefore Yaakov's primary residence was with her. Once she passed away, Reuven felt his mother would be pained that her husband made his primary abode with the handmaiden of Rachel and not with her, so he moved his father's bed to Leah's tent. While this idea may have arisen from sensitivity to his mother and from an intuitive understanding, it was an inappropriate initiative.

Had Reuven used this quality properly, he could have been a king in Israel. By using it improperly, he lost his inheritance as firstborn.

The Quality of Modesty

> "Dinah, the daughter of Leah, went out." This is what it means when it says, "The daughter of the King is all glorious within" (*Tehillim* 45:14). Rabbi Yosei said: When a woman is modest within her home, she is worthy of marrying the *kohein gadol* (the high priest) and having children who are priests. As it says, "The daughter of the King is all glorious within." If she respects herself within the home, "Her clothing is of embroidered gold" (ibid.), and she will marry the one about whom it is said, "You will weave the coat of fine linen" [i.e., the *kohein gadol*] (*Shemos* 28:39).
>
> Rabbi Pinchas HaKohen bar Chama said: When she is modest within her home, just like the altar atones, so she too atones for her household...and if she does thus, she will have children that are anointed with the anointing oil.
>
> (*Tanchuma, Vayishlach* 6)

Seemingly, this *midrash* would be difficult to put in the context of Leah's actions, since Leah "went out" and her daughter "went out." Yet it is indeed Leah who is rewarded with sons who become kings and priests. Clearly, her "transgression for the sake of Heaven" is considered a modest act, despite external appearances. Why?

Modesty means having one's focus on the inside, on the spiritual. It is staying within spiritual borders and focusing on God. This indeed was Leah's intention and motivation, appearances aside. Hence, she is rewarded measure for measure. She who focused internally was rewarded with sons from the tribe of Levi, who serve within the internal spiritual world of the Temple. The high priest served within the innermost sanctum of the House of God.

In fact, just as the altar atoned for the sins of the people, a modest woman will atone for her home. What is atonement? It is the correction of a negative energy produced by sin. Repentance, *teshuvah*, is fixing one's self after a sin to the point that one will not repeat that sin. But what of the negative energy left in the world by the sin itself? That is repaired through atonement, *kapparah*. Yom Kippur is the day that we not only repent and begin to change ourselves, but the day itself achieves certain atonement, repair of the negative spirituality created by sin.

The altar had the same effect. Nothing can replace the *teshuvah* of a person who sins. That is why the person who brought a sin offering had to confess his sins, and why a sacrifice was not deemed worthy unless it was brought with a sense of contrition. However, the sacrifice itself brings atonement for the sin. It fixes that which we broke with our sin. The role of the priest is to facilitate this repair.

So too the modest woman. To repair the negative effects of sin, there must be a refocusing toward the internal world. The daughter of the King repairs the broken by redirecting the focus toward God.

This was Leah's ability, whether she was inside the home or outside.

Losses and Gains

> Because she [Rachel] treated that righteous man [Yaakov] so slightingly, she was not buried together with him. Thus it says, "Therefore he will lie with you tonight," hinting, "with you will he lie in death, but not with me."
>
> (*Bereishis Rabbah* 72:3)

Rachel is criticized by our Rabbis for depreciating a night with Yaakov. Therefore she lost burial with him; Leah was buried in Chevron with Yaakov, but Rachel was buried in Beis Lechem. Yet there is another reason given for this separate burial, a reason that is more positive:

> What was Yaakov's reason for burying Rachel on the way to

Efras? Yaakov foresaw that the exiles would pass on from there. Therefore he buried her there so that she might pray for mercy for them. Thus it is written, "A voice is heard in Ramah...Rachel weeping for her children.... Thus says the Lord: Refrain your voice from weeping and your eyes from tears...for your children will come again to their own border" (*Yirmeyahu* 31:15–18).

(*Bereishis Rabbah* 82:10)

How do we reconcile these two different opinions as to why Rachel was buried separately from her husband?

The answer is to be found in the second part of the *midrash* about the losses and gains of Rachel and Leah:

Each lost [by the transaction], and each gained. Leah lost the mandrakes and gained the tribes and the birthright, while Rachel gained the mandrakes and lost the tribes and the birthright. Rabbi Shmuel ben Nachman said: One [Leah] lost mandrakes and gained [two] tribes and the privilege of burial with him; while Rachel gained mandrakes and lost the tribes and burial with him.

(*Bereishis Rabbah* 72:3)

We understand what Leah gained by her actions, but what did Rachel gain? How could gaining the mandrakes be a real gain?

One of Rachel's most dominant spiritual characteristics was *mesirus nefesh*, self-sacrifice. Even on the night of her wedding, she allowed her sister to marry Yaakov, so as not to cause her humiliation. When she was faced with her own infertility, she gave her maidservant to Yaakov in order to have children through her. She gave Leah the extra night with her husband to bring the ninth and tenth tribes of Israel into being. In so doing, Rachel set her priorities — she would do anything, sacrifice anything, including herself, for the sake of the future of the Jewish people.

This is why all of the twelve tribes born to Yaakov were like her own. She gave up the most for them to come into being. She always put them first, and that is why she was willing to give Leah this extra night with Yaakov. It was not that she devalued her husband as much as that she placed value on "her" children. She was willing to lose her "eternal resting place" with Yaakov in order to facilitate the birth of the tribes of Yissachar and Zevulun.

She was not buried with Yaakov, but she was buried in the very place where her children would need her. As they went into exile, she would be there to pray for their safety in exile and for their eventual return. And she waits on the road for us. When we will finally return from exile, she will be there to greet us.

Rachel is rewarded for her self-sacrifice with the birth of Yosef.

> God remembered Rachel, and God listened to her and opened her womb. She conceived and bore a son, and said, "God has taken away my reproach."
> She called his name Yosef; and said, "The Lord shall add to me another son."
>
> (*Bereishis* 30:22–24)

What did God remember that He rewarded her with this much desired child after years of infertility?

> She is rewarded for bringing her maidservant into her home, and for the mandrakes.
>
> (Seforno, *Bereishis* 3:22)

She was rewarded with her own child because she did all she could to bring tribes into the world even if they were not borne by her.

Rachel lost two tribes but gained the mandrakes. What are these mandrakes? What gain were they? Perhaps the mandrakes were the spiritual quality of intuition and initiative that belonged to Reuven and to his mother, Leah. This quality is a kingly one, one that King David would use to "go out" to war in service of God.

Rachel "borrowed" this quality from Leah in order to enhance her fertility. This was her gain and she was rewarded with Yosef, who, like David, was a king in Israel. But unlike David whose kingship is eternal, Yosef was a temporary king: his kingship did not last forever. His kingship is "borrowed." Hence, Yosef's descendant, King Shaul, is given his name, Shaul, which means "borrowed" (*Michtav MeEliyahu*).

The Reward

The reward for Leah was her son Yissachar. The text tells us that the reward came to her because she had given her maidservant, Zilpah, to Yaakov.

The commentaries note that the name *Yissachar* has two *shin*s, indicating that there is a double reward.

> Two rewards: one the reward for the mandrakes. The other the reward for "I gave my handmaiden to my husband."
>
> (Rashbam, *Bereishis* 30:18)

There is another way to understand the two *shin*s — the word *sachar*, "reward," reverberates in our minds when we remember the verse:

> Thus says the Lord: A voice is heard in Ramah, lamentation, and bitter weeping; Rachel weeping for her children, refused to be comforted for her children, because they were not. Thus says the Lord: Refrain your voice from weeping and your eyes from tears; for your work shall be rewarded, says the Lord; and they shall come again from the land of the enemy. And there is hope for your future, says the Lord, for your children will come again to their own border.
>
> (*Yirmeyahu* 30:15)

The reward of the birth of yet another tribe in Israel is credited to two mothers — Leah and Rachel. For although this child of Torah is a reward for the initiative of Leah, he is equally the reward for the *mesirus nefesh*, the self-sacrifice, of Rachel.

The Gift of Inquiry

The initiative of Leah gave birth to the gift of inquiry and investigation. Whenever we engage in the study of Torah, whenever we ask a question and search for an answer, we develop this inherited spiritual quality within ourselves.

I ask, therefore I am — a Jew. And the more we ask, the more we learn. The more we learn, the more questions we have. It is an endless sea of inquisitiveness that keeps us going. So ask a Jew a question, and remember, it isn't always the answer that counts.

Life in Exile

Are We Really Free to Choose?

W here there's a will there's a way — so the saying goes. We go about our daily lives assuming that we can make choices and that our will can determine the day, but is that true? Can a person determine his own destiny by exercising his own will, or does God decide the course of history and the course of our lives? And if the latter is true, how does the exercise of free will accord with the predetermined fate that God has already chosen for us?

Yosef and His Brothers

It is well known that Yosef appeared to be the favorite son of our patriarch, Yaakov. Yaakov gave Yosef a linen coat, which provoked the jealousy of his brothers. In addition, Yosef told his brothers that he dreamed he would be a king over them, and that they would bow down to him. Telling his brothers of his dreams caused them to hate him even more.

When Yosef was seventeen years old, his brothers were in Shechem, shepherding Yaakov's sheep. The patriarch sent Yosef to see how they fared, and Yosef ended up being sold into slavery. Yosef was taken to Egypt, where he was in bondage for many years, but eventually he rose to the position of viceroy of Egypt. This position allowed him to bring his family to Egypt during a devastating famine.

This was the beginning of the Egyptian exile. Subsequently, in a step-by-step process, Yosef's family became enslaved.

The story, however, is not so simple:

And he [Yaakov] said to him [Yosef], "Please go, see whether it is well with your brothers and well with the flocks, and bring me word again." So he sent him out of the valley of Chevron, and he came to Shechem.

(Bereishis 37:14)

"The valley of Chevron" — Was not Chevron a hill, as it says, "They went up into the south and they came to Chevron" *(Bemidbar* 13:22)? Alluding to the deep [profound] counsel of the righteous one buried in Chevron [Avraham], to fulfill what was told to Avraham when the covenant was made "between the pieces," "Your offering shall be aliens..." *(Bereishis* 15:13).

(Rashi)

The Torah states that Yosef was sent from the valley of Chevron to Shechem. Rashi asks why the Torah describes Chevron as a "valley" when we know that Chevron is on a mountain, and he answers that the Hebrew word for "valley," *emek*, has the same root as the Hebrew word *amok*, which means "deep." The Torah is not speaking of a valley, but of the wisdom that comes from the depths of Chevron, i.e., the wisdom of Avraham, who was buried in Chevron. What is deep is the prophecy given to Avraham that Avraham's seed would be exiled. Yosef was sent "out of the depths of Chevron" because the Egyptian exile was about to begin through Yosef's descent into Egypt. Therefore, the activities of Yaakov, Yosef, and the brothers were the fulfillment of the prophecy that the Jewish people would be enslaved in Egypt, during an exile that was preordained and predestined.

It happened, as the sun was about to set, that a deep sleep fell upon Avram; and behold — a dread! Great darkness fell upon him. And He said to Avram, "Know with certainty that your offspring shall be aliens in a land not their own — and they will serve them, and they will oppress them — four hundred years. But also the nation that they will serve, I shall judge, and afterwards they will leave with great wealth."

(Bereishis 15:12–14)

This leaves us with a question: Why did the Jewish people end up in exile? Was it because of a series of decisions made by Yaakov, Yosef, and his brothers, or was it preordained, with every step along the way being a

Divine decree designed to lead to the exile foretold to Avraham?

Twenty-two years after Yosef was sold by his brothers, the brothers approached the viceroy of Egypt (who was Yosef, but they didn't know it) and bowed down to him. In an emotional scene, Yosef revealed his true identity to them. The brothers were shocked and feared an angry reaction, but Yosef said:

> And now it was not you that sent me here, but God; and He has made me a father to Pharaoh, and lord of all his house, and a ruler throughout all the land of Egypt.
>
> *(Bereishis* 45:8)

Did Yosef speak this way because he was a very forgiving person, or were these words a theological statement? If Yosef actually believed his own words, the implication is that the brothers were merely God's puppets, instruments of the Divine will to bring Yosef to Egypt and thereby to begin the Egyptian exile prophesied to Avraham.

> Do not wonder, saying: How could a person do all that he pleases and be in control of his actions? Is there anything in this world that can be performed without the Creator's authority and against His will?... Know that God performs everything according to His will, even though we are in control of our actions. For example, just as the Creator willed that fire and air should ascend upward and that water and earth should descend downward and that the sphere should revolve in a circle, and the rest of the creatures behave as they do because God desires it to be thus, so He willed that man should have freedom to act, and that all his actions should be within his power. No one will force him or push him. Rather, he himself, using the mind that God gave him, can do all that he wants to do.
>
> (Rambam, *Hilchos Teshuvah* 5:4)

Interestingly, this statement of Rambam appears in his section on the laws of repentance (*Hilchos Teshuvah*). We might expect Rambam to expound on the concept of free will when he wrote about the principles of the Torah (*Hilchos Yesodei HaTorah* or *Hilchos Dei'os*), but instead he discusses it in the fifth chapter on the laws of repentance. Rambam was no doubt addressing a problem people might have with the concept of sin and the need for repentance: "But, God, You made me the way I am. You put the evil inclination (*yetzer hara*) in me, You put desires in me, You put me in a situation I couldn't handle. How could you expect me to repent when I am not in control?" Rambam's answer: You can repent because you have free will to do good or evil. Your actions are in your own hands.

In other words, God created us with negative desires that oppose His goals for man, but He also gave us the free will to reject those negative desires. And yet God controls the world and there is nothing in this world that can be performed without the Creator's authority or against His will.

There is an intrinsic conflict between the concept of free will and the idea that God is always in control. How can we resolve this conflict?

> You might say, doesn't the Holy One, blessed be He, know everything that will happen? Before it happens, does He not know who will be righteous and who evil? And if He knows who will be righteous, it would be impossible for [that person] not to be righteous. Know that the answer to this question is wider than the land and deeper than the sea.... You must know and understand that a human being cannot understand His Creator...as the prophet states, "My [God's] thoughts are not your thoughts and your ways are not My ways" (*Yeshayahu* 55:8). Therefore, we cannot know how the Holy One, blessed be He, knows His created beings and their deeds, but we do know, without a doubt, that the actions of man are in the hands of man.
>
> (Rambam, *Hilchos Teshuvah* 5:5)

Volumes of philosophical treatises have been written on the subject of free will, and many Jewish philosophers have expounded on the conflict between free will and Divine will. In this essay, we will not attempt to cover all of the various approaches, but instead, we will focus on a *midrash* in *Tanchuma Vayeishev* that deals with the subject, dividing it into three parts.

Punishment or Pretext?

"Yosef was brought down to Egypt" (*Bereishis* 39:1) — as it is written, "Go and see the workings of God, His awesome actions (*nora alilah*) upon man" (*Tehillim* 66:5). Rabbi Yehoshua ben Korcha said, "Even those awful things that He brings on us, He brings using a pretext [*alilah*]." Come and see: When the Holy One, blessed be He, created the world on the first day, He created the angel of death. How do we know? Rabbi Berechya said, "Because it says, 'Darkness was on the face of the earth' (*Bereishis* 1:2) — this is the angel of death, who darkens the face of the creatures. Man was created on the sixth day and the false accusation [*alilah*] was hung on him that he brought death to the world, as it says, 'On the day you eat of it, you will surely die' (ibid. 2:17)."

To what is this similar? To a man who wanted to divorce his wife. When he went home, he wrote a *get* [bill of divorce], entered the house with the *get* in his hands, and sought a pretext [*alilah*] to give it to her. He said to her, "Make me a drink." When he took the drink from her hands, he said to her, "Here is your *get*." She said to him, "What is my sin?" He said, "Leave my house because you mixed me a lukewarm drink." She said to him, "You knew I would bring you a lukewarm drink, since you wrote the *get* and brought it in your hand."

Here, too: Adam said to the Holy One, blessed be He, "Master of the Universe, even before You created the world two thousand years ago, the Torah was a nursling in Your Hands, as it says, 'Then I was by Him as a nursling, and I was daily His delight, playing always before Him' (*Mishlei* 8:30). Two thousand years ago! And this Torah says: 'When a man dies in a tent...' (*Vayikra* 19:14). If You had not established mortality for Your creatures, You would not have written thus. But You come to put the accusation [*alilah*] on me." As it says, "You [impose] awesome actions [*alilah*] on man."

(*Tanchuma Vayeishev* 4)

The same word, *alilah*, is translated in several different ways. It means actions, false accusations, and pretexts! This is the key to understanding the *midrash*, and we will return to it later.

On the sixth day of creation, God created the first human beings, Adam and Chavah. He put them in the Garden of Eden and gave them one mitzvah: not to eat of the Tree of Knowledge of Good and Evil. They were warned, "On the day you eat of it, you will surely die" (*Bereishis* 2:17). And indeed, when they ate of the forbidden fruit, mortality came into the world.

Yet the Midrash proposes that God decreed death upon the world on the first day of creation, well before Adam was created. Was a false accusation (*alilah*) hung on Adam? In other words, was Adam and Chavah's sin a pretext for God's preordained decree?

This is similar, continues the Midrash, to a man who had already made up his mind to divorce his wife and then looked for a pretext. With the bill of divorce (*get*) already in hand, he asked his wife to make him a hot drink, knowing that the drink she would serve would be lukewarm because she always brought him a lukewarm drink. When she brought him the usual (lukewarm) beverage, he used the drink as an excuse (*alilah*) to divorce her.

The situations are parallel because just as the man in the story already had the bill of divorce in hand, so too did God already have the Torah in which many laws dealing with death are written. Just as the man in the story knew his wife would bring lukewarm drink, God knew that Adam would eat from the Tree of Knowledge of Good and Evil, for, knowing his nature, He knew he would sin. Then God used Adam's sin as a pretext (*alilah*) for the mortality that he preordained.

Man Plans and God Laughs

We feel as if we alone are in charge of our surroundings and masters of our destinies. We assume that we use our free will to make decisions that determine our future. But, as the Yiddish saying goes, "Man plans and God laughs." We can plan and decide and determine all we want, but in the final analysis God directs creation toward His goals.

So what choice do we really have? Is our feeling of free will and determination merely an illusion? We have the ability to choose right or left, but both paths lead to the place where God wants us to be:

Go and see the workings of God, His awesome actions (*alilah*) on man.

(*Tehillim* 66:5)

We do not determine our destinations; we merely choose how to get there, and our decisions will become the road-marker for the destination God set for us. True, the way God carries out each individual "program" is indeed wondrous to behold, but, still, if we will inevitably end up where He wants us to be, what does free will have to do with our lives?

Everything is in the hands of Heaven, except for fear of Heaven.

(*Berachos* 33b)

What we can decide, and do decide, is whether to be God's partner to do good or God's tool to do the opposite. What actually happens may not be a consequence of our human activities, but the kind of person we become is a choice that we control absolutely. For example, if a person decides to pull a trigger and, God forbid, kill another person, the decision to kill is a free-will decision of the murderer. However, only God decrees death, and if the murderer's victim is not fated to die, the gun will jam, the shooter will miss, or the victim will be hurt but not killed. If, on the other hand, God decrees death on a person, and nobody makes a free will decision to kill that person, death will befall him in another way.

We see a similar idea in the Purim story. King Achashveirosh gave permission to Haman to exterminate every Jew in Persia, man, woman, and child. Mordechai came to Queen Esther to tell her that she must approach the king to ask for a cancellation of the evil decree, and he told her:

For if you remain silent at this time, then relief and deliverance shall arise for the Jews from elsewhere, but you and your father's house shall perish. And who knows whether you have attained royalty for such a time as this?

(*Esther* 4:14)

Mordechai told Esther that there would be a salvation for the Jewish people, with or without her. She was being given an opportunity to be part of that salvation, through a free-will choice to be God's partner in the unfolding of

His plan for the redemption and survival of the Jewish people. The decision to be God's partner involved tremendous danger and self-sacrifice, and if she chose to risk her life to save her people, she would be remembered forever. If not, the Jews would be saved another way, but Esther and her father's house would be relegated to oblivion.

The unfolding of God's plan for the universe is generally not in our hands, but the role that we play is of our own choosing.

> When you build a new house, you shall make a parapet for your roof, so that you do not bring blood upon your house, if any faller will fall from there.
>
> *(Devarim* 22:8)

> "If any faller will fall" — This man deserved to fall [for this reason he called a faller], and nevertheless let not his death be brought about through you, for good things are brought about through the agency of a good man and bad things are brought about through the agency of a bad man.
>
> *(Rashi)*

Our free will is manifested in the material world through a Divine system whereby God brings about merits through those who are meritorious and negative occurrences through the agency of those who are not meritorious. Our choice is to be meritorious or, God forbid, the opposite. Despite the choices that we make, however, God's plan will be carried out.

Adam's Argument

Understanding these principles sheds a new light on the *midrash* about Adam. The *midrash* uses a parable, and we can now understand the key to the parable. The wife is, like Adam, the victim of a predestined plan; the husband, like God, had already prepared the bill of divorce. The lukewarm drink is the pretext, as is the Tree of Knowledge of Good and Evil, and the bill of divorce is the equivalent of Adam's banishment from the Garden of Eden. The wife's argument is the same as Adam's: "You came with the *get* already in your pocket! You knew I would bring you lukewarm drink, because you know my nature. This was a setup!"

Adam felt manipulated by God. How can we understand his feeling of manipulation? Did God really impose His preordained will onto Adam and Chavah?

The key to this puzzling question lies in the word *alilah*. The Hebrew language is very precise. In all languages in the world, words are merely symbols of the items they represent. These words are chosen at random and can be changed as society wishes. For instance, we call a table "table" and a chair "chair," but if we would agree to change the symbol, we could call a chair "table" with no harm done. However, the Hebrew language is different because the essence of the item is reflected in the word itself and therefore words are precise in both their meaning and their connotations. For example, the word *Torah* means instructions, the word *horeh* means parent, and *moreh* means teacher. We see clearly how all of these words are related in meaning.

But sometimes words that are based on the same root have different translations. In such cases, one must study the root of the word more deeply to understand how these "offspring" words are related. In our *midrash*, the word *alilah* was used to mean "false accusation," "pretext," and "actions." It would seem, at first glance, that there is no relationship between a false accusation and a miracle. Yet there must be a common thread, a similar underlying meaning, because word choice in the Torah is never random.

> That you may tell in the ears of your son, and of your son's son, the things I have done in Egypt, and my signs which I have done [*hisalalti*] among them, that they may know that I am the Lord.
>
> (*Shemos* 10:2)

Here, the root word *alilah* refers to the miracles and wonders and the plagues that God did for the Jewish people in Egypt.

> And lo, he has laid accusing speeches [*alilos*] against her, saying, "I have not found your daughter to be a virgin," and yet these are the tokens of my daughter's virginity.
>
> (*Devarim* 22:17)

Here, the root word *alilah* refers to a false accusation made by a man against his new bride. How can we reconcile the usage of *alilah* for such drastically different ideas?

Rav Shimshon Refael Hirsch explains that the word *alilah* comes from the root word *olel*. *Olel* is a small child who is in a state of development, a toddler. Every day the child changes and progresses. An *alilah*, then, is not an isolated event, but a series of actions and deeds that result in a person's development or a revelation of oneself through a progressive series of individual actions.

We can understand more clearly by looking at another Hebrew word, "*lehisolel*." The word *lehisolel* is in the reflexive verbal conjugation, i.e., the action always comes back on the one who acts. *Lehisolel*, then, would mean someone who acts in a progressive series of events on another person with no respect to that person, but only to reflect back on himself. These actions are a way of imposing his power on another person, as in the case in *Devarim* when the man falsely accused his wife. The husband is treating his new wife as a mechanism through which to reveal his own power. According to his whim, having no respect at all for his wife, he slanders her and falsely accuses her (Rav Shimshon Refael Hirsch on *Devarim* 27:17).

When one person imposes his power on another, this is abusive. However, when the imposition of power comes from God, i.e., when God uses His actions on man to reveal Himself, this is called a wonder. In this case, the word *lehisolel* means to impose Himself using awesome actions.

We can now understand why the verse quoted in the Midrash is read in two different ways: "See the awesome actions that come through God" or "See the imposition of God's power on you." From God's perspective, death was brought into the world using the events of the world as they happen. There was indeed free will for the human beings, but God's goal was primary. There is an overall plan for the world, but it is man who creates the reality through his actions.

From Adam's perspective, however, death was brought about through an *alilah*, a false accusation. Adam felt "manipulated" by God because he was not the total creator of his own destiny. Adam experienced the sense of God imposing His power on him. In fact, Adam had a point; God did impose His will on man, because He had always intended for death to come to the world.

Who's in Charge?

Let's imagine a hypothetical situation. Suppose your child's bedtime is approaching, and, at the same time, he is trying your patience. As any parent knows, the excuse you are going to use to send him to bed isn't the real reason you are sending him to bed. You might say, "I've had enough — you're going to bed right now!" But, in truth, the child was going to be sent to bed anyway. Did he really do whatever it was that tried your patience? Yes, he did. Were you going to send him to bed anyway because he needs enough rest to feel good and be productive the next day? Yes. Does he feel manipulated? Yes. Was he responsible? Yes.

Adam cried, "I feel manipulated, I feel used. You have used me to bring death into the world, when it was preordained!" Was this true? Yes, but Adam's argument is also a failure to take responsibility. God brings merits into the world through the meritorious, and He brings evil into the world through the wicked. Death was going to enter the world regardless of Adam's actions, but, nevertheless, it was Adam's choice and Adam's act that provided the channel for death's entry into the world. One might argue, "Well, God knew that Adam would sin, and even gave him a mitzvah so that he could sin, and it's not fair to expect otherwise!" However, our Sages never said that Adam was predestined to fail. Nor was the wife predestined to bring luke-warm drink to her husband. Nothing at all prevented her from bringing a hot cup of tea instead. She acted with complete free will.

Moral Battlefield

The Midrash in *Tanchuma Vayeishev* continues:

So too, you find that the Holy One, blessed be He, said to Moshe, "Surely, [not] one man (*ha'ish*) of these men of this evil generation shall see the good land" (*Devarim* 1:35). "*Ha'ish*" refers to Moshe, as it says, "The man (*ha'ish*) Moshe was humble" (*Bemidbar* 12:3). "*Ha'ish*" refers specifically to Moshe. And also it says, "Now you will see what I will do to Pharaoh" (*Shemos*

6:1) — you will see in the war against Pharaoh, but you will not see in the war against the thirty-one kings [of the land of Canaan]. But when he [Moshe] said, "Listen, you rebellious ones" (*Bemidbar* 20:10), God said to him, "Therefore you will not bring this congregation into the land." As it is stated, "You [impose] accusations (*alilah*) on man."

The second part of the *midrash* gives a completely different analysis of free will. In "An Essay on Free Will" (*Michtav MeEliyahu*, vol. 1), Rav Dessler explains that when two armies are locked together in battle, the real battle takes place only at the battlefront. Each side's territories behind the lines are not the battlefields; the real fighting takes place at the point of actual confrontation. When one side wins a victory at the front and pushes the enemy back, the location of the battlefront changes. The actual fighting takes place in only one location at any given time.

So, too, continues Rav Dessler, we as individuals have a battlefield — a moral battlefield with only one point of actual confrontation. This point (Rav Dessler calls this the "free-will point") is the place where there's a confrontation between truth and fiction, good and evil, right and wrong, and it is at this point only where free will exists. The free-will battle occurs specifically where there is a struggle in our lives. In areas where we don't struggle, i.e., the "territories behind the lines," there is no free will.

For example, for a person raised in a Torah home, there is no temptation to eat forbidden foods. It is simply not an issue for him. On the other hand, a beginner in Torah, someone who attached himself to the Torah later in life, will not find it easy to give up foods that he is used to eating. It will be a struggle, sometimes an intense one. Since a person raised in the Torah lifestyle is not tempted to eat forbidden foods, for him, this is not a free-will decision. It is territory behind the lines of the battlefield. But for a late beginner, the intense struggle is indeed a free-will point.

Each moral decision made leads a person to a new battlefront, and hence a new struggle and free-will point. If the decision made is good and in line with the Torah, then the new free-will point will be at a higher level, since more moral territory will have been conquered. If the decision made is not in line with the Torah, then it is as if the person has lost the moral battlefront and the new struggle will be at a lower level.

This explains the dictum of our Rabbis, "One mitzvah leads to another; one sin leads to another" (*Devarim Rabbah* 6:4). Each decision made leads to another decision that leads to another. Territory that is beyond the battlefront — i.e., beyond the ability of the individual — is not within the free will of the individual, nor is territory that he has "conquered" so well that it no longer presents a struggle for him.

We can now understand the second part of our *midrash*.

When God appeared to Moshe at the burning bush and commanded him to go to Egypt to speak to Pharaoh, Moshe objected, saying, "I am a man of uncircumcised lips." In response to this refusal, God told Moshe that he, Moshe, would not be allowed to enter the Land of Israel.

> Rabbi Shmuel bar Nachman said: All seven days at the bush, the Holy One, blessed be He, was trying to convince Moshe to go on His mission to Egypt. [After the seven days] the Holy One, blessed be He, said to him, "Moshe, you say, 'Send by the hand of whomever You will send' — on your life, I will clip you by your wings." When did He punish him? All seven days of the month of Adar [before his death], Moshe begged and prayed that he be allowed to enter the Land of Israel. On the seventh day, He said to him, "You will not cross over the Jordan" (*Devarim* 3:27).
>
> (*Vayikra Rabbah* 11:6)

Some time after the burning bush incident, Moshe and Aharon appeared before Pharaoh in his court to demand that the Jewish people be allowed to exit Egypt. Pharaoh became angry and made the labor harder for the Jewish people, forcing them not only to build structures for him, but also to gather straw and make their own bricks.

> Moshe returned to the Lord, and said, "Lord, why have You dealt ill with this people? Why did You send me? For since I came to Pharaoh to speak in Your name, he has done evil to this people; and You have not delivered Your people at all."
>
> (*Shemos* 5:22)

God responded:

> Now you will see what I will do to Pharaoh, for with a strong

hand shall he let them go and with a strong hand will he drive them out of his land.

(Shemos 6:1–2)

Once again, the *midrash* states that Moshe's punishment for his accusation of God was that he was not be allowed into the Land of Israel:

"Now you will see what I will do to Pharaoh" — you will see in the war against Pharoah, but you will not see in the war against the thirty-one kings [of the Land of Israel].

(Tanchuma Vayeishev)

Three years later, after the Jews had received the Torah and were ready to enter the promised land, Moshe sent spies to spy out the land. He did so at the request of the nation, without God's command. When the spies returned with a negative report, the Jews refused to go up to the Land of Israel and conquer it. They were punished; none of them would be allowed to enter the Land of Israel, and specifically Moshe would not be permitted entry.

So, too, you find that the Holy One, blessed be He, said to Moshe, "Surely, not one man of these men of this evil generation shall see the good land" *(Devarim* 1:35). "One man" refers to Moshe.

(Tanchuma Vayeishev)

After thirty-eight years of wandering in the desert, the miraculous well that traveled with the Jewish people was removed, and the people complained for the lack of water. Moshe was instructed to "speak to the rock, and it shall give forth water" *(Bemidbar* 20:8). Instead, however, he took his rod and hit the rock and, in his anger, said to the Children of Israel:

"Listen, you rebellious ones, shall we fetch you water from the rock?"

(Bemidbar 20:10)

God said to him, "Therefore, you will not bring this congregation into the land." As it is stated, "You [impose] accusations *(alilah)*."

(Tanchuma Vayeishev)

Moshe is punished because he didn't rise to the challenge of sanctifying God's name in the way that would enable him to enter the land (Rav Dessler, *Michtav MeEliyahu*, vol.1, p. 161). Four different times, over the span of forty-one years, Moshe did something that prevented him from being able to enter the Land of Israel. It was not just one act, or two, but a series of incidents that brought him this punishment. On each occasion, Moshe exhibited a small lack of faith, and each small deficiency in faith led to the next problem.

Bear in mind that Moshe's "lack of faith" has nothing to do with the "lack of faith" that you or I might experience. For you or me, hitting the rock might be a negligible oversight, but for Moshe Rabbeinu it was a deficiency in faith.

This pattern of behavior started at the burning bush when Moshe said he couldn't speak properly and so would be unable to bring the Jewish people out of Egypt. The Midrash says that it was from that moment in time that Moshe could not go into the Land of Israel. Later Moshe said to God, "You made it worse for this people!" Still later, Moshe sent out the spies, and perhaps that was another deficiency in faith, i.e., suggesting to the people that they didn't have to believe God when He promised to bring them into the Land. Each event progressively led to the next action, until that final action of hitting the rock.

It was not one mistake that caused Moshe to be denied entry to the Land of Israel, but the progressive series of events (*alilah*) that finally led to the refusal of God to allow his entry into the Land of Israel.

When There Is No Free Will

There are times when the Divine will has determined that a particular mission will be carried out for the building of the nation of Israel. The individual who is assigned that mission may have no free will but to carry it out, and he is compelled to act in the way God determines.

The story of Yehudah and Tamar is an example of this concept. Yehudah, whose tribe was destined to issue the kings of Israel, had three sons. The first son, Onan, married Tamar, but he sinned and died without issue. According to Jewish law, the widow of a man who died without children should marry his brother. The child they bear together will then be called the son of the deceased. (We no longer perform this kind of levirate marriage but instead we release the man through a ceremony called *chalitzah*.) And so, Tamar married Onan's brother, Eir. But Eir also sinned and died without issue.

Tamar, who knew through prophecy that she was destined to be the mother of Israel's royalty, wanted to marry Yehudah's third son, Shelah. Yehudah, however, stalled and put her off, until Tamar realized that Yehudah did not intend to give her in marriage to Shelah. She therefore disguised herself as a prostitute and waited on the road in order to entice Yehudah himself to come to her so that she could fulfill her mission as the mother of royalty.

> So she removed her widow's garb from upon her, covered herself with a veil, and wrapped herself up. Then she sat by the crossroads which is on the road toward Timnah, for she saw that Shelah had grown and she had not been given to him as a wife. When Yehudah saw her, he thought her to be a harlot, since she had covered her face. So he detoured to her by the road and said, "Come, if you please, let me consort with you," for he did not know that she was his daughter-in-law.
>
> (*Bereishis* 38:14–16)

The text contains within it a contradiction: the word "detour" implies that Yehudah saw the prostitute and turned away from her. Yet the text says, "he detoured *to* her."

> "Yehudah saw" — Rabbi Yochanan said: [Yehudah] wanted to pass by, but the Holy One, blessed be He, sent the angel that is appointed over lust. He said to Yehudah, "Where are you going?" [He answered,] "I am going to the place where kings stand, the place where great ones stand." "He detoured to her towards the road." This was against his will and not for his own benefit.
>
> (*Bereishis Rabbah* 85:8)

Yehudah did not want to go to this prostitute; his will was to turn away from her. God, however, had determined that our nation would receive kingship, and it would come from Yehudah and Tamar. Consequently God imposed His will on Yehudah by sending an angel that forced Yehudah to go to the prostitute.

The Midrash ends by saying that this was "against his will, not *letovo*, for his own benefit." Whenever the Midrash uses the word *tov*, good, it refers to the physical good. Yehudah didn't go to the "prostitute" because he had a desire for physical pleasure. He went to her because he had no choice; his free will was taken from him and he acted against his will. There was a mission crucial to the development of the Jewish people that depended on the union of Yehudah and Tamar, and God ensured that it happened.

We are ready to look at the last part of the Midrash:

> The coat of stripes caused all the tribes to descend to Egypt. Rabbi Yudan said: The Holy One, blessed be He, wanted to fulfill the decree of "Know with certainty that your offspring shall be aliens..." (*Bereishis* 15:13). Therefore, He brought about the pretext (*alilah*) including all of these things: Yaakov loved Yosef, the brothers hated him and sold him to the Ishmaelites, who brought him down to Egypt, and Yaakov heard that Yosef was alive in Egypt, and he came down with the tribes and they were enslaved there. Therefore, it says, "Yosef was brought down [*hurad*] to Egypt." Don't read, "he was brought down" [*alilah*], read "he brought down" [*heirid*] his father and the tribes to Egypt.
>
> Rabbi Tanchuma said: To what is this thing similar? To a cow that they wanted to yoke with a collar, but she refused to be yoked. What did they do? They took her son from her and pulled him down to the very place they wanted her to plow, and the calf bellowed. When the cow heard him so bellowing, she went, though it was not for her own good, for the sake of her son.
>
> So, too, the Holy One, blessed be He, wanted to fulfill the decree of "Know with certainty" and brought a pretext [*alilah*] for all these things, and they came down to Egypt and implemented the contract. Therefore it says, "Yosef was brought down to Egypt." As it is stated, "You [impose] awesome acts [*alilah*] on man."
>
> (*Tanchuma Vayeishev* 4)

In order to lure the cow to the hard labor of the plow, the farmer led her calf to the field because, as our Rabbis teach, "More than the calf wants to suckle, the mother wants to nurse" (*Pesachim* 112a). Even though the plow is not for the good of the mother, the instinct to suckle her child is greater than her instinct to avoid the hard labor. The cow goes "not for her own good" but for the interest of her child.

So too Yaakov, the "cow," is drawn to Egypt to be with Yosef, "the calf." The Egyptian exile would be arduous for Yaakov and his sons, as the plow is difficult for the calf. Yet, as the cow was drawn into hard labor because of the love for her calf, Yaakov was pulled by his love of his son into a situation that would not be good. Who is the farmer in our parable who manipulates the cow and uses the calf as a magnet? The farmer is God.

A similar *midrash* has a different ending:

> Rabbi Berechya said in the name of Rabbi Yehudah bar Shimon said: [It is similar] to a cow that they were pulling to the slaughterhouse and she would not be pulled. What did they do? They pulled her son before her and she walked after him, against her will and not in her own interest. So, too, our father Yaakov should have descended to Egypt in chains and leg irons. The Holy One, blessed be He, said, "He is my firstborn son, should I bring him down in shame? I will not allow Pharoah to think [that he will bring Yaakov down into slavery]. I will bring him down in a public way, but I will draw his son down before him and he will come after him, against his will and not for his own benefit." And He brought the Divine Presence (*Shechinah*) to Egypt with him.
>
> (*Bereishis Rabbah* 86:2)

Yosef's coat of stripes "caused" all of the tribes to descend to Egypt. When God wanted "the very deep wisdom" to begin, i.e., the prophecy of the exile in Egypt to be fulfilled, He brought about a series of events to ensure that it happened. Therefore, Yaakov loved Yosef a little more than he loved his brothers, Yosef's brothers hated him and sold him to the Ishmaelites, he was brought down to Egypt and became viceroy, Yaakov heard that Yosef was alive in Egypt, and all the Jewish people descended to Egypt and were enslaved there.

In other words, God imposed the emotions and actions upon them. Yaakov had no choice but to favor Yosef, and the brothers had no choice but to hate him. The sale had to take place. Yosef had to be brought down to Egypt and he had to become viceroy so that the twelve tribes would end up in Egypt — against their will. "Yosef went down to Egypt" means that he brought his father down, and all the tribes with him.

To what is this thing similar, asks the Midrash? To a cow!

This *midrash* has a new element to it: The cow is drawn to the slaughterhouse, a metaphor for Egypt. Yaakov was destined to go to Egypt in chains and leg irons, in humiliation and degradation. But God had mercy on him and instead He brought Yosef down first, so that Yaakov would come in honor.

When Yosef became viceroy of Egypt and was reunited with his brothers, he sent for his father and invited him to come to live there. Yosef sent wagons (*agalos*) to transport his father (the word *agalah* is a double entendre with the word *egel*, calf).

The Sefas Emes explains the *midrash* in the following way: Yaakov had reached the pinnacle of his spiritual success, yet he had one more journey to take in this world, the journey of exile. This was the beginning of the fulfillment of the prophecy of Avraham, "Your children will be strangers in a land that does not belong to them."

Taking Yaakov down in chains and leg irons refers to a spiritual descent from a very high level to a lower one, then a lower one, then a lower one, culminating in the pit of Egypt, which was the most promiscuous, materialistic, and base society. With mercy and compassion, however, God instead set up the situation — *alilah*! — so that Yaakov's "calf," Yosef, would go first and Yaakov would follow "voluntarily" in wagons. Travelling on a wagon, buffered by its wheels, one doesn't feel the descent. Therefore:

> The sale of Yosef was a merit for [the brothers] and caused [Yosef] to rule. It was a merit for his brothers and for his father's entire house, for he sustained them with bread during the years of famine. Therefore, he was sold by their hand, for [God] brings about merit through the meritorious.
>
> (*Bemidbar Rabbah* 13)

> I drew them with human cords, with leading strings of love....
>
> (*Hoshea* 11:4)

Things are not always what they appear to be. What appeared to be hatred, what appeared to be a would-be murder and sale of a brother, was really a manifestation of God pulling "with leading strings of love" in order to bring Yaakov down to Egypt in the kindest way possible. In fact, the brothers were puppets at the end of God's string, doing God's will, though they did not know it. God chose them as the mechanism through which He showed kindness to Yaakov because they themselves were meritorious.

It is true that there are other ways to understand this story and the brothers' role in it, but we cannot ignore the statement of this *midrash* that the sale of Yosef was to their credit. For God used the brothers to save the Yaakov and his household — as well as the whole world — from starvation.

Where There's a Will There's a Way

We look around the world and we are confounded by the chaos that we see. Nations fight nations, the Jewish world is muddled in confusion, our own country, Israel, is faced with impossible choices, and there seems to be no end to our troubles.

Yet the world is not abandoned, and we are not alone. There is a Divine plan, our destination has been set, and God continues to draw us "with stings of love." We will reach God's final goal, which is the final redemption, but each one of us must decide what part to play: will we be God's partner to effect good, or will we not? Will we be meritorious, or the opposite? Each choice we make along the way will lead us to another choice, so let us choose well.

Crying Out in Solitude

O ur Rabbis teach that the heart of King David contained in it the heart of every Jew, and that his *Tehillim* express every joy, pain, sorrow, and delight ever experienced. How did he know our hearts? How was he able to compose a book in which every person can find himself somewhere?

We might assume that King David's days were filled with honor and repose, with dignity and majesty. Yet when we read his life story, and even more his Psalms, we learn that he knew sorrow well.

> A *maskil* of David; a prayer when he was in the cave. My voice cries out to God, with my voice I make my supplication to the Lord. I pour out my complaint before Him; I declare my trouble before Him. When my spirit envelops me, You know my path. In the path where I walk they have secretly laid a snare for me. I look on my right hand, and behold, but there is no man who knows me; no refuge remains to me; no man cares for my soul. I cry to you, O Lord; I say, "You are my refuge and my portion in the land of the living." Attend to my cry, for I am impoverished; save me from my persecutors, for they are too strong for me. Bring my soul out of prison that I may give thanks to Your name; the righteous shall be crowned through me; for You shall deal bountifully with me.
>
> (*Tehillim*, ch. 142)

The fact that a person of King David's stature made a record of his pain suggests why he might have had to know such pain. A record is clearly meant for future generations. In fact, the simple existence of David's Psalms indicates how critical it is that we find meaning in our own pain. With his words, we have a way to express the kind of suffering that would otherwise feel indescribable, unmentionable, beyond words. From King David's life and work, we learn that great suffering has a purpose. What is that purpose? The answer is encoded in the psalm above. A close reading of the psalm offers an answer to this universal question.

The Cave

To understand Psalm 142, we must first know about the life of suffering that inspired it. We must begin by knowing the story of David's greatest foe: David's predecessor, the first king of Israel — King Shaul.

Shaul accomplished much as king. He established a unified civil administration and defended the Land of Israel against enemy nations. He was a deeply righteous person, humble before God and modest before man. This modesty, in fact, taken to an extreme would lead him to sin, to lose his kingship, and, ultimately, to develop great loathing for David.

When told by the prophet Shmuel to lead the people in war against Israel's archenemy Amalek, Shaul did not hesitate. Shaul was told that in battle, he must kill every man, woman, and child, along with all livestock. Instead of doing as he was told, he followed the will of the people, who were intent on saving the animals. Shaul thus waived his own obligation to lead. In the end, along with livestock, he spared the life of the king of Amalek himself.

In so doing, Shaul sinned against God. Punishment followed swiftly. He was told by the prophet Shmuel that the kingdom would be taken from him and given to another. Then, the Divine presence (the *Shechinah*) was removed from him, causing him great anguish. "The spirit of Hashem departed from Shaul, and he was tormented by a spirit of melancholy from Hashem" (*Shmuel I* 16:14).

Next, Shaul's successor was chosen and anointed by Shmuel the prophet in secret, his name concealed until the time of his ascension to the throne.

It was David, of course, who was anointed king of Israel; and although Shaul was not told the identity of his replacement, he suspected the truth. He witnessed David's serenity, courage, and faith in difficult times. He saw the love of the people and the palace servants for David. Even Shaul's own children adored the young shepherd. In his heart, he knew that David was his successor.

At first, Shaul wanted only to keep watch over David; he gave his daughter Michal to him in marriage, expecting that she would spy on her own husband for him. But his fear and suspicion grew deadly. Twice, Shaul came after David with a spear, planning to kill him. The formerly righteous king fell to this level because of his misplaced modesty in the war with Amalek. Because he did not assert himself as king when obligated, he lost the kingship, the Divine presence, and the loyalty of his own children. His anger raged so fiercely that it stirred him to murderous intent. However, each time he tried to kill David, David nimbly escaped.

Eventually, the young future king fled. Shaul then pursued him relentlessly, ruthlessly, chasing him from hiding place to hiding place. After two years on the run, David found himself trapped. None of his subsequent enemies would ever come as close to capturing him as King Shaul did on that day. Shaul had chased David to Ein Gedi, to a lonely mountain that rises above the Dead Sea in the Judean desert. Surrounded on all sides, David and his tiny band of followers retreated to their last hideout, deep in a dark cave.

> It was after Shaul returned from after the Pelishtim, and people told him, saying, "David is in the wilderness of Ein Gedi." Then Shaul took three thousand chosen men from all Israel and went to seek David and his men upon the rocks of the wild goats. He came to the sheepfolds by the way, where there was a cave; and Shaul went in to relieve himself; and David and his men remained in the back of the cave. And the men of David said to him, "Behold the day of which the Lord said to you, 'Behold, I will deliver your enemy into your hand, that you may do to him as it shall seem good in your eyes.'" Then David arose, and cut off the corner of Shaul's robe secretly.
>
> And it came to pass afterward that David's heart struck him because he had cut off the corner of Shaul's robe. And he said to his men, "The Lord forbid that I should do this thing to my master, the Lord's anointed, to stretch forth my hand against him, seeing as he is the anointed of the Lord." So David scolded his servants with these words and did not allow them to rise against Shaul. And Shaul rose up from the cave and went on his way.
>
> (*Shmuel* I 24:2–8)

This is the cave that David speaks of in his prayer in Psalm 142.

Shaul entered the cave where David had been hiding. David and his men identified him immediately, but Shaul did not see them. Their eyes had adjusted to the dark of the cave, while his had not.

David could have killed Shaul on that day; and in fact, his men urged him to do so, believing that this act was the fulfillment of a prophecy that David would prevail over his enemies. But David refused, saying, "The Lord forbid that I should do this thing to my master, the Lord's anointed, to stretch forth my hand against him, seeing as he is the anointed of the Lord." Instead, he cut off the corner of Shaul's cloak. At that moment, David's "heart struck him," as he realized that Shaul was still king, and that his own rule had not yet begun (Malbim). He reasoned that if merely cutting the king's garment frightened him so, harming the king himself must surely be a sin. From his trepidation, he understood that Shaul, while still king, was "the anointed of God."

Physically, David could have killed the king, but spiritually he could not. Doing anything to harm the "anointed of God" was terrifying to him. The reality was suddenly very plain: Shaul could kill him, but he could not kill Shaul.

And he was afraid.

In his fear, he called out to God:

> I look on my right hand, and behold, but there is no man who knows me; no refuge remains to me; no man cares for my soul...save me from my persecutors, for they are too strong for me.

Transition to Kingship

How does one become king? Shmuel crowned David first secretly and later in front of his family, yet his reign did not begin, in truth, until after Shaul's death. Only then was he declared king before the entire kingdom. David could not immediately assume rulership because becoming a king is a process. A person must become worthy of kingship.

> "My son, fear the Lord and be a king (*u'meloch*)" (*Mishlei* 24:21). What is implied by the expression "*u'meloch*"? It means: Proclaim Him as your king.

Another interpretation is that the word *u'meloch* means 'Make your good inclination king over your bad inclination, which is termed a king"; as it says, "And there came a great king against it and besieged it" (*Koheles* 9:14)....

"My son, fear the Lord and be a king (*u'meloch*)." Whoever fears the Holy One, blessed be He, will ultimately become a king.

(*Bemidbar Rabbah* 15:4)

The Midrash asks: What does "*u'meloch*" mean? It then offers what appears to be three answers: (1) "Fear God and make Him your King," (2) "Fear God by making your good inclination king over your evil inclination," and (3) "Fear God and you will become a king."

At first, it seems that the answers above are alternate definitions of a puzzling word in the verse. However, Rav Goldvicht, *zt"l*, understood the *midrash* as describing three stages in one process, the process necessary to acquire kingship.

The first stage is to acknowledge that God is King. One must then make a decision to be the servant of the King and to subjugate himself to His rule. "Fear God, my son, and make Him King."

Stage two is to exercise self-control by making the good inclination rule over all one's choices. This is only possible after having mastered the first stage, acknowledging God as king. A person must then make a great effort to control all of his actions and words, and will only succeed if he has awe for the King.

When he finally achieves self-control, this quality will be internalized. His self-rule will be obvious to others and his regal bearing evident, as a face reflects the inner world of a person. The Hebrew word for face is *panim*, which is connected to the word *lifnim*. *Lifnim* means inside, internal. *Panim* is the external revelation of the inside, the *lifnim*. In this last stage in the process, all will notice his inner kingship and will then acknowledge his majesty. Thus, he will become a king.

There are two models of Jewish kingship, Yehudah and Yosef, and both undergo this three-stage process.

Yehudah's name is derived from the Hebrew word *hodah*, which means "acknowledge," "admit," and "thank." *Hodah* implies that a person understands that there is someone beyond himself to whom he is obligated. If he sins, he must admit wrongdoing to God. If he is given a gift, he must acknowledge that he owes the giver by thanking him.

Leah gave her son the name *Yehudah* to express her gratitude; it was an acknowledgment of this God-given gift. Yehudah inherited this ability to see the hand of God and to acknowledge both his thanks and his obligation to his Creator. When, as an adult, Yehudah sinned against his daughter-in-law, Tamar, and she confronted him with the truth, he immediately admitted his wrongdoing, saying, "She is more righteous than I."

This ability to admit wrong comes from the recognition that God is King and that we are obligated to do His will. Yehudah's ability to acknowledge God as King and then rectify his mistake made him kingly.

Hence, when Yaakov blessed Yehudah before his death, he said, "Yehudah, your brothers will acknowledge you (*yoducha*)." Clearly, there is a connection between Yehudah's acknowledgment of God as King over him and his brothers' acknowledgment of Yehudah as king over them. Yehudah had internalized God's sovereignty so absolutely that it became obvious to all who knew him.

> "Yehudah, your brothers will acknowledge you" (*Bereishis* 49:8). You acknowledged [your part] in the incident of Tamar; your brothers shall acknowledge you as king over them.
>
> (*Bereishis Rabbah* 89:8)

Yosef, as well, became a king because of regal behavior. The defining moment in his life was when, as an eighteen-year-old slave in the house of Potifar, he resisted seduction by Potifar's wife. She tried relentlessly to entice him to intimacy, yet he steadfastly resisted her advances.

Thirteen years later, Pharaoh was impressed with Yosef's wisdom and humility and made him viceroy over Egypt.

> And Pharaoh said to Yosef, "For as much as God has shown you all this, there is none so discreet and wise as you are. You shall be over my house, and according to your word shall all my people be ruled [literally, according to your mouth shall be the kissing of all my people]; only in the throne will I be greater than you." And Pharaoh said to Yosef, "See, I have set you over all the land of Egypt."

And Pharaoh took off his ring from his hand and put it upon Yosef's hand, arrayed him in cloaks of fine linen, and put a gold chain about his neck. He made him to ride in his second chariot, and they cried before him, "*Avreich* (ruler);" and so he made him over all the land of Egypt.

(Bereishis 41:39–43)

There would seem to be little connection between Yosef's attainment of kingship and his resistance to Potifar's beautiful wife. Yet, to the Midrash, there is a clear relationship between the ornate jewelry, garb, and honor given to him as viceroy and his earlier battle against temptation:

Yosef was only given what was his. Thus, to the mouth that had not kissed in sin [Pharoah] said: "And according to your mouth shall be the kissing of all my people." His neck had not cleaved to sin; therefore [Pharaoh] "put a gold chain about his neck." His hands had not stroked in sin, therefore [Pharoah] "put it [the royal ring] upon Yosef's hand." His body had not cleaved to sin; therefore [Pharoah] "arrayed him in cloaks of fine linen." The feet that had not stepped forward to sin would step toward the royal chariot: "And he made him ride in his second chariot." Let the thought which had not yearned for sin come and be called wisdom: "And they cried before him, '*Avreich*,' " which means "father in wisdom though tender in years."

(Bereishis Rabbah 90:3)

Not only was Yosef rewarded for his righteousness, but also every part of his body that had not sinned, that had subjugated itself to the rule of the King, was rewarded with the honor of kingship. Yosef had internalized the Kingship of God and had made his good inclination king over his bad inclination. This princely behavior and inner subjugation reflected outward until even Pharaoh recognized it and crowned Yosef.

In the same way that Yehudah and Yosef internalized the rule of the King of Kings, so too David had to recognize, not just intellectually, but in his heart, that God is King and that there is no reality outside the reality of God. "*Ein od milvado* — there is no one but Him [God]" (*Devarim* 4:35). Once he absorbed that, he too would become king.

From his birth, he was prepared for this reality through *yissurim*, afflictions. As a child, he was rejected by his family. As described above, his father-in-law, Shaul, tried to kill him twice, and he lived in exile for two years. Many times, members of his own tribe came close to turning him into Shaul, and each time he escaped miraculously. In his loneliness and suffering, David realized that God is "a shield to all those who trust in Him" (*Tehillim* 18:31).

It was as Shaul entered his hiding place in the cave that David wholly and utterly internalized the reality that nothing exists but God.

> Understand what David wrote in *Tehillim* 142, "A *maskil* of David; a prayer when he was in the cave...." [The title *maskil*] comes to relate that David became enlightened when he was in the cave...and there kingship grew like a shoot and blossomed. Therefore, he then prayed: "My voice cries out to God."
>
> Who is a prince? "Someone who has no one on top of him except for the Lord his God" (*Horayos* 10a).
>
> *(Agra Dechala* 157)

The Midrash asks why this particular psalm begins with the word *maskil*. *Maskil* means "enlightened." What did David learn in the cave that enlightened him so much that he named the psalm "Enlightenment"? It was in the cave that David recognized with absolute clarity that there was no one above him except God. The only One to whom he must answer was God. Only when David understood this did his kingship begin to blossom.

What did he see in the cave that enlightened him?

> When Shaul and David were in the cave, he knew and saw that no one can rely on his money, on his wisdom, or on his strength. And on what can he rely? In his prayer, David became enlightened (*maskil*) and knew and said that nothing is good for him, except for prayer. Therefore, it says, "A *maskil* [enlightenment] of David."
>
> *(Beis Midrash, Tehillim* 142:1)

In the cave David was enlightened to the fact that he had no one to turn to but God, nothing to save him but God. This was a turning point for him — the moment when he rose to kingship.

The definition of a Jewish king is different than that of a non-Jewish one.

Whereas in the non-Jewish world a king enjoys "the Divine right of Kings" and has authority to enact laws and implement them as he wishes, a Jewish king has no such right. A Jewish king is nothing more, or less, than a servant of God. It is through attaining the spiritual status of servant of the King that he merits kingship, *malchus*.

Kingship

"Every king needs a nation" (*Pirkei DeRabbi Eliezer* 11). Every king needs a kingdom to acknowledge his rule, for without this recognition, he is not a king. This is true of God as well as of earthly rulers.

If God is to be King in this world, there must be a people that accept Him as King, who willingly embrace subservience to His rule. In the relationship between God and the Jewish people, God is King, *Melech*, and we are His kingdom, *malchus*. The King bestows from His abundance onto His servants, and His servants acknowledge His Kingship.

What is the Jewish concept of an earthly king? A Jewish king has two roles: *melech*, king to the nation of Israel, and *malchus*, subject of the King of Kings. As the king to his nation, he bestows good, making every effort to ensure the spiritual growth and physical well being of his subjects. As a subject of the Divine King, as *malchus*, he is a servant of the King of Kings and is the recipient of all good that emanates from that King.

The concept of a Jewish king is further defined by David's name. The first letter in his name is *dalet*, which means "impoverished." A Jewish king knows that he is nothing more than a poor man totally dependent on the largesse of the King above. The second letter in David's name is *vav*. *Vav* is a vertical letter that connects Heaven and earth. A Jewish king is servant to the One above and is king to those below. *Dalet* is the last letter in his name, again connoting impoverishment, for David knew that none of his strengths or talents were his own. Any accomplishments, power, wealth, or wisdom David acquired in this world were all gifts from God.

The Jewish king receives the respect of the people and must ensure the honor due to his high office. He is required, therefore, to prevent any devaluation of his position. All must stand in his presence; he may not allow them to sit (Rambam, *Hilchos Melachim* 2:5). At the same time, the king must respect all people and serve each of his subjects.

> In the same way that the text accords him great honor and all are obligated to honor him, so it commands him that his heart within him [be] lowly and empty.... He should not behave with too haughty a heart to Israel.... He should be gracious and merciful to little ones and great ones. He should go in and out with their possessions and for their good. He should have mercy on the smallest of the small.... He should say [to himself], "You are a servant of this people." And he should always act with extra humility.
>
> There is no one greater than our Teacher Moshe and he said [about himself], "And what are we?"... And he carried their burdens, their troubles, their complaints, and their grievances, and he carried them like a nursing father carries his young.
>
> (Rambam, *Hilchos Melachim* 2:6)

The king must empathize with each of his subjects and bear every man's burden, the way a father suffers his children's pain. How does the king learn to feel compassion for great and small alike? Rambam says, "His heart must be lowly and empty."

What does it mean to be lowly and empty? An empty space is a space that has room to store many things. A lowly person is one who empties out his own agenda for the agenda of God. A Jewish king earns his station because he knows he has little status as compared to the King of Kings. When he is lowly and empty he will also have room to hear others, to feel their sorrow, to be one with their hearts.

> The heart [of the king] is the heart of the entire community of Israel.
>
> (Rambam, *Hilchos Melachim* 3:6)

When David composed *Tehillim*, he wrote from his own experiences, but he also wrote of the pain and joy of each Jew and of the nation as a whole. *Tehillim*, therefore, is written on three levels: it is about David's life, the life of every Jew, and the life of the nation.

Thus, *Tehillim* is not poetry, but the diary of a struggle, the personal struggle of David to become king, to overcome his evil inclination and subjugate himself to the Kingship of God. *Tehillim* records this internal battle, which is also the battle of each Jew as he wrestles with faith and trust in God in difficult times. And it is the record of the *yissurim*, the suffering, of the nation of Israel during our long and painful exile.

Enlightenment

Psalm 142 begins with the word *maskil*, which means "enlightenment." The word suggests the state of David's mind when he uttered this prayer. Earlier, we said that the word also refers to a particular moment of clarity for David, when, in the cave, he recognized that no one could help him but God. The word *maskil* has a third implication, as well.

Before the creation of the physical world, nothing existed except God. This is to say that there was no physicality, only spirituality. In the place of the spiritual world, there is actually no room for physicality. God is infinite and physicality is limited. To create the physical world, God had to create a new reality. We call this the universe or the "place." He created this with speech. The words "let there be" began a process by which the physical evolved from the spiritual. When God said, "Let there be a firmament in the midst of the water" (*Bereishis* 1:6), the physical heaven came into existence as a reflection of the spiritual one.

In this world God created a chain, a process through which the world functions. This is called nature. He set rules for nature, but He is constantly moving the world, pouring energy into it so that it keeps functioning (Ramchal, *Sefer HaKelalim*).

Every physical object has its source in spirituality. All things, from apples to paper clips, are sustained by the constant flow of spirituality from above. Thus, everything that exists was not only created from the spiritual world, but is also constantly maintained by spirituality. Contrary to conventional wisdom, the world does not operate like a clock that is set once and keeps ticking, but exists because of this steady outpouring of abundance from the upper world. Seasons change, not merely because of the revolution of the earth, but because God guides that revolution. Winter becomes summer, and summer winter, because God directs the world. Seeds grow into plants that can be harvested because God instructs each seed to grow.

> While the earth remains, seedtime and harvest, cold and heat, summer and winter, and day and night shall not cease.
>
> *(Bereishis* 8:22)

This process of creating this world and everything in it by drawing on the higher world is called *"yeish mei'ayin."* *"Yeish"* means "something" (i.e., something physical). *"Ayin"* means "nothing" (i.e., nothing physical, in other words, something spiritual). *Yeish mei'ayin*, then, means the formation of something physical from the "nothingness" (nothing physical) of the spiritual.

Even the spirituality of this world is part of the rules of nature. All spiritual qualities are reflected in nature and expressed by nature. Furthermore, man's spiritual actions bring consequences that are part of the rules of nature. For instance, in times of national calamity, recitation of the thirteen Attributes of God brings mercy to the Jewish people. This is, in fact, the highest level and expression of nature.

But the spirituality of nature, the spirituality of this world, is not the same as the spirituality of the upper world, of the pre-created world, or of God. It is a small, transformed spirituality that is usable in a physical world.

Let us compare the spirituality of God to the power of Niagara Falls. The great energy of the Falls is untapped, raw, and unusable. In order for us to draw on the energy of the Falls to turn on a light bulb, for example, the energy must be converted to electricity through a complicated system. When the energy is converted into electrical energy and then directed toward the electric boxes in our homes, we can flick a switch and light up our living rooms. The only way we can access the energy of Niagara Falls is when it is harnessed, limited, and confined to the electric wires. But the energy we receive is nothing like the real power, the source of the energy.

When we see God's actions in this world, it is through the screen called nature. What we see is the final stage of the light bulb turning on. We can understand how the energy became electricity, but we cannot explain how the energy became energy.

The Divine energy source of all human wisdom, which is simultaneously above all human wisdom and also continuously feeds human wisdom, is known as *maskil*. Thus human wisdom is a creation *yeish mei'ayin*, something from nothing.

> Wisdom came to be from nothing (*ayin*).
>
> (*Iyov* 28:12)

Maskil, then, is the root wisdom from which all other wisdom is derived and nurtured. It is spiritual wisdom in its pure form, beyond this world and without the limitations of letters, words, or sentences. *Maskil* is located in the part of the spiritual world to which we have no access; but, when we labor in Torah, it is *maskil* that feeds our understanding, our *chochmah*.

How does a person gain wisdom? If he attempts to make himself important and grand, he will not succeed. For example, when a person discovers a new interpretation (*chiddush*) in Torah, he might be tempted to think it is his own idea. Instead, he must empty himself of his own agenda. The more a person realizes that his wisdom is connected to a higher source, the more humble he will be. The more humble he becomes, the more space he creates within himself, which, in turn, makes room for more wisdom. His self-nullification allows him to connect with *maskil*.

David began this psalm with the word *maskil* because *maskil* is about self-nullification and a realization that nothing comes from us. David was completely aware that everything he had emanated from God, including his ability to gain wisdom and to connect with the *ayin*, the spiritual world.

The story is told that the Baal Shem Tov was born to very old parents who died when he was a boy. His father, on his deathbed, imparted only one message to his son: "Fear no one but God." The young boy grew up alone, holding on tightly to that one message. He could sleep, for example, in the woods among wolves and not be afraid, because he had no fear except of God.

This is what happened to David in the cave. He realized that there is nothing in this world except God, and that He is the only One to fear. This is the beginning of wisdom.

> The beginning of wisdom is the fear of God.
>
> (*Tehillim* 111:10)

Actualizing the Message

Keser (crown) is the source of all spiritual qualities. These qualities, called *Sefiros*, are wisdom, knowledge, intuition, kindness, strength, truth, beauty, eternity, and foundation. We call the expression of these qualities *malchus* (kingship). When we visit the sick, learn Torah, or honor our parents, we draw from these spiritual qualities. In so doing, we become subjects of the King of Kings. We create a Kingship of God in this world.

Malchus has no light of its own, but rather takes the light of all the *sefiros* and reflects it back in a more intense fashion. Hence, *malchus* is the realization of *keser* in this world.

Now we understand the last line in *Tehillim* 142: "The righteous shall be crowned (*yachtiru*) through me." The king of Israel is the reflection of all spiritual qualities in the world. By seeing the king's faith in times of trouble, the righteous will learn to access their own trust in God.

Psalm 142

How often does each of us experience what David did in the cave? How often do we feel abandoned, trapped, helpless? How are we, as a nation today, alone in the world? Were it not for God, the Jewish people would have no one to turn to.

> My voice cries out to God; with my voice I make my supplication to the Lord.
>
> (*Tehillim* 142:2)

In a moment of great suffering, David uttered two different kinds of prayer: crying out (*ze'akah*) and supplication (*techinah*). Crying out is wordless prayer. When a person is in distress and frightened, he often lacks the presence of mind to speak at all, but he may just make a wordless cry for help. When that cry is directed to God, it is prayer (Rav Shimshon Pincus, *She'arim BeTefillah*). David, the fugitive, cried out in a wordless plea.

Supplication is the prayer a person says when he asks for something — not because he deserves it, but because he needs a gift from God. Like a poor man who asks a rich man for bread that he did not earn but needs to survive, David asked for God's help. He appealed not on the basis of his merits, but because he felt impoverished and in need.

Eventually, David's original wordless prayer gave way to words:

> I pour out my complaint before Him; I declare my trouble before Him.
>
> (*Tehillim* 142:3)

As an overflowing pitcher cannot contain even one additional drop of water, David's emotions could no longer be contained. His sorrow overflowed; his entreaties poured out endlessly. Ultimately, his suffering was so great that wordlessness brought him to words; then words flowed incessantly, like a wound that would not stop bleeding.

> When my spirit envelops me (*behisatef alai*), You know my path.
> In the path where I walk they have secretly laid a snare for me.
>
> (Ibid., 4)

The word *behisatef*, envelops, is the same word used in the blessing recited over putting on a tallis. A person who wears a tallis is enveloped in the Divine presence. David was enveloped with weariness, desperation. No matter which path he took, he landed in the hands of his enemies, who discovered his plans and filled his road with snares.

> I look on my right hand, and behold, but there is no man who knows me; no refuge remains to me; no man cares for my soul.
>
> (Ibid., 5)

The right hand connotes strength and support. The expression to "look to the right," means to seek the place from which help will come. David, alone in the cave, had no way out and no help from the "right." Hounded and hated by the king himself, who would take him in? Who would save him?

How often have we, the Jewish people, felt helpless, without a soul to turn to? The nations of the world condemn us, criticize us, and cast us away.

> I cry to You, O Lord; I say, "You are my refuge and my portion in the land of the living."
>
> (Ibid., 6)

This is the second time in this psalm that David cries out to God. His pain had two sources — fear for his own life and fear of harming King Shaul. He prays that he should not have to kill the king, and that the king should not kill him. Either choice was despicable to David.

God was David's portion in "the land of the living." This portion takes the form of the houses of prayer and study, where the soul can be infused with Divine inspiration. He understood that after death, the only thing that lives on is our soul and our connection to God. Facing mortal danger, then, reminded David that the only life worth living in this world is a spiritual one and that the only truly eternal acquisition that a person can attain is spirituality.

The Land of Israel is also called "the land of the living." David pined and groaned, "How I yearn for my portion in the Land of Israel, but alas, I cannot enjoy it."

> Attend to my cry, for I am impoverished; save me from my persecutors, for they are too strong for me.
>
> (Ibid., 7)

David described himself as "impoverished," because without God, he had no ally, no power, and no support.

> Bring my soul out of prison that I may give thanks to Your name; the righteous shall be crowned through me, for You shall deal bountifully with me.
>
> (Ibid., 8)

To David, the cave was a prison. Yet he wanted to leave, not because he wanted to taste freedom, but because he wanted to thank God and be a model of trust and faith for the righteous.

> "To thank God" — This is the proudest word that any man has ever spoken, and the manifestation of which we experience even today. Here we see a Jew, in flight, persecuted, hiding in a dark cave in the midst of the desert, who, in all his misery, can still speak...[about thanking God].
>
> (Rav Shimshon Refael Hirsch on *Tehillim* 142)

Each of us has a prison in which we are incarcerated. We, too, ask God to free us so that we can thank Him.

The Righteous Shall Be Crowned through Me

We, like David, are alone. Our enemies live in our midst and there is none among them we can trust. The nations of the world have been abusive in their rhetoric, isolating and threatening us. We are alone.

As individuals, we have our own tests and difficulties. As we seek to resolve our pain, we find that strategies for escape fail us. We realize that no earthly solution will solve our problems. We also learn that there is no one who truly understands us. Even with the best of intentions, our friends and loved ones cannot save us. We are alone.

If it were not for God, we would truly be alone. Knowing this is the beginning of our liberation, because we recognize that there is no hope outside of God. With His help, salvation can come as quickly as the blink of an eye, as easily as the splitting of the sea. Suffering also makes us humble. It forces us to recognize that everything we have, everything we are, even the suffering itself comes from Him. These realizations are the purpose of our suffering — to understand that we are never alone, to reach out to God, to cry out to our Creator. To acknowledge that everything we have in this world, including our pain and our redemption, emanates from God.

May it be the will of God that we, too, be released from our prisons, both personal and national. May we proclaim God King. May we be able to walk our streets safely and visit our holy sites. May our children grow to be the crown with which the righteous will adorn themselves.

Longing for Guidance

(Based on *shiurim* of Rav Chaim Goldvicht, *z"l*)

The modern world has blessed us with an unprecedented number of options and opportunities. We can choose from an assortment of lifestyles; we can choose where we live and with whom; we can choose how we work and how often. Yet, for all of this choice, we are not motivated but instead confused and gripped with indecision. We feel alone in our process, unguided, unprotected, and unsure of ourselves. We experience angst about life decisions. We crave direction, guidance, a caring mentor.

We did not always experience such confusion. There was a time when we knew with clarity that we had Divine supervision — when we were sure of what was expected of us. For forty years while the Jews traveled through the desert, the Clouds of Glory were there to protect and guide them. They never had a moment of doubt, never a question as to what they should do or where they should go.

We, too, yearn for such a cloud to guide and protect us. We, too, want to feel Divine supervision in our lives. We, too, wish to be sheltered and cared for. If only we had a cloud.

Merits for Priesthood

Moshe, the shepherd, was on Mount Chorev when he encountered a strange vision: a burning bush that would not be consumed. From the bush there came a voice, the voice of God. It told Moshe of the suffering of the Jews in Egypt and of God's plans to redeem them. Moshe's mission would be to represent God in Pharoah's court, by presenting His demand that the Jewish people be released from slavery.

For seven days, Moshe argued with God, for he did not feel competent or worthy enough for the mission. God met each of his arguments with a counterargument. Finally, He became angry at Moshe's refusal to go. He informed Moshe that Aharon, Moshe's older brother, would also go to speak to Pharoah and be a partner in Moshe's mission.

> The anger of the Lord was kindled against Moshe, and He said, "Is not Aharon the Levite your brother? I know that he can speak well. And also, behold, he comes forth to meet you; and when he sees you, he will be glad in his heart."
>
> (*Shemos* 4:14)

The text identifies Aharon as a Levite and as Moshe's brother. Since Moshe and Aharon are brothers, it would have been clear to Moshe that Aharon was a Levite. Why then does the text find it necessary to identify Aharon's tribe? Rashi tells us why this is mentioned:

> "Is not Aharon the Levite your brother?" implies that [Aharon] was destined to be a Levite and not a priest. "I intended that the priesthood should proceed from you [Moshe]. Now, however, this shall not be so, but he [Aharon] will be priest and you [Moshe] will be the Levite..."
>
> (*Rashi, Shemos* 4:13)

God punished Moshe for his refusal to stand before Pharoah by stripping him of the honor of priesthood. Moshe understood that it was a sin that cost him this honor, but he hoped the sin would be forgiven. Only when the Tabernacle was complete did Moshe realize that God's decree was irreversible and the priesthood would, in fact, go to his brother Aharon:

> All seven days of the consecration [of the Tabernacle], Moshe served as the high priest, thinking that [the priesthood] was his. On the seventh day, He [God] said to him, "It is not yours, but Aharon your brother's."
>
> (*Vayikra Rabbah* 11:6)

He then understood that his sin had not been forgiven and felt a sense of great failure and bitter disappointment. The seven days of the consecration are juxtaposed to the seven days of Moshe's refusal to stand before Pharoah. He thought himself unworthy of the task. This misplaced humility was the sin that cost Moshe the priesthood.

But why was Aharon now accorded this honor? What did he do to deserve it? The verse tells us that he could "speak well" and that he would be "glad in his heart." Perhaps these two qualities are connected to meriting the privilege of priesthood.

> "When he sees you [Moshe], he will be glad in his heart" — Not as you think, that he will be upset with you that you are elevated in greatness. [Rather, he will be glad for your new position.] From here we learn that Aharon merited the breastplate that is put on the heart.
>
> (*Rashi, Shemos* 4:14)

It would have been natural for Aharon, Moshe's older brother and a leader of the Jewish people at the time, to be jealous of his younger brother's opportunity to lead the Jews in this most crucial hour of their liberation. Yet Aharon did not feel jealousy, but only happiness when his brother's greatness was recognized. This is the reason, says Rashi, that Aharon merited priesthood, symbolized by "the breastplate that is put on the heart."

Every reward from God is a repayment for something that we have done and is always given measure for measure. It is not hard to see the literal connection between "the heart of Aharon that was happy" and "the breastplate worn on the heart." But there must also be a deeper, spiritual connection between the reward of priesthood and Aharon's glad heart. What is it?

Aharon receives another gift as well. This gift was not his alone, but shared with the Jewish people.

> Rabbi Yosei the son of Rabbi Yehudah says: Three good leaders arose for Israel, namely, Moshe, Aharon, and Miriam, and for their sake three good things were conferred upon Israel, namely, the well, the pillar of cloud, and the manna. The well [came] in the merit of Miriam; the pillar of cloud [came] in the merit of Aharon; the manna [came] in the merit of Moshe.
>
> (*Ta'anis* 9:1)

Three gifts were given in the merit of our leaders, each as a reward for some specific merit or deed performed. For Aharon, the gift was the clouds of glory. What action or characteristic makes him worthy of this honor?

Finally, there must be a connection between his happiness, the priesthood, and the Clouds of Glory. What is it?

Humility: A Balancing Act

All human beings, at birth, are given talents, dispositions, and inclinations. God gives these qualities according to the task assigned to each person in this world. Some people have a proclivity for kindness, others for honesty, others for humility or anger.

It is normal for a person to work from within his personality and make use of characteristics that are natural to him. Using inborn traits, he can choose to effect good or evil in the world. He has the free will to direct these traits in the service of God or not to do so. He can neglect to control his inclination and so cause destruction, or he can learn to control them when appropriate.

A person who perfects the ability to use the strengths and weaknesses of his personality in the appropriate way is called a tzaddik, a righteous person. He has fulfilled the mission of the human being in this world — to use God-given traits in the service of his Creator. Every person is given a different set of qualities to aid him with his job in the world. These qualities are his particular "tools of the trade" and are in part an indication of his mission and purpose. No two people are given the same talent set. It therefore follows that everyone will be deficient in some areas. Each person will have relative strengths and energies, but not all strengths and energies. However, when two people work together, each using his unique abilities, they are able to build the world.

In addition, every person houses within himself many traits and at times conflicting ones. For example, a person can be sublimely sensitive in some areas, yet callous in others. Or he could be mild-mannered in general, but aggressive in certain situations. Even our opinions can be in conflict. Since we are complex as people, there will be times when one ideal of ours will be at odds with another. For example, a person may be inspired to invite guests to his home, yet deeply resent the lack of privacy this brings. If he gives full expression to this internal conflict, as his heart desires, he will become entangled in contradiction.

A person must learn, therefore, to control himself. He must select the attribute appropriate for a particular time, place, and audience. He must balance his clashing drives, only giving expression to those actions, thoughts, or words that suit the situation.

How does a person learn to balance and control his inclinations, using them properly and containing them when necessary? How does he learn to give fitting expression to each of his qualities and use them to be a whole person? The question is a critical one, since these qualities crave expression. We must find a proper venue for our personality, talents, and drives because if we don't they will express themselves inappropriately or they will erupt inside us.

For instance, a person who has an instinct to give to others but finds no healthy and appropriate expression for this drive will end up giving in an unhealthy or inappropriate way. An artist who leaves her art unexpressed will wither inside, and this will negatively affect her ability to function in other areas of her life. Every God-given gift requires expression, yet inappropriate or stifled expression is dangerous and unhealthy.

How then do we keep the balance? The Torah provides an answer:

> He has told you, O man, what is good; and what does the Lord require of you, but to do justice, to love *chesed* (kindness), and to walk humbly with your God.
>
> (*Michah* 6:8)

From the above passage, it seems that a person who walks with God is one who defines himself by God's standards and subordinates his wishes to those of God. When God desires justice, the person walks with justice. When God desires *chesed*, the person walks with *chesed*. Each trait we have clamors for expression, so in order to walk with God, there will be times when we will have to rein in our impulses. In fact, the defining moments in the life of a Jew are precisely those times — when, instead of simply reacting, he pauses and asks himself: "Which of my many competing traits is called for now?"

Walking humbly with God means using every talent and strength we have in a positive way and restraining those energies when that is the will of God. For instance, a person who is a gifted speaker will certainly have opportunities when God desires his speech — such as in learning Torah, communicating to a child, or praying. But there will also be times when he will know that using speech would be is wrong — as in a session of gossip or slander. Therefore, a gifted speaker must learn how to restrict his speech, no matter how eloquent, in order to "walk humbly with God." The artist must express her art, but the laws of modesty will set boundaries for her creative expression. The giver must give — to the right people, at the right time, and in the right way.

Asking, "What does God want of me?" and then behaving in a fitting manner is an expression of *bitul hayeish* (self-nullification or subjugation of ego). The desire to "walk with God" defines both the questions and the answers. It directs decision making and actions. It requires us to allow our intellect to prevail over emotion and instinct, and it provides us with clarity.

This is the secret of humility.

Humility means knowing who you are — your talents, strengths, personality traits — knowing what the Torah expects of you, and then subjugating the expression of these qualities to the will of God. Humility is making personal ambition serve the truth of Torah.

Paradoxically, humility and self-nullification greatly strengthen a person — enough to tame the opposing forces in him, preventing these forces from clashing inside the person and wreaking destruction. By defining himself by "what God wants," a person has clarity about how to behave in any situation. He learns to fully express himself without misusing his traits and talents. He knows when being silent is better than speaking, when it is correct to laugh, and when it is more appropriate to cry. He resolves internal conflicts by using only those characteristics that suit the demands of the moment.

Acquisition of Torah

Humility is a necessary trait to acquire Torah.

> "Why do you run and fight (*teratzdun*), you high mountain peaks (*gavnunim*)?" (*Tehillim* 68:17). Rabbi Yosei the Galilean and Rabbi Akiva discussed this. Rabbi Yosei the Galilean applied the verse to the mountains. When the Holy One, blessed be He, came to reveal the Torah on Sinai, the mountains ran

about and contended (*ratzim u'mdayanim*)with each other, each claiming: "The Torah shall be revealed on me." One said, "I have been called," [and the other said,] "I have been called." Said God to them: "Why do you run and fight, you high mountains? You are all indeed high mountains; idol worship has been performed on the tops of all of you."

(Bereishis Rabbah 99:1)

When God announced that He would give the Torah on Sinai, each of the world's mountains argued that the Torah should be given on it. We can look at these mountains as expressing a spiritual yearning, each wanting to be central to the bringing of Torah into the world. Yet the words *on me* and *high* betray their motivation. Even spiritual aspirations must be divorced from ego. The height of these mountains testifies to their arrogance, and their requests to be chosen as a stage for the giving of the Torah attests to the self-centered nature of their desires. This self-importance is described in the Midrash as idol worship. The idol is the self.

Spiritual yearnings that are tainted with ego are called "blemished." The Hebrew word for blemish is *mum*, a word only applied to objects that could be used for holiness but have a devaluing flaw. For instance, a blemished animal is called a *baal mum*, and although it could have been used for a sacrifice had it been perfect, the blemish disqualifies it for sacrifice.

Any Divine service can be disqualified if the one performing it has a blemish. This is true even in the acquisition of Torah itself. This is how the Midrash describes the mountains who compete to be the one on which the Torah is to be given.

Bar Kapara gave the following exposition: What is the meaning of the verse, "Why do you fight (*teratzdun*), you high mountain peaks?" A Heavenly voice went out from there and said to them: Why do you desire litigation (*tirtzu din*) with Sinai? You are all full of blemishes compared with Sinai.

(Megillah 29:1)

Closeness to God is not achieved through grabbing honor, even when in the service of God. This makes one a *baal mum*. True closeness to God requires a person to put aside his ego, to be lowly and humble, as was Mount Sinai.

Clouds of Glory

The Clouds of Glory surrounded the Jewish people on all sides, protecting and guiding them. They represented the *Shechinah*, the Divine presence of God in their midst.

> When the cloud was taken up from the Tabernacle, after that the children of Israel journeyed; and in the place where the cloud abode, there the children of Israel encamped. At the commandment of the Lord the children of Israel journeyed, and at the commandment of the Lord they encamped: as long as the cloud abode upon the Tabernacle they remained encamped.
>
> When the cloud remained upon the Tabernacle for many days, then the children of Israel kept the charge of the Lord and did not journey. So it was, when the cloud was a few days upon the Tabernacle; according to the commandment of God, the children of Israel remained encamped and by the commandment of God they journeyed.
>
> So it was, when the cloud abode from evening to the morning, and the cloud was taken up in the morning, then they journeyed; whether it was by day or by night that the cloud was taken up, they journeyed.
>
> Or whether it was two days, or a month, or a year that the cloud stayed upon the Tabernacle, remaining on it, the people of Israel abode in their tents, and journeyed not; but when it was taken up, they journeyed. At the commandment of the Lord they rested in the tents, and at the commandment of the Lord they journeyed; they kept the charge of the Lord, at the commandment of the Lord by the hand of Moshe.
>
> *(Bemidbar* 9:17–23)

The clouds were God's way of leading His people where they were supposed to go and protecting them every step of the way. Yet there is another important message in the clouds.

Reading the description of the encampment and travels of the Jewish nation, we are struck by the repetition. The words "by the commandment of

God" are repeated seven times. The word "journey" or "did not journey" is mentioned nine times, while "encamped" is mentioned six times. In general, we also have a sense that these verses could have been condensed into two sentences: The Jewish nation traveled when the cloud lifted, and camped when the cloud rested, whether for a short time or a long time. In so doing, they obeyed the word of God.

The Ramban teaches that this repetition shows us that the nation subjugated itself to the will of God, even when their desires differed from His.

> [Sometimes] the "cloud tarried upon the Tabernacle many days," and the place [where they camped] was not good in their eyes. Therefore they very much desired and wanted to journey away from there. They were nevertheless not to transgress the will of God; this being the meaning of the verse, "and the children of Israel kept the charge of the Lord and did not journey." That is to say that [it was only] because of their awe of God and because they kept the charge of His command that they did not journey. Similarly if the cloud was there only a few days, for instance two or three days, and the people were very tired because their strength had weakened in the way, they would nonetheless fulfill the will of God and walk by order of the cloud.
>
> (*Ramban, Bemidbar* 19:20)

The clouds not only provided Divine protection, they were also an instrument of informing the people of Divine will. Therefore, following the clouds meant that the Jewish people were acting according to the will of God, and not their own desires. They moved when He indicated that it was time to move and camped where they were supposed to camp whether they liked it or not.

Like Ramban, Seforno reads the repetition as teaching us how much the Jewish people subjugated themselves to the will of God. But Seforno emphasizes that even when the desires of the people matched the will of the Divine, they were still motivated to act by His will, not their own (note how Seforno interweaves the verse into his commentary to explain his point):

> "When the cloud remained upon the Tabernacle for many days"... Sometimes the encampment would be in a pleasant place for them and their cattle, and the cloud would rest there many days. [But] "at the commandment of the Lord they

encamped" — not because they loved that place. "At the commandment of the Lord [they] journeyed" — [God's will would direct] when they would leave that good place. [Not because of their own desires, but because of God's.]

(Seforno, Bemidbar 9:20)

This subservience was an expression of *bitul*, self-nullification.

Aharon, the Sanctuary, and the Priesthood

The Tabernacle was built as the "home" for the Divine Presence, the *Shechinah*. What kind of home does God require? What kind of place does the Divine Presence need? The *Shechinah* can only dwell in a place of *bitul*, a place where the heart has been emptied of arrogance and self-focus.

"Every man in whom is haughtiness of spirit," the Holy One, blessed be He, declares, "I and he cannot both dwell in the world."

(Sotah 5b)

The Torah teaches us that God's greatness is beyond human comprehension. He is all knowing, all-powerful, and eternal. Yet His *Shechinah* rests only on those individuals and nations that are humble.

Thus says the high and lofty One who inhabits eternity, whose name is holy: "I dwell on high and in a holy place, yet [I am] with he who is of a contrite and humble spirit, to revive the spirit of the humble and revive the heart of the contrite ones."

(Yeshayahu 57:15)

A person who wants to be a vessel of the *Shechinah* must subjugate his own ego and make room for the *Shechinah* to enter. This is why the Tabernacle was built with the voluntary contributions of the Jewish people.

And they came, everyone whose heart stirred him up and everyone whom his spirit made willing, and they brought the Lord's offering for the work of the Tent of Meeting, for all its service and for the holy garments. And they came, both men and women, as many as were willing hearted, and brought bracelets, earrings, rings, and bracelets, all jewels of gold; and every man who offered an offering of gold to the Lord. And every man with whom was found blue, purple, scarlet, fine linen, goats' hair, red skins of rams, and goats' skins, brought them. Everyone who offered an offering of silver and bronze brought the Lord's offering.

(*Shemos* 35:21–25)

The human being naturally desires gold, silver, material wealth. Giving away our physical possessions expresses willingness to self-negate. When a person donates his possessions to build the Tabernacle or gives of his funds to buy a sacrifice, he overrides his own desires and makes room for the *Shechinah* to define him and dwell within him. A parallel in today's world would be the giving of *tzedakah*. A person who works hard for his money finds it difficult to give it away, even to needy causes. Doing so expresses his will to take what is "his" and give it to God.

When a person is not willing to do God's will and instead follows his own desires to sin, he has failed to create the space needed for God to dwell in his heart. When he is ready to return to God, he brings a sacrifice. The Ramban explains the idea behind sacrifice in the Temple.

Since man's deeds are accomplished through thought, speech, and action, therefore God commanded that when man sins and brings an offering, he should lay his hands upon it [the animal] in contrast to the [evil] deed [committed]. He should confess his sins verbally in contrast to his [evil] speech, and he should burn the innards and the kidneys [of the offering] in fire because they are the instruments of thought and desire in the human being. He should burn the legs [of the offering] since they correspond to the hands and feet of a person, which do all his work. He should sprinkle the blood upon the altar, which is analogous to the blood in his body.

All these acts are performed so that when they are done, a person should realize that he has sinned against his God with his body and soul, and that his blood should really have been spilled and his body burned. Were it not for the loving kindness of the

Creator, who took from him a substitute and ransom, namely this offering, so that its blood should be in place of his blood, its life in place of his life, and that the chief limbs from the offering should be in place of the chief parts of his body, [he would die from his sin]. The portion [given from the sin offering to the priests] is in order to support the teachers of the Torah, so that they pray on his behalf. The reason for the daily public offering is that it is impossible for the public [as a whole] to continually avoid sin.

(Ramban, Vayikra 1:9)

We are placed in this world to serve God. This is our purpose and mission. When we fail in this mission in any way, it is a sin. The sacrifice comes to remind a person of his role in Divine service — to completely give over his life to God.

The foundation of the Tabernacle is self-negation and the message of the sacrifices in the Tabernacle was self-sacrifice. The one who performs the service must also be a person who lives a life of creating space for the *Shechinah*.

Why was Aharon rewarded with priesthood when he rejoiced at his brother Moshe's elevated status? Aharon was not sad nor resentful that God had chosen Moshe. In fact, his ego was not engaged at all. He felt complete joy, with no reservations. This act of joy in seeing the mantle of leadership given to his younger brother was not only an acceptance of God's will but an expression of *bitul hayeish*, self-nullification. Unlike the mountains that wanted the Torah given "on me," Aharon was deeply happy when God appointed Moshe as leader. And this happiness earned him the priesthood.

Happy with His Lot

What is the nature of the happiness that Aharon experienced?

Who is rich? One who is happy with his portion in life, as it says, "When you eat of the labor of your hands, you are happy and all is well with you" (*Tehillim* 128:2).

(Avos 4:1)

The meaning of this *mishnah* is clear — happiness is a frame of mind. It is acceptance of your life as it is given to you. Yet the proof text from *Tehillim* implies something else. A person who works hard appreciates that which he earned through his labor and that makes him happy. In contrast, a free gift, something that is not earned, is not wholly appreciated, nor is it a source of the same degree of happiness. Only when a person labors does he enjoy true ownership of the thing he has labored for. The joy of truly earning brings a sense of satisfaction.

How then do we appreciate a gift? When we receive gifts, we do not feel the same appreciation as when we work and are compensated for our labor. However, it is possible to earn a gift because all gifts are really credit. The giver gives with the expectation and hope that the receiver will justify the grant, that he will use the gift appropriately and well. Indeed, the gift leaves the recipient with the uncomfortable sense that he is now in debt.

The way to pay off the debt is to make full use of that gift; when a person does this, he gains ownership. Using the gift well brings a joy like that of earning.

This is true in *avodas Hashem*, service of God, as well. When we are given a gift from God — talent, energy, strength, a personality trait — it is a free gift, and so we are "in debt."

How can we repay the debt we owe God? All the struggles of life that we experience are "tests" from Heaven to allow us to use our gifts properly, to justify them to the Giver. By using our strengths and talents appropriately, we earn them. In this earning, there is joy, the joy of ownership.

When Aharon came to meet Moshe with happiness in his heart, he was rewarded with the gift of priesthood. The verse tells us why Aharon was suited for the priesthood: "I know he can speak well," i.e., he has the gift of communication. He is able to speak lovingly and clearly to others. A priest is the intermediary between the nation and God, a conduit of peace. The tool of his trade is his ability to communicate love between the nation and God. To do that, he too must feel love and joy for his fellow Jew and for God.

The power of speech is a gift from God, a talent given by the Creator. It is a necessary tool for a priest, but it did not earn Aharon the priesthood. He earned it when he came out to greet Moshe. "And also, behold, he comes forth to meet you; and when he sees you, he will be glad in his heart" (*Shemos* 4:14).

The word *behold* implies that God is pointing out why he earned this gift. His joy for his brother's greatness and his complete lack of jealousy at the elevation of his brother to a position of leadership earned him the priesthood. In feeling love for his brother, and in communicating this love, he used his gift well. The natural extension and manifestation of this joy was in his attainment of the priesthood.

> The heart that rejoices in the greatness of his brother will wear the *urim* and *tumim* [the breastplate worn by the high priest], as it says: "They will be on the heart of Aharon" (*Shemos* 28:9).
>
> (*Tanchuma, Shemos* 27)

Earning the Clouds of Glory

As we said before, there are two aspects of the Clouds of Glory: God's guidance of the Jewish people and the self-negation of the nation in serving God. The two are related to each other. God endows us with His wisdom, guidance, and gifts. We respond by taking those gifts and guidance and using them, in turn, to serve God. When we do, we are rewarded with more gifts, more opportunities to use our talents, strengths, and energies.

In the desert, it was Aharon who taught this lesson to the Jewish people. He did not feel jealousy of his younger brother's elevated position. Why? Because Aharon asked himself: *What does God want? If God wants Moshe to be the leader, that is what I want.* In the merit of this self-negation, the Jewish people are given the Clouds of Glory, which represent the same idea.

We see a pattern: Aharon was given the gift of communication and the ability to make peace. He used these gifts appropriately when he came out to greet his brother with joy. In this joy, he demonstrated his self-negation, and, as a result, he merited the Clouds of Glory. These clouds require us to put our own desires on hold and to follow the will of God. The more we do that, the more God is there for us. It is a gift that earns us more of the same.

Sukkos

During the holiday of Sukkos, we dwell for seven days in our sukkah. This sukkah represents the Clouds of Glory. Here, too, there is a double message. God is always there to protect us, and we can rely on that. We live outside in flimsy, impermanent huts that represent the fragility of our lives. We acknowledge that God is our guide, our protector. We rededicate ourselves to His service by using all of our talents and energies to serve Him, subjugating our will to His. We live under His roof.

We Dwell in His Shadow

Today, we no longer have a Cloud of Glory to guide us, and it is more difficult for us to know God's will. Sitting in the sukkah reminds us that His will is knowable nevertheless. It is no longer as simple as standing at Sinai and experiencing clear revelation. Instead, we must work hard to understand our role in this world. We must gain ownership of our "gifts." By studying His Torah, by reflecting on our own strengths, energies, and talents, by praying for clarity, we will be given *siyatta diShmaya* (Heavenly assistance) in determining the path we should take.

When we understand who we are and what our contributions should be, when we utilize our energies to serve God, we will earn the very gifts He has given us and merit His continued protection and guidance. For we, too, are guarded and directed by the Holy One, blessed be He.

> He who dwells in the secret place of the Most High, who abides under the shadow of the Almighty, will say to the Lord, "My refuge and my fortress, my God, in whom I trust...." He shall cover you with His feathers, and under His wings shall you find refuge; His truth shall be your shield and buckler. You shall not be afraid of the terror by night, nor of the arrow that flies by day, nor of the pestilence that walks in darkness, or of the destroyer that lays waste at moon.... Because You, O Lord, are my refuge....
>
> (*Tehillim* 91:1–9)

Lowliness, Sin, and Transformation

The story of the conquest of Israel begins with the story of a remarkable woman, a woman whose bravery and faith carries her
from the most debased profession in the world to a place of
honor among the Jewish people. When we meet her first, Rachav is a prostitute; by the end of the story, she has become a convert to Judaism, accepted by
all, and the wife of Yehoshua the leader of his generation.

How does Rachav make this transformation? How does she go from a life
of depravity to one of high moral and spiritual character? What message does
she teach us about *teshuvah* (repentance) and its potential? What hope does
she give us about changing our lives?

Let us read the story of her contribution to the conquest of Israel:

> Yehoshua the son of Nun sent from Shittim two men to spy se-
> cretly, saying, "Go view the land of Yericho." And they went,
> and came to the house of a harlot named Rachav, and they
> lodged there.
>
> It was told to the king of Yericho, saying, "Behold, men
> came here tonight of the people of Israel to search out the
> country."
>
> The king of Yericho sent to Rachav, saying, "Bring forth the
> men who have come to you, who have entered into your house;
> for they have come to search out all the country."
>
> The woman took the two men and hid them, and said, "Yes,
> men came to me, but I did not know from where they were from.
> And it came to pass about the time of the closing of the gate, when
> it was dark, that the men went out. Where the men went I know
> not. Pursue after them quickly, for you shall overtake them."

But she had brought them up to the roof of the house and hid them with the stalks of flax, which she had laid in order upon the roof. And the men pursued after them on the way to the Jordan River, to the fords; and as soon as the pursuers had left the city, the city gates were closed.

Before they lay down, she came up to them upon the roof. She said to the men, "I know that the Lord has given you the land, and that your terror has fallen upon us, and that all the inhabitants of the land faint because of you. For we have heard how the Lord dried up the water of the Red Sea for you when you came out of Egypt, and what you did to the two kings of the Emorites who were on the other side of the Jordan, Sichon and Og, whom you completely destroyed. As soon as we heard these things, our hearts melted, nor did courage remain in any man because of you; for the Lord your God, He is God in heaven above and on earth below. Now therefore, I pray you, swear to me by the Lord, since I have shown you kindness, that you will also show kindness to my father's house. Give me a true sign that you will keep alive my father, my mother, my brothers, my sisters, and all that they have, and save our lives from death."

The men answered her, "Our life for yours, if you do not utter our business. It shall be, when the Lord has given us the land, that we will deal kindly and truly with you."

Then she let them down by a rope through the window, for her house was upon the town wall, and she lived upon the wall. She said to them, "Go to the mountain, lest the pursuers meet you; and hide yourselves there for three days, until the pursuers return; and afterwards you may go on your way."

And the men said to her, "We will be guiltless with respect to this oath of yours that you have made us swear. Behold, when we come to the land, you shall bind this line of scarlet thread in the window from which you let us down; and you shall bring your father, your mother, your brothers, and all your father's household home to you. Whoever shall go out of the doors of your house to the street, his blood shall be upon his head, and we will be guiltless. Whoever shall be with you in the house, his blood shall be on our head, if any hand be upon him. If you utter our business, then we will be absolved of your oath which you have made us swear."

She said, "According to your words, so be it." And she sent them away, and they departed; and she bound the scarlet line in the window.

And they went, and came to the mountain, and stayed there three days, until the pursuers returned; and the pursuers sought them throughout all the way but did not find them. So the two men returned, and descended from the mountain, and passed over, and came to Yehoshua the son of Nun, and told him all the things that had befallen them. They said to Yehoshua, "Truly the Lord has delivered to our hands all the land, for all the inhabitants of the country faint because of us."

(Yehoshua ch. 2)

Now Yericho was completely closed up because of the people of Israel; none went out and none came in. And the Lord said to Yehoshua, "See, I have given to your hand Yericho, and its king, and the mighty men of valor...."

[Yehoshua said to the people,] "The city shall be devoted [to God], it and all who are in it, to the Lord; only Rachav the harlot shall live, she and all who are with her in the house, because she hid the messengers whom we sent."...

They completely destroyed all that was in the city, all the men and women, all the young and old, all the oxen, sheep, and donkeys, with the sword. But Yehoshua had said to the two men who had spied out the country, "Go to the harlot's house and bring out from there the woman and all that she has, as you swore to her." The young men who were spies went in and brought out Rachav, her father, her mother, her brothers, and all that she had; and they brought out all her family and left them outside the camp of Israel.

They burned the city and all that was in it; only the silver, the gold, the utensils of bronze and iron, they put in the treasury of the house of the Lord. But Yehoshua granted life to Rachav the harlot, her father's household, and all that she had. She lives in

Israel to this day, because she hid the messengers whom Yehoshua sent to spy out Yericho.

(Yehoshua, ch. 6)

Rope, Flax and Window

Where did Rachav find the courage to act as she did? What motivated her? As she herself testified, everyone was afraid of the Jews, yet the king and his men sought to capture them, not to capitulate. This despite the fact that everyone had heard of the miracles associated with their previous conquest. What made Rachav different?

To understand the answer to these questions, we must understand Rachav's position in her society. She was a woman who knew the hearts of the strong and the prominent, the rich and the powerful, visited by princes and kings, a woman who was intimate with all.

> There was no prince or ruler who did not know Rachav the harlot. It was said: She was ten years old when the Israelites departed from Egypt, and she was a harlot the whole of the forty years spent by the Israelites in the wilderness.
>
> *(Zevachim* 116b)

The elite of her society boasted to her of their accomplishments, as powerful men are likely to do; and when the Jews closed in on the Land of Israel, it was Rachav in whom these same powerful men confided their fears.

> "It came to pass, when all the kings of the Emorites...and all the kings of the Canaanites...heard that the Lord had dried up the waters of the Jordan for the people of Israel, until they had passed over, that their heart melted. Nor was there any spirit left in them anymore, because of the people of Israel" (*Yehoshua* 5:1). And Rachav the harlot also said to Yehoshua's [spies], "Nor did courage remain in any man" — she meant that they even lost their manhood [from their fear].
>
> *(Zevachim* 116b)

Accordingly, Rachav had access to the morale of the entire country. She knew the leadership and knew that their daring had failed them (*Malbim*, *Yehoshua* 2:11). Difficult times require courageous leadership, and with this sorely lacking on the eve of conquest, how could her nation succeed?

It was precisely this information that the spies sent by Yehoshua sought when they came to Rachav's home. They knew that God would grant them victory, but they also knew that a war of conquest had to be fought by natural means. They came on a search mission to Canaan, to learn about the mood of the people and their level of confidence.

Soon after the spies arrived at the house of Rachav, their presence was detected and the king sought their capture. He sent a message to Rachav demanding that she hand them over to his men; instead, she hid them and lied to the king's messengers. "I do not know where they are," she said, sending the messengers on an impossible mission to find the very people she had secreted away.

In addition to hiding them, Rachav freely offered the spies the information they had come to spy out. She told them that the people of the land had heard about miracles that God had wrought for the Jewish nation during the exodus from Egypt. They had heard about the victory of the Jews over the Emorite kings and recognized that it was God's hand that was behind these victories. "As soon as we heard these things, our hearts melted, nor did courage remain in any man because of you; for the Lord your God, He is God in heaven above and on earth below."

With these words, the spies' mission was completed; now they knew that the inhabitants of the land feared the Jews. They also understood the effects of a weakened morale on a nation at war and were ready to return to their leader Yehoshua with the good news.

At this point, Rachav aided them in their escape, but before doing so, she solicited their help. She asked that they save her and her family, and the spies agreed. It is at this juncture that we begin to see Rachav's motivation. Our Sages teach that her change of heart and loyalties was not merely the result of fear or the desire for personal salvation, but instead came from a deep submission to God and the aspiration to change her life.

> Then she let them down by a rope through the window, for her house was upon the town wall, and she lived upon the wall.
>
> (*Yehoshua* 2:15)

> She let them down with the same rope and window that her pa-
> trons would come to her. She said, "Master of the Universe,
> with these I have sinned, with these forgive me."
>
> *(Rashi, Yehoshua 2:15)*

She set out to make amends for her sinful life by using the very things that she had used to act corruptly. This is a key to her repentance.

The above *Rashi* continues,

> At the age of fifty, she became a proselyte. She said: "May I be
> forgiven as a reward for the rope, window, and flax" (*Zevachim*
> 116b). She said, "Master of the Universe, with three things I
> have sinned, with three forgive me: with the rope, the flax, and
> the window." Because her patrons would ascend to her using a
> rope to climb through the window and lower themselves that
> way as well. Also, she would hide them in the flax. And with
> these same things, she merited to save the messengers.

What is the meaning of the Midrash? Why was it so important for Rachav to use exactly those things with which she sinned to do a complete repentance, *teshuvah*, and transform her life to a meritorious one?

Repentance

> Resh Lakish said: Great is repentance, for because of it premed-
> itated sins are accounted as errors, as it says, "Return, Israel,
> unto the Lord your God, for you have stumbled in your iniquity
> (*avonos*)" (*Hoshea* 14:2). "Iniquity" [connotes] premeditation,
> and yet he [the prophet] calls it "stumbling." Resh Lakish
> [also] said that repentance is so great that premeditated sins are
> accounted as though they were *merits*, as it says, "When the
> wicked turns from his wickedness and does that which is lawful
> and right, he shall live thereby" (*Yechezkel* 33:19).
>
> That is no contradiction: one refers to a case [of repen-
> tance] from love, the other to [repentance] from awe.
>
> *(Yoma* 86b)

The Talmud tells us two contradictory things and then tries to resolve them. The first thing we are told is that repentance changes the status of a sin. A person who sins in an intentional manner, conscious of what he does and even rebellious against God, can repent. In so doing, he downgrades the sin to the level of an accidental sin, one that was not premeditated, but the result of error (or "stumbling"). In this case, he will, of course, be judged and punished much less severely than he would have been.

The second thing the Talmud teaches is that when a person repents, his intentional sins actually become merits! No longer is there any minus in the account, but rather a plus. The sinner lives by his former iniquity.

The Talmud resolves the seeming contradiction by stating that there are two different kinds of repentance. The first kind is repentance done out of fear of God. The second kind emanates from love of God. Repentance from fear enables a person to downgrade his sins, but repentance from love overturns the sin completely, transforming them to actual merits.

Why the difference?

Awe of God expresses itself in introspection and self-control. It is as if a person is saying to himself: "I do not want to do anything to hurt my Master, so I will refrain from any action that might offend Him." In this relationship, God is King, and we are His servants. By definition, there is distance in the relationship.

The Ramban teaches that the source of all negative precepts is awe of God. All the mitzvos that tell us what not to do are rooted in our desire to refrain from displeasing God.

Rav Goldvicht explains how this awe manifests itself in the *baal teshuvah*, the one who repents of his sin. The repentant says to himself, "I failed. I do not want to repeat this failure, and so I must hold back, stay away from my own lusts that caused me to offend my Creator." Sin activates within him dormant forces and powers that come alive at the moment of the sin. Therefore, the goal of the *baal teshuvah* is to control these forces by withdrawing from the physical world that brought him to sin.

Love of God functions differently. Love is the desire to bestow goodness on the other. In this relationship, we are the children and God is the parent. We say to our God, "What can we do for You? What can we give You?"

The Ramban teaches that all positive mitzvos are expressions of our love of God. These mitzvos tell us what we can give our Creator, how to bestow upon Him that which will please Him.

How does this love manifest itself in the *baal teshuvah*? Again Rav Goldvicht explains that the repentant says to himself, "I failed. In that failure is a dormant power, a *koach*, that can bring pleasure to the very One before Whom I have sinned. I will discard the sin, but keep that power and use it to serve Him."

Every sin has a *koach* (power), an energy that motivates it. That energy is a neutral force that can be used positively or negatively. Using it negatively is called sin. Using it positively is called mitzvah.

When we sin, we discover a latent energy that perhaps we were unaware of, and that discovery reveals potential for good. When acting on that potential, we are repenting from love.

For instance, a person who speaks *lashon hara*, negative speech, sins gravely before God. A *baal teshuvah* who repents from awe will realize how destructive his words are and will stop speaking them. He may even withdraw from people altogether, knowing that being in their company leads him astray. This is repentance from awe.

On the other hand, the repentant might ask himself: *What is the energy behind my sin? Why do I speak these inappropriate words?* He may come to realize that it is his love of people and desire for closeness to them that brings him to speak even words he shouldn't. Silence does not bring intimacy nor does it express love, so in an effort to bond with his friend, he spoke improperly.

Having discovered the energy of his sin, he might now be able to use it differently. Perhaps he will learn with his friend, or teach, or work with others on a community project. The sin becomes the vehicle for holiness, since it allows him to harness an energy, previously abused, and use it for good.

Now we can understand the different approaches in this *gemara*. When a person repents from awe, he downgrades his intentional sin to one that is "stumbling," error. However, when he repents from love, he discovers and uses the energy of the sin in a positive way. Hence his sin has actually brought merit to him.

Of course, no one would want to sin just to make that discovery. However, sometimes there are things about ourselves we only discover through our mistakes.

Rav Goldvicht compares this to a car accident. No one intentionally has an accident, but if insurance money arrives, sometimes even an accident has beneficial consequences!

It is a two-step process. First, a person must repent from awe. He must stop the sin. Only then can he repent from love and use the energy of the sin in a holy way.

> Depart from evil, and do good.
>
> *(Tehillim* 34:15)

Depart from evil — this is repentance from awe. Do good — this is repentance from love. Turn the evil into a vessel for good.

Energy

Every *koach* or quality in a person is, by definition, neutral. There are no bad or good qualities. Rather, how a person uses a quality determines its value. A good metaphor for this principle is water. Water is a tremendous source of energy. We cannot live without water — it is a basis of life. We need it for drinking and to make things grow. It provides us with energy and power. Yet water can be extremely destructive. It can cause floods, drown people, and bring colossal destruction.

> When David dug the Pits, the Deep rose up and threatened to submerge the world, whereupon David inscribed the [Ineffable] Name upon a [pottery] shard, and cast it into the Deep, and it subsided sixteen thousand cubits. When he saw that it had subsided to such a great extent, he said, "The nearer it is to the earth, the better the earth can be kept watered." He uttered the fifteen Songs of Ascent and the Deep reascended fifteen thousand cubits and remained one thousand cubits [beneath the earth's surface].
>
> *(Sukkah* 53b)

Tunneling into the earth to secure the foundation of the Temple, David dug too deeply. Suddenly, water surged upward, threatening to flood the world. David used a pottery shard to tame the waters and make them recede, but the water retreated too far. The world would not survive with so danger-ously little water. At that point, David had to do something to return the water to a healthy, sustainable level that would allow the world to endure.

Too much water can flood the world. Too little can deprive it of all life. Ei-ther state is fatal; only a delicate balance of forces, not too much or too little, will sustain life.

Human appetites, like water, must be kept in balance. They are given to us to sustain us and to help us grow, but too much appetite can lead us astray. Without desire, the world would not progress. Technology would not be de-veloped. Cities would not be built. Progress in society would not be made. On an individual level, we would not marry, work, discover, or learn new things. Yet there is appropriate use of desires and inappropriate use. One must use water and appetite for good, for holiness, and not for the opposite.

Yom Kippur and Sukkos

Both aspects of *teshuvah*, from awe and from love, are required of us in the month of Tishrei. We reflect on our actions, admit our sins, and move forward to separate from them. This process culminates on Yom Kippur, when we withdraw from the physical world and refrain from its pleasures, for it was the physical world that tempted us to act in inappropriate ways. Although Juda-ism is not an ascetic religion, on Yom Kippur, we remove ourselves from the lusts that saturate our lives. We stand before God as angels, as beings who are not tempted by physicality. It is a day to "depart from evil," to do *teshuvah* from awe.

Yet immediately after Yom Kippur, we go outside to begin building a sukkah. By doing this we assert that we will take the energy of sin and use it for the good. It is the aspect of "do good," of *teshuvah* from love, which drives us to take what we learned about ourselves and elevate it for the service of God.

The *sechach* (organic material that forms the roof of the sukkah) symbol-izes this idea. Instead of tossing our tree trimmings away as waste, we use them to complete our holy sukkahs. What seems unusable to others is em-ployed in the service of God, just like the energy of sin when directed to per-form a mitzvah. No lust or desire is negative in and of itself. Rather we must learn to take what appears to be useless and work with it to build our lives.

In ancient times, we performed a beautiful ceremony in the Beis HaMikdash called the *nisuch hamayim*. In this ceremony, water was drawn from the spring of Shiloach and transported to the Sanctuary, where it was poured on the altar. This water libation was a very joyful ritual, and it is said that whoever did not see the Simchas Beis HaSho'eivah, the celebration of the drawing of the waters, never saw true joy in his life.

What was the source of this joy? Rav Goldvicht explained that the happiness of the *nisuch hamayim* was coupled with the custom of *tashlich*, which we still do today. On Rosh HaShanah, we go to a body of flowing water, reach into our pockets, pull out crumbs of bread or dust or lint, and throw them into the water. The dust or crumbs we find represent our sins that we want to dispose of, so beginning the year in purity.

In ancient times, the nearest body of water to the Beis HaMikdash was the spring of Shiloach. Jews would descend to the spring from the city of Jerusalem and "discard" their sins there.

Later, however, at the celebration of the Simchas Beis HaSho'eivah, the Jews would descend to the same spring, collect the water, and pour it on the altar. As mentioned earlier, water symbolizes energy, energy that can be used for good or its opposite. On Rosh HaShanah, we discard our sins, but at the Simchas Beis HaSho'eivah, we retrieve the energy of those sins and use it as a "sacrifice" to God.

This is *teshuvah* from love.

Transformation from Impurity to Holiness

Rachav's prayer expressed her desire not only to stop her sinful ways but to use the very same force that drove her to sin in a positive way. She sinned with three things: the rope, the flax, and the window. Now she would use these things to serve God. She hid the spies in the stalks of flax on the roof, so the king's men would not discover them. Later, she helped them to escape through the window, using the same rope she had used to give entry and exit to her patrons.

Certainly the Midrash is giving us an insight into her full repentance from love. Discarding the sin but keeping the *koach* that propelled her to it, she now used her strengths to save Jewish lives.

Every sinful action begins with allowing our eyes to see and our minds to think about that which is forbidden.

> You should not seek after your own heart and your own eyes, which incline you to go astray (literally, "which you stray after").
>
> (*Bemidbar* 15:39)

> The eye sees, the heart desires, and the body sins.
>
> (*Rashi, Bemidbar* 15:39)

There are three steps to sin: sight, desire, and action. The verse in *Bemidbar* puts the heart before the eyes, yet Rashi reverses the two: the eyes see, the heart desires. That is because we allow ourselves to see that which we desire to see. The heart leads the eyes; the eyes, in turn, lead the heart. And together, when focused on that which is forbidden, they lead us to improper action.

This is the significance of the flax and the rope. The Maharal (*Chiddushei Aggados* 4:74) points out that of the three things that Rachav used to sin and then to expiate her sin, two were made of the same substance, flax. She hid the spies in the flax on her roof, and then she lowered them from the window by means of the rope, also of flax. Flax is the raw material and rope is the end product, just as desire is the beginning of sin and action is its product. The window represents sight, seeing what is forbidden to us; the flax represents the desire and forbidden thoughts; the rope binds the two together in action.

For forty years, Rachav had allowed her heart and eyes to dictate her actions. She behaved according to her own desires and thoughts. Her heart dictated to her eyes what to see, and together they led her to sinful actions.

Yet when she heard of the miracles that God did for the Jewish people, she made a change. Others heard what she did about the victories of the nation, but it did not change their perspective. They saw what they wanted to see. Only Rachav internalized the message. Only she allowed herself to see the truth and forced her heart to listen. Her heart perceived, her eyes saw, her ears heard, and she feared God.

The very eyes and heart that had led her astray brought her to recognition of God.

There is another *midrash* similar to the one quoted above, yet slightly different. The differences are instructive:

> She said, "Master of the Universe, I have sinned with three
> things: family purity, *challah*, and candle lighting. With these
> three things, forgive me: with a rope, a window, and a wall, as it
> says, 'Then she let them down by a rope through the window;
> for her house was upon the town wall, and she lived upon the
> wall.' "
>
> (*Mechilta, Yisro*)

This *midrash* also speaks about three sins Rahav committed and the three things with which she repented. Instead of flax, though, a wall is the third component of her atonement. In addition, this *midrash* juxtaposes her three acts of repentance with the three mitzvos given to women. Each of these mitzvos corresponds to one of Rachav's sins. The energy, *koach*, used in each is the same, yet Rachav had misused it for forty years in prostitution.

> Raw flax must be processed to be useful. It must be woven into
> cloth or rope. The Hebrew word for cloth, *bad*, is derived ety-
> mologically from the root word *badad*. *Badad* means alone. Ev-
> erything that is alone in the world desires connection. This is
> why flax waits to be woven. Rope, or cloth, created from strands
> of flax is the connection.
>
> (Maharal, *Chiddushei Aggados 4:72*)

Every person who is alone desires companionship and connection. One of the most powerful forms of connection is the union of husband and wife. But many seek to fulfill their desire for union and connection in inappropriate ways. Such was Rachav's life before her repentance. She created the illusion of closeness through physical intimacy, yet there was no holiness in those unions.

But it was this ability to connect that was her strength as well. Our Rabbis teach that the desire for connection that all humans have is the same *koach* needed to desire a relationship with God.

When the Men of the Great Assembly asked God to nullify the human desire for idol worship, Rabbi Yitzchak wanted them to neutralize strong physical desire, as well. He argued that physical desire need only be experienced at the time of procreation. This would prevent a lot of sin, since controlling physical desire is difficult. Rabbi Yehudah argued that physical desire was as vital to the world as rain, because from it comes the love of God. Therefore, it could not be nullified (*Zohar*, part 1, p. 148a).

> To unite with Torah is the goal of every Jew, and it comes from the same human desire to create connection in a relationship. It is not enough to learn Torah intellectually, because this does not create a complete connection. The Torah must penetrate all the emotions and energies of a Jew.
>
> (Rav Wolbe, *Alei Shur*, vol. II, p. 432)

The flax yearns to be cloth. Man and woman yearn for connection with one another. The Jews yearns to connect completely with God.

Rachav knew the *koach* of physical desire. She used it for forty years to gain entry to the psyche of kings and nobles. But then, when repenting, she took the energy of her sin, the knowledge of intimate connection, and redirected it, using it to connect with God and the Jewish people.

She knew that she had sinned in regard to *challah*, family purity, and lighting of candles. These same mitzvos are what typified the life of our matriarchs.

> The entire time that Sarah was alive, there was a candle that was lit from *erev Shabbos* to *erev Shabbos*, blessing was present in the dough [of her bread], and a cloud was [present] on the tent. When she died, they all stopped, and when Rivkah came, they returned.
>
> (*Rashi, Bereishis* 24:67)

> The candle is the light of spirituality that illuminates the Jewish home. The blessing in the dough represents our ability to transform the physicality into spirituality. The cloud on the tent is the cloud of the Divine presence, the *Shechinah*, that hovered there in the merit of family purity.
>
> (Maharal, *Chiddushei Aggados* 4:72)

Juxtaposed with these spiritual acquisitions, light, blessing, and the Divine presence — mainstays in the homes of our matriarchs — are the window, the rope, and the wall used by Rachav to do *teshuvah*. Perhaps the window that brings light into a home corresponds to the light of the Shabbos candles. The rope, strands of flax woven together, is like the *challah*. And the wall, which provides protection to the inhabitants of a home, is like the Divine presence which provides protection for us.

Rachav wanted to correct all that she had done wrong and, by so doing, complete the process of repentance in love.

The Scarlet Thread

When Rachav asked for "kindness and truth," the spies told Rachav to put a scarlet thread in the window as a sign. When they returned to conquer the city, Rachav and her entire family would be saved, on condition that this thread appeared in the window.

What is the significance of this string of scarlet thread (*tikvas chut hashani*)?

The color scarlet appears many times in the Tanach, in two different contexts. One is the context of royalty. Scarlet was one of the colors in the garment of the *kohein* and in the coverings of the Tabernacle, and the color worn by kings:

> You shall make a screen for the door of the tent, of blue, purple, scarlet, and fine twined linen, decorated with embroidery.
>
> (*Shemos* 26:36)

> He made the eifod of gold, blue, purple, scarlet, and fine twined linen.
>
> (*Shemos* 39:2)

> You shall be clothed with scarlet and have a chain of gold around your neck, and you shall rule as the third in the kingdom.
>
> (*Daniel* 5:16)

Scarlet is also the color of sin:

> "Come now and let us reason together," said the Lord; "though your sins be as scarlet, they shall be as white as snow; though they be red like crimson, they shall be as wool."
>
> (*Yeshayahu* 1:18)

When Rachav is told to hang a scarlet thread (*tikvas hashani*) from her window, it is significant. It is both a symbol of her sin and her repentance, her royal status and her grandeur. It is a scarlet thread changed to white, as God promises us that our sins will be as white as freshly fallen snow.

One of the central sacrifices of the Yom Kippur service in the Temple also involved a scarlet thread. The day before Yom Kippur, two identical goats were chosen, one to be sacrificed in the Temple on the afternoon of Yom Kippur, and the other to be led to the desert and pushed off a cliff. A scarlet thread would be tied to the second goat's horn and an identical thread would be hung on the opening to the Temple. After the goat was pushed off the cliff, the thread in the Temple would be examined. If it had turned white, the Jews knew that their sins had been forgiven.

Such was the thread of Rachav. Her hope was that her scarlet sins would be turned to purity. This was the hope offered by repentance: repentance from awe and repentance from love. In Hebrew, the line of thread is called *tikvas chut hashani*. The word *tikvas* is actually a double entendre. It means "line" (from the word *kav*), as translated above, and "hope" (*tikvah*). The thread of scarlet that hung in her window was her lifeline, her hope. But her real hope was in the power of repentance.

Every Friday night, Jewish husbands return from synagogue and sing a chapter of *Mishlei* beginning with the verse, "A woman of valor, who can find" to their wives. The Midrash tells us that each of the verses in this chapter describes one of the great Jewish women whom we admire and aspire to emulate. One of these verses, according to the Midrash, describes Rachav:

> She is not afraid of the snow for her household, for all her household are clothed with scarlet.
>
> (*Mishlei* 31:21)

> This is Rachav…she was not afraid of them because they gave her a sign, the *tikvas chut hashani*, the scarlet thread of hope…and from her descended prophets and priests.
>
> (*Midrash Mishlei* 31)

Indeed, after Rachav converted, she married Yehoshua (*Megillah* 14b). Our Sages learn this fact from the following verse:

> Yehoshua granted life to Rachav the harlot, her father's household, and all that she had. She lives in Israel to this day, because

she hid the messengers whom Yehoshua sent to spy out Yericho.

(Yehoshua 6:25)

When the great leaders of the Jewish people saw that Yehoshua married Rachav, which " granted her life," they married her family members, "her father's household," who had converted as well.

Though her sins were like scarlet, they became white as snow, and she married in purity and became a mother in Israel, bearing daughters who married into the tribe of Levi. Among her grandchildren are prophets and priests:

> Eight prophets who were also priests descended from Rachav the harlot, namely, Neryah, Baruch, Serayah, Machseyah, Yirmeyahu, Chilkiyah, Chanamel, and Shallum. Rabbi Yehudah says: Chuldah the prophetess was also one of the descendants of Rachav the harlot. [We know this] because it is written here "the son of Tikvah" and it is written elsewhere [in connection with Rachav] "the line (*tikvah*) of scarlet thread."
>
> *(Megillah 14b)*

Why priests and prophets? Priests to show the purity of her repentance; prophets because they are seers. Because she saw with her eyes the evidence that God exists and gives kindness to those who follow Him, because she followed her eyes to do the will of God, God granted her children who "see" through visions, dreams, and prophecy.

From Rachav we learn that *teshuvah* not only heals, but can also raise us from the lowest place to the highest.

> Are not these things a logical inference? Just like she [Rachav] was from a nation about whom it was written, "Of these people...you shall not keep alive anything that breathes" (*Devarim* 20:16), [but] because she advanced herself to God, He [in turn] brought her close [to Him], Israel, who keeps the Torah, even more so.
>
> *(Yalkut Divrei HaYamim, ch. 4)*

Promises Kept

> Your lips are like a thread of scarlet, and your mouth is comely;
> your cheeks are like a piece of a pomegranate behind your veil.
>
> *(Shir HaShirim* 4:3)

Shir HaShirim speaks about the relationship between the Jewish people and God. It is a relationship of trust and of love, of promises given and promises kept. The thread of scarlet is reminiscent of the thread that Rachav tied in her window, trusting the promise of the spies that they would save her (*Rashi, Shir HaShirim* 4:3). So too, we trust God to keep His promise that if we do *teshuvah*, He will forgive us. But more than that, our sins, though they be the color of scarlet, will become as white as the snow.

Trusting God in the Dark of the Night

W

hen we read the story of the spies, it's easy to feel disdain for the children of Israel. It is, after all, a time of great sin for that generation. Yet, despite this fact, we feel empathy for them as well. They were given a particularly harsh punishment for a lapse of faith. Admittedly, the sin was serious, but they were sentenced to exile and suffering for generations to come. Doesn't this punishment far outweigh the crime?

Their sin, we are taught, was doubt. Although privileged to see God's open miracles performed in Egypt and in the desert, the Jews of the time faltered when challenged to trust God. In short, God commanded them to conquer the land of Canaan, the land promised them via their forefathers. While preparing for conquest, they decided to send out spies to determine strategy and tactics. These spies returned with a discouraging report;they said that the inhabitants and the protective walls of this land were mighty, and it would be impossible to conquer the land.

Hearing this, the Jews cried bitterly all night long. Punishment was swift — they would not be allowed into the land. In fact, they would be made to wander in the desert for forty years until the entire generation died. Only their children, those not yet twenty years of age or those not yet born to them, would enter the land.

But that wasn't all; their crying reaped another punishment. For the bitter tears of one night, they were punished with crying for generations. The Gemara states:

> "All the congregation lifted up their voices and wept" (*Bemidbar* 14:1). Rabbah said in the name of Rabbi Yochanan: That day was the Ninth of Av, and the Holy One, blessed be He, said,

"They are now weeping for nothing, but I will fix this day for them as an occasion of weeping for generations."

(*Sotah* 35a)

How could God punish crying for nothing with crying for generations? Why such a sweeping punishment for one indiscretion? It could seem unjust to us, even cruel.

The answers are in the details.

The Lord spoke to Moshe, saying, "Send men, that they may spy the land of Canaan, which I give to the people of Israel; of every tribe of their fathers shall you send a man, every one a leader among them." Moshe, by the commandment of the Lord, sent them from the wilderness of Paran; all those men were chiefs of the people of Israel....

Moshe sent them to spy out the land of Canaan, and said to them, "Go up this way southward, and go up into the mountain. See the land, what it is; and the people who live in it, whether they are strong or weak, few or many; and what the land is that they live in, whether it is good or bad; and what cities they are that they live in, whether in tents or in fortresses; and what the land is, whether it is fat or lean, whether there is wood in it or not. Be you of good courage, and bring of the fruit of the land."...

They returned from searching the land after forty days. They went and came to Moshe, and to Aharon, and to all the congregation of the people of Israel, to the wilderness of Paran, to Kadesh, and brought back word to them and to all the congregation, and showed them the fruit of the land. They told him, and said, "We came to the land where you sent us, and surely it flows with milk and honey; and this is its fruit. Nevertheless the people who live in the land are strong, and the cities are walled and very great; and moreover we saw the children of Anak there. The Amalekites live in the land of the Negev; and the Hittites, the Jebusites, and the Emorites live in the mountains; and the Canaanites live by the sea and by the side of the Jordan."

And Kalev quieted the people before Moshe and said, "Let

us go up at once and possess it, for we are well able to overcome it." But the men who went up with him said, "We are not able to go up against the people, for they are stronger than we."

They brought up an evil report of the land which they had spied to the people of Israel, saying, "The land which we have gone to spy is a land that eats up its inhabitants, and all the people that we saw in it are men of a great stature. There we saw the Nefilim, the sons of Anak, who come from the Nefilim; and we were in our own sight as grasshoppers, and so were we in their sight."

(Bemidbar, ch. 13)*

On the one hand, the spies brought back a very positive report. "We came to the land where you sent us, and surely it flows with milk and honey; and this is its fruit." Yet, on the whole, their report was negative. They said that despite the goodness of the land, strong men inhabited it and enormous walls protected the cities.

The people were torn, frightened by the seeming impossibility of the mission, until Kalev quieted them down with reassurances, "Let us go up at once and possess it, for we are well able to overcome it." Yet these words of faith were simply not strong enough to convince them. The ten spies spoke boldly and with conviction, "We are not able to go up against the people, for they are stronger than we…. [It] is a land that eats up its inhabitants."

The people cried all night long. They cried from despair, from a lack of belief that God desired their good, from fear that the exodus had led them to a worse predicament than even slavery.

Perhaps now it is easier to understand why the consequences for this night of tears had to be so grave. After all, the generation of Jews in the desert were privileged to live through the most dramatic display of open miracles in human history, a life of clear Divine intervention. After having been redeemed from Egypt with ten plagues in which they were spared but the Egyptians were punished, how could the Jews doubt God's ability and desire to care for them? After experiencing the splitting of the sea in which their enemies drowned and they walked on dry land, how could they ask themselves if God wanted them to die? Being led by Clouds of Glory, fed by manna from Heaven, and given drink from a traveling well, how did they fear entry into the Land of Israel and cry for nothing?

Crying for nothing was punished with crying for generations. We know that in the Torah, punishment is given to correct a sin and to educate the sinner. Therefore, with a closer reading, we ask ourselves a different question than we would on first encountering the story. We might ask, how was this crying for nothing to be repaired with crying for generations? What was the lesson to be learned?

Trusting God in the Night

The night of crying in the desert was the Ninth of Av. It was on this same night that, hundreds of years later, the First Temple would be burned and the Jewish people sent into exile to Babylonia. The Second Temple, as well, would be destroyed on the Ninth of Av. This time, the exile would last thousands of years. A night of crying from lack of faith led to the bitter weeping of a long, harsh exile.

Night is a time when fear overcomes reason. During the day, it's easier to think rationally and to believe in ourselves and the future. Even our relationship with God changes as the day does. During daylight hours, it is easier to know that He is with us, that His loving kindness guides us as individuals and as a nation. At night, however, fear rules, and we access Him in the mode of *din* (awe), not in *chesed* (kindness). Night is a metaphor for exile, and day for redemption.

King David, in his psalms, declared that we sing God's praises night and day, yet the song we sing during the day is different than the one we sing at night.

> To declare Your loving kindness in the morning and Your faithfulness in the night.
>
> (*Tehillim* 92:3)

Not only does God act differently toward us in the day (redemption) than He does at night (exile), but we also respond to Him differently. Every day, we recite a prayer between the Shema and the *Amidah*. At night, the prayer begins with the phrase "true and trustworthy" (*emes ve'emunah*), but during the day, we begin, instead, with the words "true and firm" (*emes veyatziv*). At night, when fears overtake us, we remind ourselves that we must nevertheless trust in God. During the day, when it is easier to believe, we declare that God stands firmly with us.

> Rabbah Bar Chanina the elder said in the name of Rav: If one does not say "True and Firm" in the morning and "True and Trustworthy" in the evening, he has not performed his obligation. For it is said, "To declare Your loving kindness in the morning and Your faithfulness in the night" (*Tehillim* 92:3).
>
> (*Berachos* 12a)

What is the relationship between the declaration of trust that we say at night, "True and Trustworthy," and the ill-fated night of crying of long ago?

Second Chances

The purpose of Creation was to give human souls the chance to choose good over evil, and so work to perfect themselves. To provide this opportunity, God created a world in which His oneness would be concealed and it would be difficult to see Him. This hiddenness creates the illusion that evil emanates from one source and good from another. The world looks fractured and God's presence is not easily detected (Ramchal, *Derech Hashem*, ch. 1).

Because of the conflict between our own desires and our desire to choose good, we feel a constant tension. We experience an endless tug-of-war between the needs of the soul and the needs of the body. Because of this struggle, we often fail to realize our soul's desire. Often, despite good intentions, we fall down on the job.

However, the kindness of God is that, in order to allow us the maximum possibilities for perfection, He often gives us an opportunity to try again; He gives us second chances.

We learn about second chances from the mitzvah of the second Pesach, Pesach Sheini. What is the law of the second Pesach? When the Temple stood, there was a mitzvah incumbent on every Jew to come to the Temple on Pesach and bring a sacrifice. However, there were times when, for some people, meeting that obligation was very difficult. God would give them a second chance, exactly one month later. Usually, people had valid reasons for failing to fulfill this responsibility; perhaps they were spiritually unclean (*tamei*) or felt the journey was too far. But even without a valid excuse, according to many opinions, people would still be given a second chance to bring their sacrifice.

On Pesach Sheini, a person could bring a sacrifice and eat it with matzah and bitter herbs, as if it were Pesach. Pesach Sheini is the second-chance mitzvah and from it we learn that, in life, God gives us all second chances.

This is an amazing idea. God offers us the chance to repent (do *teshuvah*) and to repair inappropriate behavior. He gives us the possibility of achieving atonement (*kaparah*), thereby rectifying the negative energy of our sins. Moreover, God gives us new and different opportunities to do good the second time around.

This is true for the nation as well as for the individual. Life is full of second chances. Still, a second chance never looks like the first one. It is different and often harder. While first and second chances may lead to similar results, the effects of second-tries always come with a twist.

To see what the second chance looks like, we will consider the giving of the second Tablets. After Moshe shatters the first Tablets, God says He will give him a second set:

> The Lord said to Moshe, "Cut two tablets of stone like the first, and I will write upon these tablets the words that were in the first tablets, which you broke".... He cut two tablets of stone similar to the first; and Moshe rose up early in the morning and went up to Mount Sinai, as the Lord had commanded him, and took in his hand the two tablets of stone.
>
> (*Shemos* 34:1, 4)

On first reading, it would seem that the second Tablets simply replaced the first ones. Yet we learn:

> In the end, when He gave [Moshe] the [first] tablets, he descended [the mountain] and found the [golden] calf. Immediately, he broke the tablets to reduce the shame [of Israel], and requested [from God] mercy for them. Moshe pursued every avenue above until God was appeased. Moshe said, "Master of the Universe, give them second Tablets." He said, "The first

ones were the work of My hand, and you broke them. And now, you make the second ones instead, as it says: 'Chisel for yourself second Tablets.' "

(Tanchuma, Ki Tisa 23)

God sculpts the first Tablets with stones "from above," but Moshe must sculpt the second Tablets with stones from below. The first are a free gift, the second must be earned, labored for.

Rav Dessler explains (*Michtav MeEliyahu*, vol. 2, p. 45) that the first tablets represent the pure hearts of the recipients. At Sinai, the Jewish people stood before God as angels do, willing to do His every request. They had no personal agenda, no longings or desire to do anything but the will of God. They were like Adam before the sin. Adam had no evil inclination: it was external to him in the form of the snake. Until Adam sinned, the Divine presence hovered in the Garden of Eden; after he sinned, it departed. Until he sinned, the evil inclination was external to him; after the sin, the evil inclination became part of him.

However, at Sinai, the Divine presence returned in its full glory. The Torah was given with no boundaries or limitations. God was easily perceived by all; there was no dissonance between the reality of His being and the ability of the Jews of the time to understand Him.

The second Tablets were carved and etched by Moshe. This is to teach us that we must etch the Torah in our hearts. At this second giving, the children of Israel received the Torah as people, not as angels — as people who struggle and sometimes fail. This is similar to Adam after the sin, after the evil inclination entered him and became part of his psyche. The second time around, the gift of Torah is more limited, since we are more limited. Now, the Divine presence is not easily accessed but is discerned only through our labor and toil in learning Torah. Moreover, our understanding of God is fragmented. We do not see Him as One, we view Him as if we were looking through a fractured mirror.

The first Tablets were chiseled by God and broken by man. Man carved the second Tablets, and if they are to remain unbroken, he will have to labor and earn his right to them.

The Jews were given a second chance — a second set of Tablets — but this time they would have to prove their worthiness and their willingness to earn the Torah. This time, it would be about a struggle of human beings, not about a gift to angels.

Second chances are different from first chances; nevertheless, they offer us an opportunity to achieve a level of holiness equal to that of the first.

The First and Second Temples

The First Temple stood about four hundred years; when the Jews sinned, God sent an enemy to destroy it and exile the Jews to Babylon. Seventy years later, the Jewish people were permitted to return to their land and to build the Second Temple.

The purpose of both the First and Second Temples was the same: to bring closeness between the Jewish people and God. Even so, there were many differences between the two experiences. King Shlomo, a sovereign king in Israel, built the First Temple in a time of economic and physical security. He oversaw construction of an ornate building, rich with gold and tapestries. Daily miracles took place in the Temple. Fire descended from Heaven; there was prophecy and the Tablets rested in the ark.

The Second Temple was erected when the Land of Israel was under foreign domination. Built only with the permission of a foreign king — Darius the Second of Persia — the builders were still constantly under attack from their local enemies. They were forced to build a little at a time, stop, and build some more. They built with wood, in a simple style. There were no miracles, no prophecy, no tablets. Even the vessels were made of brass and copper, not like the gold of the First Temple.

The Second Temple did not compare to the first in splendor, grandeur, or miracles. Much of the time, we were not even an independent country, and when we were, we were never as strong or as self-sufficient as in the time of Shlomo.

But despite these differences, both Temples were holy and helped us achieve holiness. Both focused us on our service of God. Both stood as symbols of the unique relationship between God and the Jewish people.

The Second Temple afforded us a second chance to connect with God, but it was not as simple or as miraculous as our first chance. The goal was the same, but the path to that goal was arduous and more demanding.

Exile Is Also a Second Chance

Exile, along with the suffering it brings, is also a second chance to trust God.

God gave us our first chance in the desert when we were instructed to enter the land of Israel; we did not do so, but instead – doubting God – chose to send men to spy out the land. When they came back with a negative report, we cried.

What were these tears about? Crying for nothing.

What is crying? It is an external expression of internal pain. Rav Dessler (*Michtav MeEliyahu*) explains that there are two kinds of crying. There is crying for nothing and crying for something.

What, then, is crying for nothing? It is crying about a situation that could have been prevented. The congregation wept because they were afraid; and while their fear was genuine, it could have been avoided if they had trusted God. Taking faith into account, there was no reason to be afraid. Surely God would conquer the inhabitants of the land.

What could have prevented the senseless tears of the night when the spies came with a negative report? If the Jewish people had remembered that they were safe in the hands of God, if they had trusted Him to take them safely into the land and protect them from their enemies, they never would have cried. After all, had He not redeemed them from Egypt, split the sea, and rained manna from Heaven upon them?

However, instead of trusting Him, they were afraid and distressed. And they cried many tears — tears that flowed from a lack of *bitachon*, trust. This is crying for nothing: real tears expressing real anxiety, but tears that did not have to be shed, had they only trusted God.

The Jewish people stood on the border of our Holy Land and refused to enter.

> Why has the Lord brought us to this land, to fall by the sword, that our wives and our children should be a prey? Would it not be better for us to return into Egypt?
>
> (*Bemidbar* 14:3)

You murmured in your tents and said, "Because the Lord hated us, He has brought us out of the land of Egypt, to deliver us into the hand of the Emorites, to destroy us."

(Devarim 1:27)

Their fear was so irrational that they believed, as the spies told them, that the inhabitants of the land were "stronger than we." In the Hebrew, the words are *"chazak hu mimenu." Mimenu* can mean "we" or "he." Our Rabbis explain that the spies implied that the residents of the land at the time were stronger than "He," the Almighty. They did not think they could conquer the land, because they disregarded the fact that God is all-powerful. They forgot that it is God who fights our battles, so that even a problem that seems unsolvable is not.

Nothing is impossible for God. But when we feel that God is incapable of repairing our pain or does not care about our suffering we "cry for nothing."

The children of Israel sank into an enormous lapse of *bitachon*, trust; that kind of error could only be repaired by "crying for generations." But what kind of crying repairs "crying for nothing"? Crying for something.

What is crying for something? Rav Dessler explains that this is grieving over our failure to live up to the Torah's goals. It is crying because we are not the people that God wants us to be. It is crying out because we want to get close to God and His Torah and don't know how.

This kind of crying is the beginning of repair because it involves the realization that we should improve ourselves. This is true as much for the nation as it is for the individual. As individuals, we must identify what we can change in ourselves to bring us closer to God. As a nation, we must stop chasing every fad and fashion of the Western world and pursue, instead, the eternal values of the Torah.

Then we — both collectively and as individuals — will begin the process of return to Truth.

And we must trust God. We must trust Him even though we don't see Him, even though we don't understand Him. Today, the nation must know that God can save us and that — while it seems that the odds are against us, that we are surrounded by enemies, that the nations of the world oppose us — for God, saving us is easy!

This kind of trust is expressed when we declare "Your faithfulness in the night." It is trusting God in the dark of night.

To declare Your loving kindness in the morning and Your faithfulness in the night.

(Tehillim 92:3)

"To declare Your loving kindness in the morning" refers to our first chance, the opportunity to see the hand of God in the desert, amidst endless miracles. "Your faithfulness in the night" refers to our second chance, to believe in God in the darkness of night, to trust Him in the pain of exile, to have *bitachon* that He will lead us through our most difficult suffering.

This second chance even includes the opportunity to see the hand of God in the triumphs of our enemies. Rav Dessler, writing during the catastrophe of the Holocaust, states that there is Divine consent in our enemies' successes and we must see God's hand even there (*Michtav MeEliyahu*, vol. 3, p. 274).

The Ninth of Av marks the destruction of our two Temples, the beginning of our exile. Unaware of the significance of that date on the Jewish calendar, King Ferdinand II decreed that all Jews would be expelled from Spain on that day. A historian wrote that if the Spanish authorities had known how much faith the king was instilling in the exiled Jews by expelling them on the Ninth of Av, he would never have done it (*Michtav MeEliyahu*, vol. 2, p. 48). The Jews knew from the date that "this [was] the Lord's doing" (*Tehillim* 118:23), and this knowledge strengthened them.

In the course of Jewish history, simple Jews have lived with faith and trust in God. Persecution after persecution, blood libel after blood libel, exile after exile, we have been forced to choose between our faith and our lives. Today, as well, we must learn to trust God, through the darkness of our difficulties. This predicament has made us cry for generations, and has simultaneously offered us a second chance to trust God. We, like Kalev, must declare, "Let us go up at once and possess it, for we are well able to overcome it."

Appreciation and Trust

We adjoin the Shema and the *Amidah* with the words "True and Firm" during the day and "True and Trustworthy" at night. Rashi shows us the contrast between the morning and evening versions:

In its entirety, "True and Firm" is an expression of appreciation for the loving kindness shown our forefathers, for their having been brought out of Egypt, for splitting and leading the people across the Red Sea.

The blessing "True and Trustworthy" deals with the future, with our waiting expectantly for the day when God will fulfill His faithful promise and rescue us from the hands of kings and despots, preserve our souls in life, and make us tread on the high places of our enemies. Such acts are always miracles.

(Rashi, Berachos 12a)

We declare our appreciation for the kindness of the day and our trust in the promise of the night. Our relationship of trust is based on our previous experiences of redemption.

"True and Trustworthy" is a declaration that, despite the dark, we believe that God is watching out for us. We are like the child who, afraid of the dark of night, crawls into his parent's bed, is enveloped in his parent's embrace, and feels safe.

It is our second chance, harder than the first, but of equal promise.

Template of History

There is a story told about a man who lived in a time of persecution of the Jewish people. Before the trouble began, he had a home and a family. When persecuters destroyed his house, making him a refugee, he said to God, "I lost my home, but I still love You."

When they killed his wife, again he prayed, "I don't have a home and I don't have a wife, but I still love You."

When his first child was lost, he cried out to his Creator, "I have no home and no wife and my child is gone, but I still love You."

With the loss of each subsequent child, in his grief, he cried, "I still love You."

Finally, when there was no one left, he turned once again to the Master of the Universe and said, "I lost my home and I still loved You. I lost my wife and I still loved you. One by one, I lost my children, but I still loved You. Now that

I have nothing and no one left, I can devote my entire life to loving You."
    This is trusting God in the dark of the night.

Conclusion

The night of crying for nothing is long over. The time for trusting God in the darkness is here; it is our second chance. Let us not waste our tears on fear, but use them for repentance. Let us cry for something — for our distance from God, for our yearning for redemption. And through the darkness of our exile, let us trust that our Creator wants only good for us and will ultimately bring us home.

God Hides, We Seek

Every year in the month of Adar, the Jewish people are commanded to read the Purim story, as recorded in *Megillas Esther* (the Book of Esther) in its entirety. The Book of Esther was the last of the twenty-four holy books to be included in the Tanach and is unique because it is the only book where God's Name is never explicitly mentioned in print. The absence of God's Name in *Megillas Esther* is a reflection of the "hiddenness" of God's providence and direction in the Purim miracle itself (in contrast, for example, to the open fireworks of the Egyptian plagues or the splitting of the Red Sea). However, there is a clue about God's "behind-the-scenes" rescue of the Jewish people: *Megillas Esther* is named after the heroine of the story, Esther, whose name means "hidden" (*Chullin* 139b).

The quality of hiddenness, or *tzenius* (modesty), is a Jewish characteristic which has been handed down from parent to child, from individual to collective, and from generation to generation. Queen Esther inherited hiddenness from her ancestors to such an extent that she was named for it, and we, too, have inherited this quality. Throughout Jewish history, the ability to look away from the external, splashy, and showy, and focus instead on the internal, hidden, and pure has been essential to our survival.

It is no coincidence that Esther, who represents modesty and hiddenness, became the redeemer as well as the queen of the Jewish people. Throughout our history, those chosen by God to occupy a position of redeemer or royalty of Israel have been, like Esther, modest, self-sacrificing, and humble. But there is an additional quality required of Jewish leaders: When our patriarchs and matriarchs, kings and redeemers, experience feelings of insecurity and abandonment, caused by an apparent absence of God's Presence, they do not despair or give up. Rather, when God appears to be hiding, our holy leaders set about seeking Him.

Esther's Ancestry

Queen Esther's life was the ultimate expression of the genetic spiritual development of royalty combined with modesty, which began with Sarah:

> Why did Esther merit to rule 127 provinces? For the Holy One, blessed be He, said, "Let Esther come and rule 127 provinces, [for she is] the daughter of Sarah, who lived 127 years."
>
> *(Esther Rabbah* 1:8)

One hundred and twenty-seven is not a common number. It's mentioned only twice in the Tanach — once describing the years of Sarah's life, and once describing the number of provinces over which Esther ruled. The *midrash*, then, is stating that there is a fundamental connection between the quality of Sarah's 127 years in this world and Esther's reign as the queen over 127 provinces. What did Sarah and her descendant, Esther, have in common? Sarah was, of course, modest:

> They said to him [Avraham], "Where is Sarah, your wife?" He said, "Here, in the tent."
>
> *(Bereishis* 18:9)

> "Here, in the tent" — [implying] "she is modest."
>
> *(Rashi, Bereishis* 18:9)

In addition, Sarah and Esther were each abducted, forcefully taken to the palace of a king, and seemingly abandoned there (it happened to Sarah twice; see *Bereishis* 12:15 and 20:2). Something happened to them as a result of these tragedies that gave them the potential to generate quantum spiritual leaps for their people. Sarah and Avraham developed as individuals who dedicated their lives to serving God — allowing no obstacles to interfere. In the days of the Purim story, Queen Esther led the way for the Jewish people to complete what they had started at Mount Sinai by accepting the Torah without the open revelation of Godliness which the Jews experienced at Sinai, and this was accomplished by total self-sacrifice.

It would appear that abandonment is crucial to the process of redemption, both for the individual and the nation. The relationship between abandonment and redemption is made crystal clear in the Midrash:

> Rabbi Berechyah said in the name of Rabbi Levi: God said to
> Israel, "You cried and said, 'We are orphans with no Father'
> (*Eichah* 5:3). I swear that even the redeemer [Esther] that I will
> send you in Media in the future will be without father and
> mother."
>
> *(Esther Rabbah 6:2)*

As the Jewish people went into exile to Babylon, they cried out to God,
"We have no Father! We feel abandoned!" God responded that He would
send a redeemer who would be not only fatherless, but motherless as well.
This redeemer was to be Queen Esther.

Although Esther was an orphan from the time of her birth, she had a lineage worthy of royalty. She was a descendant of King Shaul, who in turn was a
descendant of Rachel. From them she inherited the royal quality of modesty:

> The reward for Rachel's modesty was that she merited that
> Shaul descended from her. The reward for Shaul's modesty was
> that he merited that Esther descended from him.
>
> *(Megillah* 13b)

Queen Esther's life was a link in the chain of descent of Sarah and Rachel
and Shaul, and the common denominator of this chain was the quality of modesty. Why does the oral Torah make a point of informing us of Esther's lineage? What was the connection between Esther's ancestry and the Purim miracle? In what way does the feeling of abandonment qualify someone to be a redeemer of the Jewish people? And, finally, how does all this affect our identity
as Jews today?

Modesty

> And the Lord God formed the man of dust from the ground,
> and He blew into his nostrils the soul of life; and man became a
> living being.
>
> *(Bereishis* 2:7)

Man was created from the dust of the earth, and after his body was
formed God blew into him a soul, part of His own holy breath. Man's body is

thus of the earth and physical, and his soul is of the breath of God and spiritual. A tug-of-war is constantly going on — what the body wants, the soul does not want. What the soul needs, the body doesn't want to access. The more a person attaches himself to the physical, external world, the more he suppresses sensitivity toward his Godly soul. The more a person connects with his spiritual, internal self, the more he strengthens his Godly soul. When this happens, his interest in the physical and external wanes.

The natural pull, as we all know, is towards what the body wants, which is the physical. It's easy to focus on material necessities and desires, and difficult to focus on the spiritual part of ourselves. In addition to that natural pull to the physical that we constantly fight and the more difficult focus on our spiritual life, there is another pull. It involves finding the balance between one's public self and one's private self. The public persona is the side of ourselves we allow the world to view. This is a natural pull — we all want to be seen, heard, and noticed. The private person is, on the other hand, our true self-definition and essence, and it is there, in the private world, that our connection with God is nurtured.

Staying within spiritual borders, maintaining a hiddenness from the external world, and reserving one's private self for God is called *tzenius*, modesty. *Tzenius* is a spiritual state which is not visible or noticeable to other people. The more spiritual it is, the more hidden it is; the more hidden it is, the more spiritual it is.

The person who functions in the physical world requires protection from the pull of the external so that he doesn't lose contact with his essential self. Without protection, the pull to the physical and public becomes overwhelming. In other words, the more we are out there in the physicality of the world, the more we need to protect our inner life. Modesty allows us to consistently maintain our internal focus and thereby strengthen sensitivity to our internal essence. The stronger the spiritual borders, the less the physical world is able to intrude and affect us.

This idea is illustrated in the Torah with the story of the clothing given to Adam and Chavah (although clothing is only one expression of *tzenius*):

> They were both naked, the man and his wife, and they were not ashamed.

> *(Bereishis 2:25)*

In the beginning, Adam and Chavah did not wear clothes. Before their sin, they lived in the Garden of Eden in a heightened state of spiritual awareness. Their entire existence was focused on connecting to God, and they experienced no pull toward the physical or external. They were not embarrassed by the physical world or by their nakedness because their thoughts were exclusively internal and Godly, and nothing distracted them from their spiritual service.

After eating from the Tree of Knowledge of Good and Evil, however, Adam and Chavah began to feel a great pull toward the material world. Now highly sensitive to the physical, they became aware of their nakedness and were embarrassed.

> Then the eyes of both of them were opened and they realized that they were naked; and they sewed together a fig leaf and made themselves aprons.
>
> *(Bereishis 3:7)*

No longer able to dwell in the totally spiritual world of the Garden of Eden, they were sent into the external world. The Torah tells us that before they were banished from the Garden of Eden, God made clothes for them. This clothing provided protection against the pull to the external, and allowed them to live within the material world while focusing on their spirituality as well.

Hiddenness

There is another spiritual state that is somewhat parallel to *tzenius*, and that is *hester*, hiddenness. *Hester* is the hiddenness of God when He withdraws His Presence from this world and is no longer "visible." Before the destruction of the First Temple, God revealed Himself through prophecy and open miracles, but after the destruction He "withdrew" into a hidden and private place. Obviously, there is no place on earth vacant of Godliness, but since the destruction of the First Temple, we can't "see" God; and as He withdraws Himself, the physical world becomes much more prominent and noticeable, while the spiritual reality becomes less visible and less accessible. It may even appear to us that God has withdrawn Himself altogether and has abandoned the world. This state is called "hiddenness within hiddenness" (*hester besoch hester*).

Rabbi Moshe Chaim Luzzatto, the Ramchal, explains that God withdraws to this place of *hester* in order to prepare us for a new and higher spiritual level. In other words, God's hiddenness is the preparation for us to reach a greater level of spirituality than we could achieve if God's Presence was plainly manifest. As an example, the Ramchal cites Yaakov's mourning for the loss of his son Yosef. For twenty-two years, God was hidden to Yaakov, for Yaakov was in mourning and received no prophecy. But although God was hidden, He had not abandoned Yaakov — He was preparing Yosef and the Jewish people for a new level of greatness.

There is an interplay between God's withdrawal into a hidden place and *tzenius*, our own sense of withdrawing to a private, internal world, for modesty is the quality required as the response to God's hiddenness. We can understand this interrelationship by examining the life of Esther, who was chosen as the redeemer of Israel because of her humility (*Or Chadash*, p. 51).

Kings and Queens

In the time of our patriarchs, it was always the youngest that became the leader because he was more modest, more in tune spiritually. Yitzchak was greater than Yishmael. Yaakov superceded Eisav. Although our two great matriarchs, Rachel and Leah, were both leaders, Rachel, the younger one, was the greater of the two. The Maharal explains that by nature, the younger child is the more spiritual child because the one who clings to the inside of the womb longer is the one who wants to remain inside the spiritual world for a longer time. The one who pushes to get out first, so to speak, is the one who is in a hurry to get into the external world. Rachel, the younger, was more spiritual than Leah, the elder. (Maharal, *Nesivos Olam* II, *Netiv HaTzenius*, ch. 1)This was also true of the twin brothers Yaakov and Eisav. Eisav, who was born first, was the more expansive, "outward" person and was described as "the man of the fields." Yaakov, the younger brother, was the more spiritual, internal person, a man who "dwelled in tents."

Rachel is called the "smaller" or younger daughter to teach us of her integrity. She was private and internally focused, so much so that when she realized on her wedding night that her father intended to put Leah under the *chuppah* in place of herself, she made an extraordinarily generous decision. Rachel and Yaakov had suspected that the wicked Lavan would attempt such a switch, so they made up a code, some words to exchange under the *chuppah*. Realizing that Leah would be horribly embarrassed in public when Yaakov said his part of the code and Leah couldn't respond, Rachel gave Leah the code. This righteous act earned Rachel no accolades and no praise, because no one knew about it except Rachel herself, Leah, and Yaakov. Her self-sacrifice and kindness was a hidden, modest deed. What was her reward? That this ability to remain modest would be inherited not only by her immediate descendants, but by all of the Jewish people:

> The reward for Rachel's modesty was that she merited that Shaul descended from her. The reward for Shaul's modesty was that he merited that Esther descended from him.
>
> (*Megillah* 13b)

The ability to remain modest, to exist within spiritual boundaries, was not only a reward for Rachel, but a necessary trait for Jewish survival — otherwise we would lose our raison d'être as God's kingdom of priests and become gobbled up in the material "rat race." Modesty is not a static spiritual inheritance; in each generation it develops and expands. It grows with every generation because the *hester*, God's withdrawal from the world, grows with every generation. The less visible God is in the world, the more a person must focus internally to be with Him, and so the modesty of Rachel was inherited by her children and evolved exponentially until the birth of her grandson Shaul.

Shaul was a farmer from a nonprominent family of the small tribe of Binyamin. Shmuel was the leading prophet of the day, and despite the fact that he banished idolatry and infused religious service with vitality, the people wanted a king, like all the nations of the world had. Why would the people want a king when they had a tremendous prophet like Shmuel to lead them? They wanted the pomp and circumstance, the royalty, the robes — in short, they wanted to be out there, to be seen, to be visible. Shmuel objected: Why desire the external when you have the internal? You have prophecy, so what do you want kingship for? You're asking for a relationship that is less than the relationship you have now!

God, however, said to give them a king. Who did He give them as a king?

> Now God had revealed in Shmuel's ear, one day before Shaul had come, saying, "At this time tomorrow I will send a man [Shaul] to you from the land of Binyamin; you shall anoint him to be ruler over My people Israel...."
>
> *(Shmuel* I 9:15–16)

Shaul, despite being a very tall man, was a most private and humble individual who saw himself as being "small":

> Shaul answered, saying, "But I am only a Benjamite, from the smallest of the tribes of Israel, and furthermore my family is the youngest of all the families of the tribe of Binyamin; why, then, have you spoken to me in this way [i.e., that I am to become king]?"
>
> *(Shmuel* I 9:21)

Shaul was anointed king in a private coronation ceremony, after which he returned to his farm.

> Shaul's uncle said to him and his attendant, "Where did you go?"
>
> He replied: "To look for the donkeys, but when we saw that they were gone we went to Shmuel."
>
> Shaul's uncle said, "Tell me now what Shmuel said to you."
>
> Shaul answered his uncle, "He told us that the donkeys had been found." But he did not tell him about the matter of the kingship of which Shmuel had spoken.
>
> *(Shmuel* I 10:14–16)

Shmuel told Shaul he was to be the king of Israel, but Shaul returned home to plow the field and declined to mention the kingship to his uncle!

Later, when Shmuel held a public coronation ceremony, he set up a test to demonstrate publicly who was God's choice to be the king of Israel, and it came down to the tribe of Binyamin, and the family of Kish, and eventually to Shaul the son of Kish. But Shaul was nowhere to be found!

> [Eventually] Shaul the son of Kish was singled out. They searched for him, but he was not found. They then asked God further, "Has the man arrived here as yet?" And God replied, "He is hidden among the baggage." They ran and took him from there, and he stood in the midst of the people. He was taller than any of the people from his shoulder upward.
>
> *(Shmuel* I 10:21–24)

Hidden among the baggage — that was not kingly, that was not pomp and circumstance. Shaul did not hide among the baggage because he was too shy to appear in public. He hid among the baggage because he knew that despite the fact that God had appointed him king, there is only one real King: God Himself.

The first king of Israel was very different from the king the Jewish people wanted. They asked for a king like all the nations of the world had; they asked for pomp and circumstance and royalty. A king of Israel, however, is a person who knows that everything comes from God. A king in Israel is merely a servant of God. God gave the people the exact opposite of what they wanted, someone who was so modest and so humble that he belittled any external expression of kingship.

Although the House of Shaul was not meant to be the eternal dynasty of kingship, it was meant to lay the groundwork for the kingship of David, which is eternal. The kingship of the House of David was founded on the modesty, humility, and hiddenness of Shaul.

Shaul's granddaughter, Queen Esther, was also royalty. Unlike her ancestor Shaul, she lived in a majestic court, a place of utter physicality and externality. But despite the allure and dazzle of the wealth of Achashveirosh, Esther, like King Shaul, knew that it was crucial to focus inward, to remain within spiritual borders, because when the external pull is overwhelming, a king or queen might lose his way and imagine that he is actually in charge. When God is hidden, we, too, must be hidden, that is, modest, so that we can recognize the true King.

> Where is Esther found in the Torah? "And I will surely hide *(haster astir)* My face" *(Devarim* 31:18).
>
> *(Chullin* 139b)

The verse "I will surely hide My face" refers to those times when God will be angry with the Jewish people for abandoning His covenant. As a result of their trangressions, many evils and troubles will befall them. God will hide His face and His people will be devoured. Our rabbis saw the fulfillment of this prophecy in the Persian exile, when the Jews strayed from Torah, pulled by the materialism of the general society. Punishment followed — an evil ruler and an evil decree of genocide. God's face was hidden, and the Jews suffered. Esther herself was in some ways both the symbol of God's hiddenness and the response of His people to their suffering.

Esther lived when God Himself was hidden to the maximum extent possible, so much so that the Name of God does not appear in the the Book of Esther. The Jewish people had enjoyed prophecy for hundreds of years, but after the destruction of the First Temple, no longer did large numbers of prophets travel throughout the Land to reveal the Divine intention to the people, and therefore there was no clarity of God's rulership over the world. Today, we are a people who have lived without prophets for 2,500 years, but in Queen Esther's time, the hiddenness of Divine revelation was relatively new and still shocking. This dramatic change, together with Haman's plot to commit genocide against the Jewish people, seemed to indicate that God had completely abandoned Esther and her people.

What is the connection between abandonment and modesty? We said earlier that modesty serves as a protection against the pull toward the external. Modesty, the focus on internality, also has a deeper dimension. In addition to being a response to God's hiddenness, modesty is itself a goal. When God hides Himself, causing us to feel abandoned, what do we do? We look for Him! We turn away from what appears to be a threatening and dangerous world; we withdraw and turn inward to seek God. When we seek God, we find Him. No longer does God appear to us in prophetic revelation as a free gift, so to speak. When God hides Himself, we must make an effort to search for Him, and the result of this effort is that our relationship with Him is on a higher and more intense spiritual level.

Esther and Sarah

This is precisely the lesson that Esther learned from her grandmother Sarah. Sarah's life was 127 years, and each one of the 127 years was equally wholehearted with God:

> The lifetime of Sarah was one hundred years, twenty years, and seven years. [These were] the years of Sarah's life.
>
> *(Bereishis* 23:1)

> "The years of Sarah's life" — they were all equally good.
>
> *(Rashi, Bereishis* 23:1)

Rashi is commenting on the repetition, "[These were] the years of Sarah's life." He explains that this indicates that every year in her life was equally good, despite the changes that various ages bring to a person. Yet when we look at the life of Sarah we see that all of her years were not equal. There were hardships in Sarah's life. In addition to her long years of infertility, there were other incidents in her life that were extremely difficult and painful. Avraham and Sarah went down to Egypt, where Sarah was spotted by Pharaoh's soldiers and taken by force into Pharaoh's harem. The Midrash reveals how Avraham and Sarah responded to Sarah's kidnapping:

> "The officers of Pharaoh saw Sarah and praised her to Pharaoh" *(Bereishis* 12:15).
>
> When Avraham saw [that they had taken her], he began to cry and pray before the Holy One, blessed be He. He said, "Master of the Universe, is this the trust that I trusted in You? Please act according to Your mercy and Your kindness. Please do not shame me and cause me to lose hope."
>
> And Sarah cried out and said, "Master of the Universe, I knew nothing, but when [Avraham] told me that You said, 'Go forth,' I believed Your words. And now I remain alone, without my father or my mother or my husband. And this evil one [Pharaoh] will abuse me. Act for the sake of Your great name, and because I trusted in Your words."
>
> And the Holy One, blessed be He, answered her, "I swear,

nothing bad will happen to you or your husband."

(Tanchuma, Lech Lecha 5)

This is strikingly similar to what happened to Esther hundreds of years later. When she was taken against her will into the harem of Achashveirosh, Esther remembered her grandmother's imprisonment. Not only did she remember, but she also identified completely with Sarah's suffering and her wholeheartedness with God despite the sense of isolation.

> Why did Esther merit to rule 127 provinces? For the Holy One, blessed be He, said, "Let Esther come and rule 127 provinces, [for she is] the daughter of Sarah, who lived 127 years."
>
> (Esther Rabbah 1:8)

When the Midrash states that Esther ruled over 127 provinces as a reward for Sarah's 127 years, the implication is that just as Sarah's life of 127 years was lived in complete wholeheartedness with God — despite her sense of abandonment, suffering, and aloneness — so, too, was Esther completely wholehearted with God. Esther learned from her grandmother Sarah to live with total awe and trust in God even in a state of Divine withdrawal (*hester*).

When Sarah felt herself to be completely alone and vulnerable, what did she do? She turned to God. She sought a relationship with God from the depths of her isolation. Esther did exactly the same thing; although it appeared that God had abandoned her, she did not give up. Instead, she looked for Him.

Abandonment

Esther's feeling of abandonment, however, was different from Sarah's in two respects. First, Esther's sense of abandonment was so much greater, having occurred at the youngest possible age, from birth:

> "For she had no father and mother" (*Esther* 2:7). Her mother conceived her, her father died [right after her mother became pregnant], and as soon as she was born her mother died.
>
> (Esther Rabbah 6:5)

Not only did Esther have no mother or father, but she also had no memory of a mother and father. She had no memory of a loving mother responding to her cries in the middle of the night; she had no memory of being held in a mother's tender arms. That's *hester besoch hester*, hiddenness within hiddenness.

In addition, Esther's abandonment and "exile" was much lengthier than Sarah's:

> To the chief Musician upon the dawning of the evening star, a Psalm of David. My God, my God, why have You forsaken me? Why so far from helping me, from the words of my cry of distress? O my God, I cry in the daytime, but You do not hear me, and in the night season, and I have no rest.
>
> (*Tehillim* 22:1–3)

> "My God, my God, why have You forsaken me?" Esther said this before the Holy One, blessed be He: Why have You changed the order of the world and the order of the matriarchs against me? Sarah was taken into captivity by Pharaoh for one night. He was afflicted, as was his entire household. I, when I am given over to the arms of this evildoer all of these years — why do You not do miracles for me?... I have kept all of the mitzvos that You have given me: family purity, *challah*, and candles. Even though I am in the house of this evildoer, I have not transgressed even one of them."
>
> (*Midrash Shochar Tov* 22)

Esther spent nine years in exile (first in the king's harem, then as queen in Achashveirosh's palace) before Haman became a threat to the Jewish people. She had no understanding of why this was happening to her, no sense of purpose in her pain. After the miraculous redemption, the Jewish people were saved and everyone was happy, but Esther was still captive in the palace of the evil king, where she remained for the rest of her life. Sarah's pain and sense of abandonment was intense, but she had to withstand only one night in Pharaoh's palace. Esther had to survive years and years of it, living in Shushan, deep in the external, far away from spirituality. How did she do it?

Esther survived by retreating to her most private place, to her inner essence. Her sense of abandonment caused her to withdraw from the external world and to focus entirely on the internal, and there she found God. Despite residing in the palace of Achashveirosh, surrounded by materialism and externality, she lived alone, intimate in her meeting place with God.

God Hides and We Seek

Just as Sarah was the role model for Esther when she felt abandoned, Esther is the role model for us when we feel abandoned. When we were led, chained and degraded by our captors, into the Babylonian exile, and we called out to God, God promised to send a redeemer who had no father and no mother, someone who could redeem us from the deepest, darkest place in Media.

Our redeemer, Esther, would be the one to teach us that despite the outrageous externality of the exile, we can live within spiritual boundaries, with God. Esther would also teach us that in our sense of abandonment, we can surely find God if we but look, and that it is in this deepest of exiles, this greatest sense of loss, that our response must be to withdraw to the spiritual. If God is hidden, we must respond by using every possible effort to find Him.

It's not an accident that *tzenius*, the great ability to withdraw and focus on the internal, is connected with *malchus*, kingship. Rachel's children were kings and queens: Yosef was king in Egypt; Shaul and Esther, the descendants of Binyamin, were king and queen. The Jewish model of kingship is one who says, "There is a greater King than I, and I am but His servant."

Esther descended from Binyamin, but Yosef, who ruled over Egypt, is considered her spiritual ancestor (since Yosef and Binyamin were both Rachel's children). In many ways Yosef's life paralleled Esther's: they were both abandoned by their families but achieved greatness; they both functioned in a non-Jewish royal court, yet remained loyal to their people and their God; both lived deep within a world of promiscuity and materialism, yet remained pure and modest.

When Yosef was called to interpret the dreams of Pharaoh, he first made a disclaimer: "It's not me who interprets dreams, it's God." When the wife of Potifar attempted to seduce him, he withdrew and ran away. So too, Esther knew, "It's not me, it's God," and, therefore, when it was necessary to risk her life and enter the chamber of Achashveirosh unbidden, Esther first fasted for three days and put ashes in her hair. This was not the behavior of a woman who thinks, "If I impress the king, I will be successful." This is the behavior of a woman who relies on no mortal, but turns only to God for help.

> "And Esther wore royalty" (*Esther* 5:1) — she wore the Divine Spirit.
>
> (*Megillah* 13:2)

When Esther approached Achashveirosh, she knew who the real King was. The Vilna Gaon taught that every time we see the word *hamelech*, the king, in the Megillah, without the name Achashveirosh connected to it, it refers to God, the King of Kings. It was God Himself who was pulling the strings in the Purim story, and Esther knew it. So although God appeared to have been absent from Shushan, although He appeared to have abandoned His people, Esther wore "His clothes," so to speak; she functioned within the true reality, knowing that God was not only present, but running the show. "Wearing God's clothes" is what Esther did to survive her long and weary confinement in the palace, and this is also precisely what we, the Jewish people, have done to survive the suffering and pain of our own harsh exile.

> Just as when Av begins, we decrease joy, so, too, when Adar begins, we increase joy.
>
> (*Taanis* 29:1)

The words "just as" connote an equality between the two halves of this statement of our Sages. They teach us that there is a connection between the decreasing joy of Av, the month when we mourn the destruction of our Temples and the beginning of our exile, and the increasing joy of Adar, the month when we recount the redemption of the Jews in the dark exile of Shushan. There cannot be an Adar without an Av because there is no redemption without exile: one does not seek God without first experiencing His absence. The seeds of Adar are planted in Av because the sense of loss is itself what brings us to seek God; the sense of abandonment caused by exile is what forces us to look inward to our spiritual essence, and there we find God.

Those of us who live in Israel and face terror daily can relate to this in a very personal way. The tension and fear we frequently experience, anticipating yet another murderous attack and its dreadful consequences, impresses upon us what we have always known: there is no one to rely on except God. In the awful sense of abandonment we feel after each tragedy, we have no choice but to retreat to our spiritual borders, where we seek God, and we find that *HaMelech*, the King, has not really left us.

Esther had no mother or father, and so she turned to her inner essence, where she found God. We also feel as if we have no mother or father, but the story of Esther teaches us that although we feel orphaned now, there will be a redemption, a dawning of the morning star. The morning star is the glimmer of light in the darkest part of the night.

> In every place that it says, "She did not have," she had [eventually]. "And Sarah was barren, she did not have a child" (*Bereishis* 11:30), she did have, [as it says], "And God remembered Sarah" (ibid. 21:1). "And Peninah had children and Chanah did not have children" (*Shmuel* I 1:2), and she had [as it says], "For God remembered Chanah...she conceived and she bore..." (*Shmuel* I 1:19–20). "Zion has no one to seek her [welfare]" (*Yirmeyahu* 30:17), and she has [as it says], "And a redeemer will come to Zion" (*Yeshayahu* 59:20). "Rejoice barren woman who did not bear children, burst out in joyous song and be glad."
>
> (*Bereishis Rabbah* 38:14)

While it's true that right now we don't have, "we don't have" is itself the very process that leads to "we have." Redemption is born out of our sense of abandonment because in our abandonment we retreat, we seek God, and we find Him.

The Midrash describes Esther's feelings as she entered the inner chamber of the king to beg him to rescind the evil decree. As her uncle gathered all the Jewish children to pray and learn, Esther beseeched the King of Kings. This is the prayer of Esther as she went into the court of Achashveirosh:

> What did Mordechai do? He gathered all the children and told them to fast, and dressed them in sackcloth and sat them down in ashes, and they cried out and wept and learned Torah. And at that time, Esther was very afraid of the evil which had grown

against the Jewish people. She took off her royal garments and her crown and made her hair disorderly and filled it with sackcloth and ashes, and she afflicted herself by fasting. She fell on her face before God and she prayed, "God, God of Israel, who has ruled since the days of old and created the world, help Your maidservant who was left orphaned, without father and mother, who is like a poor woman who begs from house to house. So too I ask for Your mercy from window to window in Achashveirosh's palace.

"And now, God, please let Your poor maidservant be successful, and save the sheep of Your flock from the enemies which have arisen against us. For You have no limitation to save with few or with many. And You, Father of orphans, please stand by the right side of this orphan who has trusted in Your kindness and let this man feel mercifully toward me, because I am afraid of him, and lower him before me, because You lower the haughty."

(Esther Rabbah 8:7)

Today, as has happened throughout most of our history, the Jewish people are threatened by both spiritual and physical harm. It is not unnatural to feel abandoned and afraid. Nevertheless, in every place where "we have not," we will have. We feel today like we have no mother and father, but this is just the darkness before the dawn. Imminently we will be privileged to greet our righteous Mashiach, but meanwhile our sense of abandonment will, as it always has, prompt us to seek God. And when we shall seek Him, we shall find Him.

Water from the Well

There are many wells in the Torah. Moshe met his wife at a well. Yaakov met his beloved Rachel at a well. Rivkah was met by Eliezer at the well. Wells were dug and wells were stopped up and then dug again. The Jews had a traveling well in the desert that provided enough water for the entire nation for forty years. What is the significance of this recurring prop in the story of the Jews? What message does it suggest to us?

We can understand this if we look first at the lives of those who merited the most remarkable of wells — the one that followed the children of Israel through the desert and slaked their thirst for forty years. This well was given to the Jewish people in the merit of Miriam. So it is surprising to find that, in addition to her, many others are credited with this well, including her brother Moshe.

When Miriam died, the Jewish people lacked water, and they came to complain to Moshe of their thirst:

> Then the people of Israel, the whole congregation, arrived at the desert of Tzin in the first month; and the people abode in Kadesh; and Miriam died there and was buried there. There was no water for the congregation, and they gathered themselves together against Moshe and against Aharon. The people quarreled with Moshe and spoke, saying, "Would God that we had died when our brothers died before the Lord! And why have you brought up the congregation of the Lord into this wilderness, that we and our cattle should die there? Why have you made us come out of Egypt, to bring us into this evil place? This is no place of seed, figs, vines, or pomegranates; nor is there any water to drink."

(Bemidbar 20:1–5)

It is from these verses that we learn that the well had been given to the Jewish people in the merit of Miriam. Immediately after her death, "there was no water." The people then complained to Moshe about their thirst — something they had not done since they journeyed to Massah and Merivah thirty-nine years earlier. The well had disappeared — transformed, by God, into a rock!

To answer their needs, Moshe was instructed by God to speak to the rock so that water would flow from it. Instead of speaking to it, Moshe erred by hitting the rock. Nevertheless, water flowed through the rock to the people. In fact, the Midrash tells us that this second reappearance was in the merit of Moshe:

> When Miriam died, the well disappeared... When Aharon died, the Clouds of Glory disappeared.... The two [the well and the cloud] returned because of the merit of Moshe.
>
> (*Ta'anis* 9a)

The Jewish people continued on their journey, and shortly thereafter, the well reappeared.

> And from there they went to Be'er; that is the well of which the Lord spoke to Moshe, "Gather the people together, and I will give them water." Then Yisrael sang this song, "Spring up, O well; sing to it." The princes dug the well, the nobles of the people excavated, with the scepter, with their staffs.
>
> (*Bemidbar* 21:16–18)

The third appearence of the well is credited to the princes, the nobles, and the lawgivers.

Thus, the well was given in the merit of Miriam, of Moshe, and of the nobles, princes, and scholars after Miriam's death. But even before Miriam was born, her great-grandfather Avraham had earned the well through his actions when he was kind to three nomads who passed by his tent in the desert of Be'er Sheva. Avraham ran after these strangers, brought them to rest under a tree, and invited them to eat and drink. As a reward for his kindness in giving drink to these angels disguised as men, God promised a well to Avraham's children:

"Please take a little water" (*Bereishis* 18:4). Rabbi Eliezer said in the name of Rabbi Simai: The Holy One, blessed be He, said to Avraham, "You said, 'Please take a little water' — on your life, I will repay your sons in the desert." As it says, "Then Israel sang this song: Spring up, O well, sing to it."

(Bereishis Rabbah 48:10)

What is this well that so many are given credit for? What is unique about Miriam's merit? What is the connection between Miriam's merit to that of Moshe, Avraham, and the princes, nobles, and lawgivers? And why, if so many people merited the well, is the well called "the Well of Miriam"?

Development and Process

Life is a process.We develop, achieve, and grow daily, monthly, yearly. In so doing, we are constantly laying the foundation for the next stage. We never finish, because as we accomplish each of our goals, our achievements become merely the backdrop to future aspirations.

When we arrive at one objective, we realize that where we are is, in fact, the point of departure for where we are going. Not only is this true for us as individuals, but it is also the pattern of the world. Our Rabbis teach that God created the world to endure for six thousand years. This six thousand years is divided into three distinct periods, each with its own essential quality and nature:

> The *Tanna Devei Eliyahu* taught: The world is to exist for six thousand years. The first two thousand years are *Tohu* (empty, chaotic); the next two thousand years are the period of the Torah; and the following two thousand years are the period of the Mashiach. Through our many sins, a number of these [years] have already passed [and the Mashiach is not yet here].
>
> From when are the two thousand years of the Torah to be reckoned? Shall we say from the giving of the Torah at Mount Sinai? In that case, you will find that there are not quite two thousand years from then until now (i.e., the year 4,000 after creation). If you compute the years (from the creation to the giving of the Torah), you will find that they comprise two thousand

and a part of the third thousand. The period is therefore to be reckoned from the time when Avraham and Sarah had made souls in Charan, for we have a tradition that Avraham was at the time fifty-two years old.

(*Sanhedrin* 97a)

The first two thousand years were a state of existence called *Tohu*, chaos. This state of chaos does not refer to the primordial condition of the universe. Rather, it is a description of the human condition at the time. In this period, there were no moral values, no spiritual leadership, and no religious teachings. This is not to say that there were no religious figures or opportunities for growth. In fact, a few individuals, Chanoch, Mesushalech, Sheim, and Ever, learned and walked in righteousness; however, these individuals had no impact on the world beyond themselves: not on their families, their communities, or the general society in which they lived. Their righteousness affected them alone.

The next two thousand years are depicted as years of Torah. The Gemara tells us that this period began when Avraham, at fifty-two years old, brought many people to the teachings of monotheism; it ended 172 years after the destruction of the Temple with the death of Rav (the last *Tanna* in the time of the Mishnah). This period of Torah includes the period of the patriarchs and matriarchs, the slavery in Egypt, the giving of the Torah, the conquest of the Land of Israel, the building and destruction of two Temples in Jerusalem, the Roman exile, and all the *Tannaim* (Rabbinic authorities mentioned in the Mishneh). The era is characterized by the dissemination of Torah values, knowledge of God, and moral teachings.

The last two thousand years, which are now coming to an end, are called the Days of Mashiach. This period began in approximately 242 C.E., and will lead us to an era of complete harmony between heaven and earth. During this last era, all the mitzvos and Torah scholarship of the Jewish people and their exiles and persecutions are all necessary precursors to the bringing of the Mashiach.

Each period in world history is indispensable because it becomes the foundation for the next era. Without the two thousand years of Torah, there could not be the two thousand years that lead to Mashiach. In addition, the generation of each era proceeds in small steps, slowly achieving the goals of that stage in history. The Jews who lived in the years of Torah were not able to disseminate Torah values all at once, but only over many centuries. Likewise the coming of Mashiach is not a single event, but something we have been working towards for thousands of years. It is a slow but sure process and it is happening, even though we do not always see it. Finally, each of us has a small, but important, role in the process.

While we are busy with our lives, we may not be aware of the stage of development that we are responsible for advancing. Nevertheless, this focus is what is necessary to prepare the world for the next stage.

To use a metaphor, there can be no Shabbos without *erev Shabbos*. Without the shopping, cooking, cleaning, and flurry of activity on Friday, we would never be ready for the day of rest. Likewise, our attention to Torah and mitzvos is the preparation for the Messianic era.

Development of Torah

Since we cannot understand history except from a distance, let us examine the middle two thousand years to understand this developmental process better.

While the Jews at Sinai had the privilege of hearing God's voice, experiencing the thunder and lightning and the shofar call at Sinai, the patriarchs had no such clear visual or auditory experience. While the nation in the desert was taught the Torah by Moshe during forty years of a miracle-filled life, the patriarchs had to discover God and His Torah in isolation. Not only were they alone in their process, but also each one had to create his own mechanism for this discovery.

How did they do this? How did they learn, integrate, and discover Torah without a teacher?

> There were ten generations from Noach until Avraham, and what can we learn from this? It teaches that all these generations angered Him and not one of them went in God's ways, until our father Avraham came and went in God's ways, as it says: "Because Avraham obeyed My voice and kept My charge, My commandments, My statutes, and My laws" (*Bereishis* 26:5).

> From here we learn that God made Avraham's two kidneys like
> two wise sages who made him wise and advised him and taught
> him wisdom all night long, as it says, "I bless God who advised
> me and even at nights my kidneys taught me" (*Tehillim* 15:7).
>
> (*Avos DeRabbi Nassan* 33:1)

In Midrashic literature, the kidneys are the seat of wisdom (as they are in Chinese medicine!). What the Midrash is teaching us is that Avraham listened to his inner voice, his inner wisdom; and his inner wisdom led him to God. In other words, planted deep within Avraham's psyche — in every person's psyche — is truth. However, most people do not listen to this truth. Most people block it out with a variety of distractions. The result is that they cannot hear that which their hearts tell them.

The Midrash teaches that there were ten generations from Noach to Avraham, but no one heard God because no one was listening. Only Avraham listened to the wisdom within his "kidneys" and so he alone heard the voice of his Master.

How does a person hear the truth? By removing the blockages that separate him from his inner wisdom. Because our patriarchs were not given a direct revelation, like the one offered the Jewish people at Sinai, all three had to find Torah on their own. The Torah alludes to this process when it tells us that each patriarch dug a well.

Digging a well is an allusion to the act of dislodging the blockages of the heart (*Shem MiShmuel*, *Parashas Toldos* 5678). What is a well? A well is a source of water hidden deep below the ground. To find water, one must dig out the earth that blocks its flow. The earth represents obstructions, the issues and confusion that keep a person from the truth. The water is the deepest wisdom each person holds in his heart. It is a wisdom waiting to be discovered, like water beneath the ground that waits to be uncovered.

Digging a well, then, is equivalent to discovering our inner wisdom. It is not creating something new, but simply removing the obstructions we have accumulated in our lives to reveal a wisdom that has always existed in us.

What is the core of every Jew? Torah.

Each of the patriarchs dug his own well, finding his own particular inner wisdom. Each used a "shovel" — Avraham dug with the shovel of *chesed* and discovered a well of spirituality and connection to God. Yitzchak used the shovel of *gevurah*, strength, and Yaakov the shovel of *emes*, truth.

While each patriarch set the stage for his son, he could not save him from doing his own spiritual work. Yitzchak had to redig the wells of his father and Yaakov had to unblock a well.

> Yitzchak dug again the wells of water that they had dug in the days of Avraham his father, for the Philistines had stopped them up after the death of Avraham, and he called their names after the names by which his father had called them.
>
> (*Bereishis* 21:18)

> And it came to pass, when Yaakov saw Rachel the daughter of Lavan, his mother's brother, and the sheep of Lavan, his mother's brother, that Yaakov went near, rolled the stone from the well's mouth, and watered the flock of Lavan, his mother's brother.
>
> (*Bereishis* 29:10)

To what does this redigging and unblocking allude? Each patriarch succeeded in digging a well and thus effecting change in himself; yet after his death that well did not remain open. It was stopped up with the misguided philosophy and idolatry of the Philistines. Therefore, the well of Avraham had to be redug by Yitzchak, and the well of Yitzchak had to be uncovered (in the metaphysical sense) by Yaakov.

The Biale Rebbe explains that the job of the patriarchs was not to change the world, but rather to prepare the world for change. If not for this spiritual tilling, the world could not have readied itself for the giving of the Torah. It would have been impossible to move directly from the state of *Tohu*, confusion and moral chaos to revelation (*Mevaser Tov*, vol. 1). Everything we do is done in stages. Preparation for each stage is crucial to the success of any project. Just as we need erev Shabbos to prepare for Shabbos, we need this world to prepare for the next world.

The Torah of our patriarchs prepared the world for the giving of the Torah at Sinai, and that was their task. Each time a patriarch dug a well, he was preparing the ground for the well of his son. Each son had to redig the well to prepare for his son. But it wasn't until the giving of the Torah at Sinai that the larger world was affected. The Biale Rebbe compares the difference between these two eras, *Tohu* and Torah, to the difference between fragrance and taste. Fragrance is not as powerful as taste. Fragrance provides a sense of the object, but not its essence; it refreshes the soul, but not the body (which is why we do not say a *berachah* after smelling fragrances). Eating, on the other hand, gives the body nourishment and produces long-term metabolic changes. Taste is "real," the essence of the object itself.

The Torah of the patriarchs was like a fragrance in that it could not nourish the world. And the revelation at Sinai was like taste; it created a fundamental change in the world, and people would never be the same. Thus, the fragrance of the patriarchs prepared the world for the taste of Sinai; it gave the world a sense of Torah. It was similar to a simmering Shabbos *cholent,* which tantalizes would-be eaters with its delicious aroma, but is in no way as satisfying as the taste itself!

Even the giving of the Torah was not the end of the process. Until the Torah was learned, argued, and renewed with *chiddushim* (new interpretations), it was not complete. Therefore, the Gemara did not mark the close of the two-thousand-year period of Torah after the giving of the Torah, but only after the learning of it. It follows, then, that the era ends with the death of Rav, the last *Tanna* in the Mishnaic period. The *Tannaim* were the rabbis who learned Torah in the great yeshivos of Israel and Babylonia. When we quote *Chazal* (our rabbis), we are referring to these great leaders and Torah scholars.

The three stages of Torah development are alluded to in the verses that tell of the renewal of Miriam's well:

> The princes dug the well, the nobles of the people excavated, with the scepter, with their staffs.
>
> (*Bemidbar* 21:18)

The Or HaChaim explains that the princes are the patriarchs. They dug wells, making the water available to drink, preparing the world for the next stage. Moshe, the elders, the prophets, and the Men of the Great Assembly are the nobles. Finally, the Torah scholars of all generations are the ones with scepters and staffs.

Each stage of Torah prepared the way for the next. The giving of the Torah by Moshe was incomplete until it was learned and absorbed. It had to be passed down from generation to generation, reinvigorated with questions and debates. And the process is still unfinished; every Jew who learns the Torah digs a well himself.

Miriam's Well

What was Miriam's role in this process of "digging wells"? After all, the well is attributed to so many others, yet it is called "the Well of Miriam."

Miriam was not a giver of Torah, nor was she a Torah scholar. Her actions are best described as preparing the way for Torah to enter the world because, had it not been for Miriam, Moshe the lawgiver would never have been born:

> A man from the House of Levi went and took a wife, a daughter of Levi.
>
> *(Shemos* 2:1)

The wording of this verse is odd: the "man went…and took." This is not the typical language that the Torah uses to describe marriage, prompting the Rabbis to say that the verse describes a second "taking" into marriage. Amram had separated from his wife and remarried her.

> He had lived apart from her because of Pharaoh's decree, and he took her back on the advice of his daughter who said to him, "Your decree is harsher than Pharaoh's. Pharaoh decreed on the males, and you are including the females." So he returned and made with her a second "taking to wife."
>
> *(Rashi, Shemos* 2:1)

After having two children, Amram had separated from his wife, Yocheved, because of a new decree of Pharaoh to cast any Jewish male child into the Nile River. He could not bear to bring children into the world only to have them destroyed. His daughter Miriam opposed him, saying that separation from his wife would prevent even the birth of female children, and urged him to remarry her mother. When Amram heeded her advice, Yocheved, his wife, indeed conceived, and gave birth to Moshe. Were it not for Miriam's wisdom, initiative, and trust in God, Moshe would not have been born.

Three months later, when Yocheved could no longer hide her baby from the Egyptian authorities, she took Moshe, hid him in a basket, and put him in the river. Miriam then stationed herself by the river to protect him as best she could and to help assure his future:

His sister stood afar off to know what would be done with him.

(Shemos 2:4)

When the daughter of Pharaoh saw the child, she knew he was a Hebrew, yet decided to take him into the palace and raise him as her son. However, she needed a wet-nurse, and again, it was Miriam who saw to the sustenance of her baby brother, Moshe:

His sister said to the daughter of Pharaoh, "Shall I go and call for you a nurse from the Hebrews so that she may suckle the child for you?"

(Shemos 2:7)

Miriam brought Moshe's mother to feed him. Moshe not only benefited from the milk of his mother, but was also taught about his origins, his people, and his God. He grew up in the house of Pharaoh but was always aware of who he was as a Jew. Thus, when he grew to be a young man, he identified with the misery of the Jewish slaves. He defended them and sought to quiet their oppressors.

Just as the patriarchs prepared the world for the giving of the Torah, Miriam prepared Moshe to receive the Torah and to become the lawgiver of the Jewish people. By coaching her father to remarry her mother, by taking Moshe to the Nile and watching over him until he was in good hands, by arranging for his physical and spiritual development, Miriam paved the way for the world to receive the Torah.

Miriam did so because she possessed the quality of great yearning, *hishtokekus* (*Shem MiShmuel, Parashas Chukas* 5679). What is yearning? It is best understood in the context of the male-female relationship. A woman yearns for her husband. She craves a relationship with him. This desire for connection is described in the very beginning of the Torah: After the sin of eating of the fruit of the tree, Chavah was told, "Your yearning (*teshukasech*) shall be to your husband" (*Bereishis* 3:16).

Yearning is expressed by the willingness to do whatever is necessary to facilitate the relationship. In Kabbalistic thought, everything in the world is either male or female. Male is portrayed as raw potential, and female as actualizing potential. Male is "from above to below," while female is "from below to above," taking the potential and transforming it into a concrete reality, as can be seen in the formation of a baby.

Miriam was the epitome of "from below to above." Her goal was never her own greatness, but rather to bring Torah into the world. It was a goal born of yearning and she did all that was in her power to make it happen. In this, she laid the groundwork for Torah, and she was rewarded with a well.

Building a world and bringing Torah into it is a step-by-step process. In that process, each step is important; not one can be skipped, because each step prepares the world for the next one. Miriam is the yearning that sustains the process. For without her longing, her *hishtokekus*, her willingness to make it happen, with no concerns for her own glory, the well of Torah would have never been dug.

Greater Is the Promise to the Women

> Greater is the promise made by the Holy One, blessed be He, to the women than [is His promise] to the men, for it says, "Rise up, you calm women, you confident daughters. Give ear to my speech" (*Yeshayahu* 32:9). Rav said to Rabbi Chiya, "How do women earn merit? By making their children go to the synagogue to learn Torah and their husbands to the *beis midrash* to learn Mishnah, and waiting for their husbands until they return from the *beis midrash*."
>
> (*Berachos* 17a)

The reward for the women is greater than for the men! Why should it be greater? We can understand that it could be the same, that both men and women should be rewarded for their particular role in Torah. But why should the women get more reward? And why should women be rewarded for their "supporting role" more than men are for their learning of Torah, a "starring role," of sorts?

As Miriam was the moving force behind the receiving of the Torah by Moshe, so Jewish women are the moving forces behind their husbands and children. It is the yearning of the women and their willingness to do whatever necessary to enable their children to be educated and their husbands to learn that actualizes the potential of that learning. A woman takes on extra work, be it responsibilities or carpools, a job outside the home or more chores in the home. She often sacrifices her own career and personal goals, or postpones them, so that she can focus on building a home of Torah. She makes extraordinary sacrifices and often has less immediate pleasure in her tasks than her family does. She does this willingly, lovingly, because of her yearning for the continuity of Torah and because of her longing for children whose lives revolve around Torah. And whatever Torah is learned by her husband and children is drawn from the well that she, the Jewish woman, has dug.

There is a story told about a devout chassid of the Bnei Yissachar (Rav Tzvi Elimelech Spira of Dinov). Year after year, the chassid went to his beloved rebbe for holidays and special times of learning. Year after year, he left his wife at home to run the household and care for the children. Though this was very hard for her, being left alone to tend the little ones all by herself, she suffered it silently, knowing that this is the way of the chassidim. Yet one time, as her husband prepared for his trip, she gave him permission to go on two conditions. The first condition was that he would promise her half of his reward for going to the rebbe. The second condition was that he must tell his rebbe the first condition.

The chassid journeyed far away to the rebbe, the Bnei Yissachar, and as he had promised, he told the Rebbe the whole story and the conditions his wife had imposed on him. When the chassid had finished his story, the Rebbe said, "You fool, you should have asked her for half of the portion of her great mitzvah in letting you go, for her portion is greater than yours! She remains at home alone watching young children and this is very difficult indeed. And in the end, she gets nothing out of your journey. You come here and enjoy the great spiritual pleasures of being with the other chassidim and of learning Torah. You suffer nothing and sacrifice nothing for this pleasure. But your wife, she sacrifices and suffers and she has no joy of learning in exchange for her sacrifice. Her reward is much greater than yours!" (as told by the Biale Rebbe in *Mevaser Tov*, vol. 1).

The reward of the women is greater because their willingness to sacrifice to bring Torah into the world is greater.

It is important to remember that although sometimes yearning brings immediate effects, more often it results in baby steps. Yet, no matter how small, each step is essential. It is a long and slow process, but as long as we yearn for the Torah, we enable Torah to enter the world.

The Yearning of Parents

Jewish parents yearn for their children's growth in Torah. Mothers say a special prayer when they light their Shabbos candles asking God to guide their children and their children's children in the path of Torah. Fathers envelope their sons in their talleisim, hoping that their children will be enveloped by their love of Torah. Daily, we beseech God, "May we and our offspring and the offspring of Your people, the House of Israel — all of us — know Your Name and study Your Torah." Our most fervent dream is that our children continue walking in the ways of our ancestors.

I'd like to share a personal story about the yearning of parents for their children's Torah. It is more about my husband than me, but illustrative of the power of *hishtokekus*. When our children were little, my husband and I had different parenting styles. I was the firm one, and my husband more the gentle coach. Every morning, when waking the children for school, our boys would have a terrible time waking up and getting out of bed. We tried everything, from multiple wake-up calls to the lure of fresh, hot pancakes. Finally, I decided that waking up was their own responsibility, and they would have to take the consequences. The response they would get in school upon their late arrival would be the best teacher. My husband, however, continued his efforts. Every morning when waking the boys, he would plead, use his best powers of persuasion, offer treats, and inevitably promise to drive them to school — anything as long is they would get up for learning. Sometimes this worked, and other times it did not.

Years later, when my sons were grown and learning in *yeshivah gedolah* (post–high school yeshivah), one son said to me, "I remember when Abba used to come to our room and beg us to go to cheder. Sometimes I just couldn't get myself to move. Still, I always knew what was important to Abba. I always knew that he wanted me to learn, to grow in Torah, and I knew he would do whatever it took to help me get there. Even today, now that I am grown and learning well, there are times when I can't concentrate on the *shiur* or when I lose patience with study, but I always remember Abba's face and his words; knowing what matters to him helps me move forward."

An Ongoing Process

The purpose of the world was not realized after the first two thousand years of *Tohu* (chaos), nor after the next two thousand of Torah. In addition, the Torah was not given in a single event. The revelation at Sinai was just the beginning of a process of the giving of the Torah — a process of learning, questioning, and integrating — and one that continues until today.

We, as individuals, cannot realize all of our goals and dreams in one generation, or two. Nor are we expected to do so. Our children will complete what we were not able to, and their children will finish what our children cannot. Step by step, we will dig our wells of spirituality and fill the world with Torah. What will fire the engine of growth? What will keep us and our children and grandchildren moving forward? Our unending yearning for Torah.

Footsteps of the Mashiach

L ife today for the Jewish people is often confusing. We experience a cycle of devastation and miracle, disillusionment and hope, God concealed and God witnessed.

We live on a seesaw: rejoicing, mourning; feeling grateful, then abandoned; celebration, lamentation. God's love witnessed; His anger endured. There is a flash of light, and then deep darkness.

We are walking in the footsteps of Mashiach.

From the beginning of time, God has prepared the world for Mashiach in strange and perplexing ways. When examined, these events make us uncomfortable; they seem improper. Apparently, God willed it that Mashiach would come by a circuitous route. Let us discover why.

Seeds of Mashiach

After the destruction of Sedom, Lot and his two daughters were the only survivors. They escaped through the agency of an angel of God and stayed in a cave near Sedom. That night, the daughters of Lot, thinking that the world had been destroyed, plotted to repopulate it:

> The older one said to the younger, "Come, let us make our father drink wine, and we will lie with him, that we may preserve the seed of our father." They made their father drink wine that night; and the firstborn went in and lay with her father; and he perceived not when she lay down, nor when she arose.
>
> It came to pass on the next day that the firstborn said to the younger: "Behold, I lay last night with my father; let us make

him drink wine this night also, and you go in and lie with him, that we may preserve the seed of our father."

They made their father drink wine that night also; and the younger arose and lay with him; and he perceived not when she lay down, nor when she arose. Thus were both the daughters of Lot with child by their father.

The firstborn bore a son and called his name Moav; he is the father of the Moavites to this day. The younger, she also bore a son, and called his name Benammi; he is the father of the Ammonites to this day.

(Bereishis 19:31–38)

The children conceived in this incestuous relationship were the forebears of two women who converted to Judaism and became mothers of kings: Rus the Moavite, who was the grandmother of King David, and Naamah the Ammonite, who married King Shlomo.

The proceedings in the cave are couched in very unusual language. Twice the daughters of Lot make reference to a desire to "preserve seed," rather than using the more common expression of wanting to "bear children." The use of the word *seed* prompts the Midrash to comment.

Rabbi Tanchuma said in Shmuel's name: It is not written [in the text of the Torah], "that we will preserve a child of our father," but that "we will preserve the seed," that is — the seed that comes from a different place. What place is that? That is [the place of] the king Mashiach.

(Bereishis Rabbah 51:8)

The daughters of Lot thought they were repopulating the world with the seed of their father. The truth is that the world had not been destroyed, only Sedom and Amorah, so that there was no need to propagate. But although their intention was repopulation, God had different intentions. This seed, which the Midrash tells us came from a "different place," would later father the King of Israel and, ultimately, the Mashiach.

The intentions of the daughters of Lot, in fact, were not only different than those of God, but also less than honorable:

Rabbi Shimon said: The first conception of Moav was not with a noble motive but in a spirit of immorality.

(Bereishis Rabbah 51:10)

One would think that the Mashiach would be born of the purest people and the purest intentions. Yet God ordained it differently.

Many years later, another strange encounter brought the world closer to Mashiach. As we discussed in the essay "Are We Really Free to Choose?" Yehudah, son of Yaakov, had three sons. The oldest son, Eir, married a woman named Tamar. Eir sinned and died as a result, leaving Tamar childless. Jewish law prescribes that, in such a case, the wife must marry her husband's brother and their child will be called by the name of the deceased husband. Therefore, Yehudah gave his second son Onan to Tamar as a husband. Onan sinned like his brother before him, again leaving Tamar childless. Yehudah hesitated to give his third son, Shelah, to Tamar and urged her to wait. But as time progressed, it was clear to Tamar that this marriage would not happen, so she conceived a plan. She dressed up like a prostitute and stood on the road to seduce Yehudah.

> She took off her widow's garments, covered herself with a veil, wrapped herself, and sat in an open place (*pesach einayim*), which is by the way to Timnah; for she saw that Shelah was grown, and she was not given to him for his wife.
>
> When Yehudah saw her, he thought her to be a harlot because she had covered her face. He turned to her by the way and said: "Come, I beg you; let me come to you; " for he knew not that she was his daughter-in-law.
>
> (Bereishis 38:14–16)

And compelled by Divine decree, Yehudah succumbed to Tamar's plan:

> Rabbi Yochanan said: He wished to go on, but the Holy One, blessed be He, made the angel who is in charge of desire appear before him, and he [the angel] said to him: "Where are you going, Yehudah? Whence then are kings to arise, whence are redeemers to arise?" Thereupon, and "he turned in to her" — despite himself and against his wish.
>
> (Bereishis Rabbah 85:8)

Out of this encounter were born twins (one for each of Tamar's husbands) named Zerach and Peretz. Peretz would become the ancestor of David and the King Mashiach for whom we are waiting.

Tamar's intentions were to act for the sake of Heaven, and as she went about fulfilling her bizarre plan, she prayed:

> [Tamar] covered herself with her veil, wrapped herself, and sat in Pesach Einayim (literally, "open eyes"). Rabbi Ami said: We have searched through the whole of Scripture and found no place called Pesach Einayim. What then is the meaning of Pesach Einayim? It teaches that she lifted up her eyes to the gate (*pesach*) to which all eyes (*einayim*) are directed and prayed: "May it be Your will that I do not leave this house with nothing."
>
> (*Bereishis Rabbah* 85:7)

Tamar, like the daughters of Lot, entered into a relationship that would seem inappropriate. This time, however, the Midrash testifies to her pure intentions to build the house of Yehudah. Her plans coincided with God's, and He aided her by "pushing" Yehudah toward her in order to build up the Kingship of the House of David that will eventually lead to Mashiach.

A third incident completes the strange pattern that established the Davidic Dynasty. Rus the Moavite married Machlon, of the tribe of Yehudah, in Moav. He died, leaving her childless. She followed her mother-in-law, Naomi, back to Israel and converted to Judaism. Following her mother-in-law's instructions, she pursued marriage with a relative named Boaz. The purpose of this marriage was to have a child to propagate her deceased husband's seed.

> When Boaz had eaten and drunk, and his heart was merry, he went to lie down at the end of the heap of grain; and she came softly, uncovered his feet, and laid herself down. It came to pass at midnight that the man was startled and turned over; and, behold, a woman lay at his feet. He said, "Who are you?"
>
> She answered, "I am Ruth your maidservant; spread your skirt over your maidservant, for you are next of kin."
>
> (*Rus* 3:7–9)

In this chapter in the building of the House of David and King Mashiach is an event where both parties acted completely for the sake of Heaven:

> The first conception of Moav was not with a noble motive but in a spirit of immorality. His descendants did not act thus, but with a noble motive, as it says, "She went down to the threshing floor and did according to all that her mother-in-law bade her."
>
> *(Bereishis Rabbah* 51:10)

Even so, going to a stranger's field in the middle of the night certainly looked immodest. Boaz himself was shaken by her presence. "The man was startled" (*Rus* 3:1) and urged her to leave quickly lest she be discovered and the incident misunderstood:

> She lay at his feet until the morning; and she rose up before one could recognize another. He said, "Let it not be known that a woman came to the threshing floor."
>
> *(Rus* 3:14)

There must be an explanation for the bizarre origins of Mashiach: in an incestuous relationship with immoral intentions, in a righteous woman disguising herself as a prostitute, and in a conversation in a stranger's field in the middle of the night.

What could be the reason for these dubious encounters?

Pattern in the Creation of the World

In his philosophical treatise, *Daas Tevunos*, Rabbi Moshe Chaim Luzzatto describes the pattern of the world. This is a brief summary:

On the first day of creation, God created light. This light was not a physical light, because the sun and moon, the two great luminaries, were created on the fourth day. Rather, the light of the first day was a spiritual light, the source of all good.

Since the purpose of creation was to give human souls an opportunity to choose good and evil and hence to perfect themselves, God had to create a situation in which there would be free will. Such a situation would require the possibility of evil and the choice between good and evil. Light (spiritual good) with no darkness (evil) would not afford such a choice, so God hid the light.

The concealment of light is the source of all evil and imperfection in the world. The result of this concealment is that the oneness of God is not obvious. It appears that evil emanates from one source, and good from another. The world looks fractured and God's presence is not easily detected.

However, God did not conceal the light so that it should remain concealed, but that it would be revealed by human beings. In so doing, evil would dissipate and the good would shine forth.

How would we achieve this? When we behave in the way that God desires us to behave, we banish the darkness and reveal the secreted light of God. We then perfect ourselves — and this is the purpose of His creation.

If we could consistently do what God desires of us, then He would no longer hide Himself and His light, and the world would reach a state of perfection. God's oneness would be revealed, and the world would enter a period of reward for Divine service, because the entire purpose of the concealment is that we should reveal that which is hidden.

If we do not choose to reveal the hidden light, then God manifests Himself in an even darker exile. Indeed, that is the state the world is in now. The exile of God gets deeper and deeper. Our Rabbis proclaimed:

> There is no day whose curse is not greater than the day before, as it is stated: "In the morning you will say, 'Would it were evening!' In the evening you will say, 'Would it were morning!' " (*Devarim* 28:67). Which morning [will they long for]?... [The morning] which has gone.
>
> (*Sotah* 49a)

Since the world seems darker every day, we constantly yearn for the day before, when life was a little better.

The concealment of the light is called *hester panim* (concealment of face). *Hester panim* is when God's "face" is hidden, not easily perceived in this world. We have a difficult time "seeing" God. The revelation of the light is called *gilui panim* (revelation of face). In this mode, the presence of God is perceptible, for His "face" is revealed.

The modes of *gilui panim* and *hester panim* operate jointly in the world. There is no area in which they do not both operate. In addition, neither mode ever functions in a way that excludes the other. Even during times when we sense the light of God's countenance, there are pockets of light that are hidden from us. And during times when we experience the concealment of God, we have flashes of revelation. *Gilui panim* and *hester panim* are intertwined in history and in our lives.

For example, when the Jews were in the desert and God's presence was manifest through the daily miracles of the well, the manna, and the cloud, there were times when the nation felt abandoned and complained bitterly to Moshe about the lack of water or meat. This was because there were pockets of darkness in a time dominated by clarity and light.

Conversely, in the darkest periods of Jewish history, there have been revealed miracles. Survivors of the Holocaust tell stories of miracles experienced in the shadowy depths of the death camps. In modern Israel, the War of Independence and the Six Day War were won despite all odds. In more recent years, there have been many terrorist actions that were miraculously thwarted.

By recognizing the patterns of the world, we can begin to understand why Mashiach has such mysterious beginnings. Just as plants grow in sunlight while their roots develop in darkness, so Mashiach will blossom in full view, but his origins are established in obscurity. The duality of this growth is part of the organic process of Creation as well as of history.

Pattern in the History of the World

Just like there is a pattern in the creation of the world, there is a pattern in the history of the world. There are two distinct periods of world history: the period in which God is for the most part hidden but destined to be revealed and the period subsequent to His revelation. The first period of time is the one in which we find ourselves now, and it is limited to the first six thousand years of the world. The second period is the time of the Redemption, the Messianic era.

We know that in the Messianic era, God's light will be totally apparent and His presence felt. How then does God deal with us in this first period of history, the period of concealment? While God is hidden, during the first six thousand years of history, He runs the world in a way that brings about events that will lead us to the Messianic era, the period of perfection and revelation.

In order to move the world in this direction, God employs two qualities that He established when He forged the foundations of the earth. The first, the order of reward and punishment, consists of a balanced state of good and evil, in which actions are recompensed accordingly. This order is called *mishpat*, justice. Using this quality, God presides in judgment over all men.

The second quality is that of Divine sovereignty (*shlitah u'memshalah hayechidis*). This quality is the perfection of all creation through the power of God, even when it is not deserving of it. The source of this quality is God's goodness and it never stops directing us toward the good.

The order of justice is revealed and manifest — that is to say that we understand the theory of how it functions, even though in reality, it operates in secrecy. The order of Divine sovereignty, on the other hand, is hidden and concealed — which means we don't understand why God does the things He does, although we do know they are for our good. In fact, sometimes, He conceals His intent to such an extent that the world seems to be abandoned and man feels he is suffering great punishment for his sins. Actually, in some way that remains incomprehensible to us, God is moving the world forward towards Mashiach and perfection.

Just as the concealment of God's light and the revelation of God's light operate jointly at all times in the world, so do the systems of reward and punishment and Divine sovereignty. An example of this intertwining can be found in the story of Yosef. For twenty-two years, Yaakov believed that his son Yosef was dead, and he was in mourning for him. During this time, Yaakov had no prophecy because prophecy can only be received in joy. But the worst suffering for Yaakov was that he believed that the lineage of the Jewish people would not come through him. Yaakov knew through a previous prophecy that if he would have twelve worthy sons, they would become the tribes of Israel and he would be the father of the Jewish people. When one son was apparently dead, Yaakov assumed he was not worthy of the role to which he had been assigned.

But the entire time that Yaakov despaired over his separation from Yosef, assuming that he, Yaakov, was unworthy and therefore being punished, God was secretly "turning the wheels" to bring about a reward for Yaakov's righteousness. God was moving events forward toward that goal, making Yosef king of Egypt. God was directing the process to give Yaakov what he deserved, to live out the final years of his life in tranquility.

This process, of course, was hidden from Yaakov. Rabbi Moshe Chaim Luzzatto explains that it is axiomatic: when God wishes to accord good to a person or the world, the whole time that He is generating that good, He does so in secret; therefore, the good is always preceded by suffering:

> Three goodly gifts were given by the Holy One, Blessed be He, to Israel, and and all were given only through suffering.
>
> (*Berachos* 5a)

These three gifts are the land of Israel, Torah, and the World to Come. Clearly these are gifts, and they are clearly good gifts. Yet the secrecy in which they are being prepared for us causes us great suffering.

This pattern of history is expressed on every level of creation by the phrase, "and there was evening and there was morning" (*Bereishis* 1:8). Day follows night, and night follows day. Night is the time of *din*, of reward and punishment, which can only come because God's countenance is shrouded in darkness. Therefore, night is a frightening time, because it is the time of strict judgment, and we lack merits to receive God's goodness. Night is also synonymous with exile and the suffering that it brings. Day, on the other hand, is the time of the revelation of God's sovereignty. It is less frightening because, although we have a limited ability to comprehend God's ways, we are aware that He is giving us more than we deserve and moving us towards redemption.

The Pattern in the Coming of Mashiach

It is now night, as we presently live in a time when God is concealed, waiting to be revealed. History is moving toward the Messianic era, and God is directing history.

Yet there are two ways that the Mashiach can come: hastened, or in his own time, as the prophet says, "I, the Lord, will hasten it in its time" (*Yeshayahu* 60:22).

> Rabbi Alexendri said: Rabbi Yehoshua the son of Levi asked [about a contradiction]: It is written; "in its time," and it is written, "I will hasten." [Which is it — hastened or in its time?] "Hastened" — if they merit it. "In its own time" — if they do not merit it.
>
> (*Sanhedrin* 78:1)

Since God set up a system of reward and punishment in order to move us towards perfection, we could hasten the Messianic era by acting in accordance with the Torah.

This would mean that redemption would be brought about by the revealed system of judgment. Redemption would come early, even before the six thousand years end. This would mean a hastened redemption.

However, should we fail to bring about a hastened redemption, God will bring about the redemption in the planned time. He is constantly moving the world toward this Messianic era, toward perfection, through the events of the hour. As He does this, His method of bringing us towards redemption is totally concealed. While He is preparing the good, we feel that we and the world have been abandoned.

Our Rabbis teach that this pre-Messianic period will be very painful and liken it to the birth pangs of a woman in labor. Why? All change is painful, but the bigger the difference between the earlier status and later status, the greater the pain. A birthing mother feels pain because the birthing process brings about a change from lifelessness to life. This transition is agonizing. So, too, is the transition from normative life in this world to the perfected life of the Messianic era. The birth pangs of Mashiach are painful for they are the result of the transition from our current reality to a new and unimagined reality (Maharal, *Netzach Yisrael*, ch. 36).

Cultivating Mashiach

From the very beginning, the seeds of Mashiach were planted in two places, one revealed, the other concealed. The revealed seed was planted in Avraham's son Yitzchak, the concealed seed in Avraham's nephew Lot (*Sefer HaLikkutim*, *Parashas Vayeira*, ch. 18, quoting the Arizal). Both seedlings were tended by Avraham (*Bereishis Rabbah* 51:11), but they grew differently. One remained fallow, hidden, and uncultivated. The other was revealed, growing, and blossoming. Only years later would these two seeds be grafted together. They would converge in David, King of Israel.

As we know, Lot passed on the hidden seed to his own daughters. The whole unseemly affair took place in a dark cave. Under the cover of such darkness, God saw to it that these women, both with less than Godly motives, would bring about His will. The Midrash says that the seed planted within them came "from a different place — the place of the king Mashiach." While the daughters intended to bring life into this world, God was planning for a different life, life in the Messianic era.

Years after the story of Lot and his daughters, this same seed was "found" in Rus and Naamah. What does the word *found* mean in this context?

> "Arise; take your wife and your two daughters that are found" (*Bereishis* 19:15). Toviah ben Rabbi Yitzchak said: Two "finds" [would spring from them], Rus the Moabitess and Naamah the Ammonitess. Rabbi Yitzchak commented: "I have found David My servant" (*Tehillim* 89:21). Where did I find him? In Sedom.
>
> (*Bereishis Rabbah* 41:5)

The Midrash starts by quoting the angel of God who comes to rescue Lot from the destruction of Sedom. The angel tells Lot to take his two daughters "that are found." These extraneous words prompt the Midrash to explain what was found. Rus and Naamah were the two "finds," as was David. No one would have expected to find the origins of the illustrious David or his foremothers in the birthplace of Lot's family, the depraved city of Sedom.

Finding something implies that it was lost or unexpected and then discovered. That Rus and Naamah would later be "found" and brought to the Jewish people was completely unforeseen. They were daughters of promiscuous, immoral nations, Moav and Ammon, and yet were chosen to be among the family of Jewish kings. Rus becomes the grandmother of David, and Naamah marries King Shlomo and becomes the mother of King Rechavam, who inherits his father's throne. That David, the King of Israel and ancestor of Mashiach, would be "found" was also a surprise; no one who knew his lineage and his history would have ever assumed that David would be king.

Yet God had planted the seed that "came from a different place" long before David was born; it was simply concealed until it was time for the seed to blossom.

The revealed line of Mashiach proceeded as expected. Yitzchak fathered Yaakov. Yaakov fathered Yehudah. All the tribes knew that kings and Mashiach would come from the tribe of Yehudah. No secrets here.

Both messianic lines, one originating with Lot and one with Yitzchak, operated jointly, just as *gilui panim* and *hester panim* (the revealed and hidden aspects of God) are intertwined. Even as the light of Mashiach was hidden in the seed of Lot, it shone in Yehudah. Until the end of the period of the Judges, the seed of Yehudah remained revealed and the seed of Lot remained hidden, in a kind of captivity.

The process of releasing the hidden seed from its captivity began when Rus made the decision to join the Jewish people.

> So Naomi returned, and Rus the Moabitess, her daughter-in-law, with her, who returned from the country of Moav; and they came to Beis Lechem at the beginning of the barley harvest.
>
> (*Rus* 1:22)

The words "who returned from the country of Moav" are not needed, as the beginning of the verse speaks about the return of Naomi and Rus. These extra words do not refer to the physical return of Rus to Israel, for, being of Moavite origin, she had never been there before. Rather, the extra phrase conveys the fact that Rus's soul, which had been in captivity "in the country of Moav," came home to the Jewish people where it belonged (*Sefer HaToda'ah*, ch. 29).

Yet would Jewish law permit her to convert and "return" to the Jewish people? Torah law prohibits Moavites from converting to Judaism, as it says, "An Ammonite or Moavite shall not enter into the congregation of the Lord; to their tenth generation shall they not enter into the congregation of the Lord forever" (*Devarim* 23:4). Did this law apply to both men and women, or only to men?

The question was a new one, one that had never come up before, because no other Moavitess had ever desired conversion. No other Moavitess possessed the hidden seed, nor had the modesty and kindness of Rus. So the law was obscure.

Many were afraid to accept her conversion, until Boaz, the great Torah leader of his time, declared that she could indeed enter the community of God. He understood that the injunction in the Torah applied only to the men of Moav and Ammon, not the women.

> An Ammonite, and not an Ammonitess; a Moabite, and not a Moabitess.
>
> (*Kesubos* 7b)

When Rus arrived in Beis Lechem, the light of Mashiach was still hidden, waiting to be revealed. The closest relative to Rus's dead husband, and the one who had the obligation to marry her by the law of levirate marriage, refused to get involved:

> Then Boaz said [to Rus's reluctant kinsman], "On the day that you buy the field from the hand of Naomi, you must buy it also from Rus the Moabitess, the wife of the dead, to restore the name of the dead to his inheritance."
>
> The kinsman said, "I cannot redeem it for myself, lest I harm my own inheritance. Take my right of redemption for yourself, for I cannot redeem it."
>
> *(Rus 4:5)*

> He [continued]: "The former ones died only because they took them [Rus and her sister-in-law, Orpah] to wife. Shall I then go and take her? Heaven forbid that I should take her; will I not contaminate my seed? I will not introduce a disqualification into my children."
>
> *(Rus Rabbah 7:10)*

Unlike Rus's kinsman, Boaz was not afraid to marry Rus. In fact, God kept him alive until the time that he could marry her, and the day after his marriage, he died. Rus conceived on their wedding night.

> Boaz was eighty years of age and had not been remembered with children. But when that righteous woman [Naomi] prayed for him, he was immediately remembered, as it says: "And Naomi said to her daughter-in-law, 'Blessed be he of the Lord' " (*Rus* 2:20).
>
> Resh Lakish said: Rus was forty years of age and had not been remembered with children as long as she was married to Machlon [her first husband, Naomi's son]. But as soon as that righteous man [Boaz] prayed for her, she was remembered, as it is says: "You are blessed of the Lord, my daughter" (*Rus* 3:10).
>
> *(Rus Rabbah 6:2)*

Many saw Boaz's death as a sign that he had been mistaken in his rendering of the law, and that this was punishment for his sin. Many hoped there would be no child born of the union so as not to raise a question on the status of the child (*Yalkut Rus*, quoted in *Sefer HaToda'ah*, ch. 29). But God had a different plan, a plan to begin to bring the hidden seed of Mashiach to light.

When Rus gave birth to a son, only the women rejoiced in his birth. The men remained silent, unsure of the legal status of the child.

> So Boaz took Rus, and she was his wife; and when he came to her, the Lord gave her conception, and she bore a son. The women said to Naomi, "Blessed is the Lord, who has not left you this day without a redeemer, that his name may be famous in Israel! He shall be to you a restorer of your life, and a nurturer of your old age; for your daughter-in-law, who loves you, who is better to you than seven sons, bore him."
>
> (*Rus* 4:13–15)

God was moving the events towards Mashiach, but no one knew this. The seed of Mashiach had to pass through revolving stages of concealment and revelation, each stage preparing for the next.

The matter seemed forgotten and remained so for two generations. Rus's son Oved fathered Yishai. Yishai married and fathered many children. But as he aged, Yishai's own doubts nagged at him: perhaps he was not a true Jew, perhaps his great-grandmother Rus's conversion had never been good, perhaps he was a Moavite, barred from entering the community of Israel (*Yalkut HaMechiri*, *Tehillim* 118:28). He separated from his wife so as not to bring more children into the world.

His wife was a very virtuous woman and she felt great distress at being separated from her righteous husband. She desired very much to have another child with him.

> He [Yishai] was separate from his wife for three years. He had a beautiful maidservant whom he desired, and he told her, "Prepare yourself for tonight so that you will be released from slavery and be with me."
>
> The maidservant went to her mistress and said, "Save yourself and my soul and my master from Gehinnom."
>
> She said to her, "What is the reason?"

> She [the maidservant] told her everything, and she [the wife] said to her, "My daughter, what should I do, because it has been three years since my husband has approached me."
>
> She [the maidservant] said to her, "I'll give you advice. Go and prepare yourself, and I will also, and tonight, when he says to close the door, you will enter and I will leave."
>
> So they did. That night, the maidservant stood and extinguished the light and when she went to close the door, her mistress entered and she left. She [his wife] was with him...and she conceived David....
>
> (*Yalkut HaMechiri, Tehillim* 118:28)

Later in his life, David wrote, "I am your servant, the son of your maidservant," for although he was truly the son of Yishai's wife, his birth came about because of the righteous act of the maidservant (*Sefer HaShelah HaKadosh, Maseches Pesachim, Bei'ur Haggadah, drush shishi*, 32).

> After nine months, her sons [those of Yishai's wife] wanted to kill her [for adultery] and her son David.... Yishai said, "Let him be, and he will be for us a servant and a shepherd." The thing was hidden for twenty-eight years.
>
> (*Yalkut HaMechiri, Tehillim* 118:28)

David's brothers treated him harshly and never considered him their brother. They told no one that they suspected their mother of adultery or that they thought that David was the son of a man who was not their father. However, David's mother loved him, knew the truth of his birth, but also told no one. David suffered greatly from his affliction.

Did he know his suffering had a purpose? Did he intuit that through his pain, he would come to understand the suffering and loneliness and feelings of rejection of every Jew, hence preparing him for his role of king? In many of his *tehillim*, we see indications of the anguish of rejection:

> I was a stranger to my brothers and an alien to the sons of my mother. For the zeal of Your house has eaten me up and the taunts of those who taunt You are fallen upon me.
>
> (*Tehillim* 69:9)

For my father and my mother have forsaken me, but the Lord will take me in.

(Tehillim 27:10)

Behold, I was shaped in iniquity, and in sin my mother conceived me.

(Tehillim 51:7)

The stone that the builders rejected has become the cornerstone.

(Tehillim 118:22)

Who could imagine that David would be a king? Who could know that he contained within him the light of Mashiach? Certainly not his father or brothers; not even his mother considered the possibility. For twenty-eight years, David was a pariah in his home. The status of Yishai as a Jew and David as his legitimate son remained questionable until Shmuel came to anoint the king.

Shmuel the prophet asked to see each of Yishai's sons. One by one, Yishai presented them, but he did not present David, because he did not consider him one of his own. One by one, the prophet rejected the sons of Yishai as candidates for kingship; finally, Shmuel asked if there were any more youths. Yishai hesitated since David was "little." (David was twenty-nine!) So he did not offer to bring him.

> Again, Yishai made seven of his sons pass before Shmuel. Shmuel said to Yishai, "The Lord has not chosen these."
>
> Shmuel said to Yishai: "Are all your children here?"
>
> He said, "There remains still the little one, and, behold, he keeps the sheep."
>
> Shmuel said to Yishai, "Send and fetch him, for we will not sit down till he comes here."
>
> He sent and brought him in. He was red haired, with beautiful eyes, and good looking.
>
> The Lord said, "Arise, anoint him, for this is he."
>
> Then Shmuel took the horn of oil and anointed him in the midst of his brothers, and the spirit of the Lord came upon David from that day forward.
>
> (Shmuel I 16:10–13)

When Shmuel the prophet came to anoint him, Yishai and his

sons were trembling with fear, for they said, "Shmuel is coming to degrade us and to inform Israel that we have an illegitimate son." David's mother was internally happy and externally sad. When he [Shmuel] took the cup of salvation, they were all happy.

(*Yalkut HaMechiri, Tehillim* 118:28)

Later in his life, David wrote, "I lift up the cup of salvation and call out in the name of God" (*Tehillim* 116:13), because his status was clarified before the eyes of his father and his family.

"I raise the cup of salvation and call in the name of God" — It mentions two degradations that happened to David, and afterwards [each] turned into honor and glory: 1) He descended from Rus and they were doubtful, in the beginning, if she was fitting to come into the community, until the law was [clarified]: "Moabite, but not Moabitess" (*Yevamos* 96b). 2) He was an exchanged son [the result of the exchange between the maidservant and the wife of Yishai].

(*Sefer HaShelah HaKadosh, Maseches Pesachim, Bei'ur HaAggadah* 16)

Not only was David's status clarified, but Yishai's as well. When Shmuel anointed David as king of Israel, Yishai was assured that he was a Jew and not a Moavite. Everyone was happy.

David's status had been hidden, not revealed, as the light of Mashiach is shrouded in darkness. David's obscure origins belied the greatness to which he would ascend. In the same way, the strength of the hidden light of Mashiach will be greater after its revelation than the darkness that preceded it.

While the seed planted in Lot was hidden and later brought to light, the seed in Yehudah alternated between revealed and hidden as well. For the most part, it was clear that Yehudah would be king, but there were times of clouding. When Yehudah refused to give Shelah to Tamar in marriage, this could have cut off the royal line before it even got started. He did not choose the right thing, but God compelled him towards Tamar, and "he turned in to her" — "despite himself and against his wish" (*Bereishis Rabbah* 85:8).

All the while, although no one knew it, God continued moving world events towards Mashiach. This idea is expressed in the following *midrash*, which describes the sale of Yosef and the aftermath of that sale:

> "It came to pass at that time, Yehudah went down from his brothers" (*Bereishis* 38:1).... "For I know the thoughts that I think toward you, says the Lord" (*Yirmeyahu* 19:11). The tribal ancestors were engaged in selling Yosef, Yaakov was taken up with his sackcloth and fasting, and Yehudah was busy taking a wife, while the Holy One, blessed be He, was creating the light of Mashiach, thus, "It came to pass at that time" [Yehudah left his brothers after the sale of Yosef, and married].
>
> (*Bereishis Rabbah* 88:1)

While we are planning our lives and our future, while we busy ourselves with physical concerns and spiritual endeavors, God is also planning. Unbeknownst to us, He is creating the light of the Mashiach. So unaware are we of His designs that when the Messianic era will be ushered in, it will feel to us like a woman who has not labored yet has borne a child.

> Before she travailed, she brought forth.
>
> (*Yeshayahu* 66:7)

God has planned it to the last detail. He has arranged the redeemer even before the enslavement. Even before the birth of the first king to enslave Israel, God planted the seeds of the Mashiach, final redeemer.

> Before the first enslaver was born [i.e., Pharaoh], the last redeemer was born [the Mashiach, whose advent was already being prepared].
>
> (*Bereishis Rabbah* 85:1)

Today, as well, with the difficulties that we experience, we are unaware that God is preparing us for Mashiach. The prophet Yeshayahu foretells the birth of a new era:

> Before she labored, she brought forth; before her pain came, she delivered a son. Who has heard such a thing? Who has seen such things? Shall the earth be made to bring forth in one day? Or shall a nation be born in one moment? For as soon as Zion

labored, she brought forth her children. "Shall I bring to the birth, and not cause to bring forth?" says the Lord. "Shall I cause to bring forth, and shut the womb?" says your God.

Rejoice with Jerusalem, and be glad with her, all you who love her. Rejoice for joy with her, all you who mourn for her. That you may suck, and be satisfied with the breasts of her consolations; that you may drink deeply, and be delighted with the abundance of her glory. For thus says the Lord: "Behold, I will extend peace to her like a river, and the glory of the nations like a flowing stream; then shall you suck, you shall be carried upon her sides, and be dandled upon her knees. As one whom his mother comforts, so will I comfort you; and you shall be comforted in Jerusalem."

(*Yeshayahu* 66:7–10)

Redemption is on the way.

Days of Love, Days of Hate

Life has its ups and downs. There are times when it is easier to serve God, and times when it is harder. *Sefer HaYashar* calls these "the days of love" and "the days of hate."

What are the days of love? Those are the times in our lives when God appears manifest to us and when we are motivated, happy, directed; days when every mitzvah is relevant and when our service of God is focused. What are days of hate? Those are the days when we loathe getting out of bed in the morning; days when we are stuck, unmotivated; when we don't feel like praying or doing other mitzvos.

This is part of the cycle of life and part of the human experience. Everyone has harder days and easier ones. Every person has times when life feels joyful, purposeful, and hopeful, and times when depression takes hold and nothing seems to have meaning.

The key is to manage the days of hate until the days of love come around. The wisest thing to do is to maintain a focus even though it is difficult, to push yourself to do the right thing even if there is a lack of connection. If you maintain your level even in the difficult days, when the days of love return, you will appreciate them and be able to grow spiritually stronger, faster.

If you don't work hard to maintain yourself in the days of hate, you will be unprepared to grow in the days of love, because you will have to regain "lost territory" and begin the growing process from a place of decline.

We must also know that in times when God is hidden that does not mean that He is not there. He is working for our good, moving things forward for us, and bringing us closer to where we need to be in life; redemption is only prepared in the darkest of times.

According to the level of sorrow, so is the reward.

(Avos 5:27)

This is all on the level of personal test. The same idea applies to the life of the nation.

Redemption Is Clandestine

Rabbi Yochanan said: When you see a generation ever dwindling, hope for him [the Mashiach], "The afflicted people You will save" (*Shmuel* II 22:28).

Rabbi Yochanan said: When you see a generation overwhelmed by many troubles as by a river, await him, as it is written: "When the enemy shall come in like a flood, the Spirit of the Lord shall lift up a standard against him" (*Yeshayahu* 59:19), which is followed by: "The Redeemer shall come to Zion" (ibid. 60:20).

(Sanhedrin 98a)

Why does God only bring redemption in hidden ways?

If God would interact with us solely in His manifest mode of judgment, on the basis of reward and punishment, very few of us would earn redemption. But when God acts in His concealed mode of sovereignty, when He is not "limited" to reward and punishment, He can bestow upon us from His bountiful generosity and kindness, with no regard to our merits, but only for the sake of bestowing goodness.

We express this idea in our daily prayer:

A King who causes death and restores life and makes salvation sprout.

(The Daily Amidah)

This prayer refers to the resurrection of the dead in the Messianic era, but it is possible to read it a different way. Our King "kills" us, but it is in order to restore our life and make salvation sprout. The suffering we experience while God is preparing salvation for us is a necessary part of the redemptive process.

The seeds of Mashiach were planted through strange encounters: in the incestuous relationship of Lot's daughters with their father, in the seemingly promiscuous encounter between Yehudah and Tamar, and in the bizarre rendezvous of Rus and Boaz. This is because redemption must be prepared in secrecy, out of sight.

God directs the creation and His creatures toward redemption, using them as the mechanism with which to bring their own salvation — against their will (as in the case of Yehudah), without their intention to do good (as in the cave of Sedom), and overriding their modesty (with Rus and Boaz at the threshing floor in Beis Lechem).

The greatest light comes from what seem to be the darkest places.

The Footsteps of Mashiach

We live in the pre-Messianic era. We don't see him; we see his footsteps. We experience darkness and see flashes of the light to come. In these difficult times, we are comforted to know that all that we suffer is part of the birth pangs of Mashiach. At times when we are near redemption, we experience both the concealment of God and His presence, simultaneously.

Yaakov, at the end of his life, could foresee the coming trials of the Jewish people and the fear and doubt that they would surely suffer. On his deathbed, he wanted to bolster his children for the long exile ahead by disclosing when the end of days would come. God, however, was not ready to have His secret revealed. We wait for the time when He is ready. May it come speedily in our days.

In memory of
Chana Leah bas Moshe
and
Hadassah bas Moshe

and

In honor of
Rebbetzin Holly Pavlov

for the years and years of *hachnasas orchim*

In memory of
my beloved grandmother
Mary Akiva, *a"h*
(Miriam bat Mazal)

and

In honor of my dear uncle
Simon Akiva

without whose love, kindness, and support
I would not be the person I am today

Chana Akiva

In honor of our parents and grandparents

Rabbi Philip and Lilly Schwebel

for all the love and support they have given us
throughout the years

Pamela and Gary Swickley
Grace, Noa, Nili, and Erez Swickley

In loving memory and an *illuy neshamah* for my aunt

Evelyn Lees

on the occasion of her one-year *yahrtzeit*
Erev Rosh HaShanah, 29 Elul 5764 (Sept. 15, 2004)

Devorah Singer

In loving memory of true *n'shei chayil*

Chava bas Aharon — Eve Lurie
Chana bas Hersh Eliezer — Anne Sack
Shayna Zelda bas Benyamin — Cynthia Lurie
Golda bas Yitzchak — Sophie Wilkov
Yocheved bas Moshe — Yetta Michels
Rivka bas Benyamin — Rita Laser
Sara Miriam bas Shimon — Sheila Lurie
Chana bas Natan — Hannah Weitzmann

Liora Intrator

In memory of my beloved husband
Rabbi Dr. Joseph Babad, *zt"l*

and in honor of my niece
Rebbetzin Holly Pavlov

Mrs. Esther Babad

In memory of

Lester Eisner
and Ruth and Louis Gottlieb

Chava and Jay Gottlieb

תפארת בנים אבותם
In honor of our dear parents
May you merit to continue your endless dedication in
chinuch for *klal Yisrael*, and
may you continue to serve as an inspiration and an example for us all.

The Pavlov, Pokroy, and Sher Families

In honor of Leiba and Zev Rudolph for their great *chesed* and righteousness Lani Droz	In memory of dear grandmother Betty Brod, Basya bas Sarah Devorah Blumberg
In memory of Irene Silver Deborah (Walman) Berkowitz	In memory of Alison Averbach-Barr Jillian (Littell) Ezekiel
In the memory of my dear mother Dr. Katalin Blancz, Miriam bat Sarah and my dear father David ben Smuel haLevi Gabriella Chava (Hoch) Politshuk	In honor of our dear friend Eve Rosenberg Steven and Marianne Sherr
In *hakarat hatov* and deep appreciation of Rebbetzin Pavlov and She'arim Yael and Andrew White	In loving memory of my parents Bessie and Reuben Goldman and my uncle Dr. George Nadler Michelle Gabel

In honor of my wonderful **Grandma Anne Geller** Sharon (Geller) Franklin	In honor of our mentors, Rabbi Mordechai Perlman, and my Rabbanit, who changed our lives and inspire us every day Lisa, Brian, and Rina Chana Silvey
לעילוי נשמת **צבי רלי בן אליהו יהודה** Sandra Littlestone	In honor of Holly Pavlov Geraldine Goldstein
In memory of David's father Avraham ben Yaakov David and Yaffa Baslaw	In honor of two women who taught me how to love Torah and be a *bas melech*, Rebbetzin Holly Pavlov and Mrs. Judith Berenstein Batya (Lam) Goldberg
In memory of my husband Dov Noach ben Menachem Mendel דב נח בן מנחם מענדל Hadassa Siegfried	In honor of my beloved husband Asher ben David Janis Fine
In honor of the She'arim Faculty Itamar and Chevy Gabbai	In honor of Evie Weinreich — my second mom Leslie Alterman
In memory of Lilian Gritz ליבא בת פנחס Marilyn Scheinfeldt	In honor of Samuel and Helen Haber Batsheva Haber
In memory of Penina Sucherman Barbara Rosen and Dena Glaser	In honor of Rebbetzin Pavlov Barry and Aleeta Shiff
In memory of my mother Shirly Bashker (Shaindel Yaffa bas Riva) Sally Bashker	In memory of Elliot's beloved mother Sura Leah bat Rivka (Lillian Balaban) Elliot and Suzanne Balaban

In honor of Rebbetzin Pavlov Sharona and Ari Schochet	In memory of Meriam bas Feigl Sarah Judith Greenberg
In loving memory of Penina Masha Liebe bas Ze'ev Leib Halevi — wife, mother, and grandmother of the Katz, Seidle, Bowman and Wolman Families	In memory of my great-grandmother חיה רוזא בת רב יעקב הלל may her memory be blessed Karen Pichel
An *illuy neshamah* for Ira Lee Dubitsky — a beloved husband, father, and grandfather From his loving daughter Leah Malka	In memory of my beloved parents Ruchal Anya bas Avraham HaLevy, Moshe Bezalel ben Mordechai Elaina Goldstein
In honor of our loving parents Jeff and Deby Goodman and Rabbi Evan and Deborah Shore Rivka and Dov Shore	To Robin and Michael: *Mazal tov* on your engagement. May Hashem grant you a life of happiness and ברכה. Love, Nancy Hilsenrath
In memory of Moshe ben Nachum Mordechai and Kressel Housman	To Rebbetzin Holly Pavlov, an amazing Jewish woman and mentor. You are an inspiration to all of us. Love, Esther Berkowitz, Malka Delman, Vivien Feen, Rivkah and Baruch Kanefsky, Michelle Meppen and Kineret Rifkind
In honor of Rebbetzin Pavlov, We feel very proud and fortunate to be a part of She'arim! Annette, Miriam, Nina, and Rachel	In memory of Barbara Rubin — Faiga bat Chaim Amy Rubin
In honor of my sister Dena, a mother in Israel and *ba'alat chesed* Risa Schulman	In honor of Rebbetzin Holly Pavlov Love, Aileen Averbach, Tina and David Hyde, Naomi and Ben Landau, Ruth Malnick, Natalie and Eli Menaged, and Gail Pariser
In loving memory of my father Moshe ben Mordechai HaLevi הי״ד Max and Netta de Vriend	To my inspiration, my mum, Lynne Jacobs All my love, Danielle

In loving memory of Pinchus ben Yekusiel Feinstein Ami and Eric Feinstein	In honor of Rebbetzin Holly Pavlov and the wonderful, dedicated staff at She'arim. Hashem should continue to give you the strength and resources to teach and inspire Jewish women worldwide. Cecile & David Devere Chaya & Chaim Silverstone & Family
In loving memory of Yehudit bat Avraham Miriam Campanil	In loving memory of דוב בער בן עזריאל זאב

Chava and David Axelrod

Jennifer Block

Debbie Eisenstein

Devorah and Eitan Fish

Rabbi Steven and Alexis Gaffin

Erica and David Goldberg

Kimberly Graham

Jill Greene

Darrin and Karen Holender

Muriel and Tzvi Honickman

Andrea and Jonathan Kamens

Yehudis Baila Kurs

Sarah and Mayor Langer

Chana and Israel Lebow

Caroline (Sternschein) Leonard

Arleeta and Ivan Lerner

Michelle and Ari Lifschitz

Rabbi David and Elisheva Mason

The Minkin Family

Marisa Pickar

Leslie (Gold) Ruder and Family

Pamela Saltsman

Faith Sheiber

Anne J. Sperling

The Trout Family

Barbara Kal-van Zoest

Judith Weisz

Daniel and Daphna Zuckerbrod